STARTING FROM THE CHILD

FOURTH EDITION

STARTING FROM THE CHILD

Teaching and learning in the Foundation Stage

FOURTH EDITION

JULIE FISHER

Open University Press

Open University Press
McGraw-Hill Education
McGraw-Hill House
Shoppenhangers Road
Maidenhead Berkshire
England SL6 2QL

email: enquiries@openup.co.uk
world wide web: www.openup.co.uk

and Two Penn Plaza, New York, NY 10121-2289, USA

First published 1996
First published in this fourth edition 2013

Copyright © Julie Fisher 2013

A catalogue record of this book is available from the British Library

ISBN-13: 978-0-33-524651-9
ISBN-10: 0-33-524651-6
eISBN: 978-0-33-524652-6

Library of Congress Cataloging-in-Publication Data
CIP data applied for

Typesetting and e-book compilations by
RefineCatch Limited, Bungay, Suffolk
Printed and bound by CPI Group (UK) Ltd, Croydon, CR0 4YY

Praise for this book

"In the fourth edition of this book, Julie Fisher once again demonstrates a comprehensive understanding of the history of early childhood education, and the enduring principles that continue to underpin practice. She has skilfully blended these principles with contemporary research and theory in order to provide readers with deep understanding of young children as capable, competent and eager learners. Julie draws on her extensive work with practitioners to present the everyday realities and complexities of their practice, and to sound welcome notes of caution about the ways in which policy frameworks are used. She offers vignettes to illustrate key issues, provocations and challenges to stimulate thinking, and questions to engage readers with contemporary issues and dilemmas. The book also reflects deeply held convictions about the moral and ethical responsibilities we have to teach young children in ways that respect their extraordinary enthusiasm for learning.

This book will be invaluable for students of early childhood education, especially those on professional development programmes such as Early Childhood Studies, Early Years Professional Status, and Post Graduate Certificate of Education."

Professor Elizabeth Wood, University of Sheffield, UK

"The fourth edition of this classic text has been updated with recent research. This is very helpful in supporting readers but it's the underpinning philosophy that makes this a continuing classic. The title says it all. Julie takes the reader by the hand and says 'Look and listen, give these children your full and respectful attention and they will teach you how to be with them.' All the practical ideas in the book support practitioners in using their skills and knowledge to recognise early childhood as valuable in its own right – to be relished and enjoyed, not to be rushed through or seen merely as preparation for the next stage. We owe it to our children to take heed."

Helen Moylett, early years consultant and writer

"Julie Fisher's work has been a staple of Early Childhood Education since the first edition of Starting from the Child in 1996. Her fourth edition does not disappoint, and is a welcome development of her thinking. She delves in more detail, for example, into brain development, and leads her readers further into the latest scientific thinking on how children learn. She is, as ever, insightful about how adults work with children, with helpful advice about how to observe (and record) children's learning, and how to plan effectively.

Her inclusion of her own latest field work ensures that Julie's advice on early years practice remains rooted in the everyday, while making accessible a range of theoretical and scientific perspectives. This is a book for students, teachers and other early years workers seeking to find their way through the conflicting needs of a rapidly changing area of work."

Nick Swarbrick, Programme Lead for the Undergraduate Modular Programme in the School of Education, Oxford Brookes University, UK

To David
for being beside me all the way

CONTENTS

List of boxes and figures   x
Preface to the Fourth Edition   xi

1 **Competent young learners**   1
   What children know and can do

2 **Observations and conversations**   25
   Learning about individual children

3 **Planning for learning**   47
   Decisions about appropriate experiences to consolidate and
   extend learning

4 **The role of the adult**   72
   Optimizing practitioners' time with children

5 **Encouraging independence**   94
   Environments that develop children's learning autonomy

6 **Collaboration and cooperation**   117
   The importance of talking and learning with others

7 **The place of play**   137
   The status of child-initiated experiences

8 **The negotiated learning environment**   161
   Issues of ownership, power and control

9 **The assessment of children's learning**   185
   What practitioners need to know about children and their
   achievements

10 **Reflection and evaluation**   209
   What practitioners need to know about their practice, their
   provision and themselves

References   227
Index   239

BOXES AND FIGURES

Box 2.1	Example 1: Responding to children's work	29
Box 2.2	Example 2: Building independence	32
Box 3.1	Principles of early childhood education	54
Box 3.2	Differentiation in short-term plans	68
Box 5.1	Making decisions about the use of space	105
Box 5.2	Principles about using space	106
Box 5.3	Principles about gathering resources	108
Box 5.4	Planning and arranging resources	110
Box 7.1	Child-initiated activities involving learning in many curriculum areas	153
Box 7.2	A charter for play	158
Box 9.1	Example 3: Focused teaching and assessment 1	197
Box 9.2	Example 4: Focused teaching and assessment 2	197
Box 9.3	Example 5: The cross-curricular nature of learning	198
Box 10.1	Ofsted Grade descriptor for 'outstanding': quality of teaching in school	221
Figure 1.1	Maslow's hierarchy of needs	3
Figure 4.1	The balance of learning experiences 1	82
Figure 4.2	The balance of learning experiences 2	84
Figure 4.3	The balance of learning opportunities	85

PREFACE TO THE FOURTH EDITION

It is 16 years since the first edition of *Starting from the Child* was published. Much has changed in that time but more still has not. While there have been unprecedented advances in our understanding of the brain and its functioning, little else has changed dramatically in our knowledge of young children and how they learn. Researchers may have sharpened and extended our understanding but fundamentally we know that young children learn by being active explorers of the world, learning alongside and with others in social and cultural contexts that determine most of their life chances. We know that successful early childhood educators encourage children to learn through play as well as offering them adult-led experiences that extend and enrich their skills and understanding. We know that being concerned for a young child's personal, social and emotional well-being is at the heart of his or her opportunities to develop, learn and thrive in the world.

But alongside this accumulated knowledge have come initiatives from central government that have challenged – and in some cases – damaged and manipulated the messages from research about how young children learn. Over the years, *Starting from the Child* has remained an antidote to such initiatives. It has always challenged practitioners to know their children sufficiently well to resist ill-informed government guidance; to have a strong philosophy rooted in reading, research and the evidence of their own eyes in order to withstand the vagaries of ill-informed external expectations; to stand firm for the child, who they are, what they need and how they learn.

My own professional learning journey has been, and continues to be, enriched by the practitioners and the children with whom I interact on a daily basis. I hope that *Starting from the Child* continues to provoke, to reassure and to inspire those of you who are on a similar journey.

1

COMPETENT YOUNG LEARNERS

What children know and can do

Introduction

Before starting statutory schooling at the age of 5, young children have developed a range of skills, knowledge and understanding at a speed that will never again be repeated in their lives. The years from 0 to 7 are a period in human development when the capacity to learn is, in John Brierley's words (1994) 'at flood-readiness'. All the evidence shows that, in their early years, young children demonstrate a variety of skills and competences that make them natural and successful learners. However, when those same children begin their more formal education it can be a different story. Children who have been motivated and determined become disillusioned and disaffected (Barrett 1989; Smith 1995; Entwistle and Alexander 1998); children who made sense of things and had begun to form their own personal construct of the world become confused and disorientated (Donaldson 1978; 1992); children who posed a thousand and one questions become quiet and uncommunicative (Tizard and Hughes 1984; Cousins 1999; Siraj-Blatchford et al. 2002). It seems that education can inhibit some of the most prominent characteristics of competent young learners.

So how can there be such a gap between some children's learning before they begin at school or their early years setting, and the learning that follows? Is it simply a question of ratios – too many children and not enough practitioners? Are those practitioners not sufficiently knowledgeable about how young children learn and how to support that learning? Is there too much pressure from external agendas to allow practitioners to follow children's interests and preoccupations? It would seem that at the root of the dichotomy between learning and teaching lies a failure on the part of many educators to learn themselves from those who have been so successful in the teaching and learning process in the child's preschool years at home. If more time were spent observing the strategies of children as learners, prior to the constraints of the educational setting, and more notice taken of the strategies of the significant adults with whom children learn in their homes and communities, then there might be more chance of schools and other early years settings mirroring the effectiveness of children's earliest learning environments.

The influence of experience on heredity

The development of every child is the result of a unique interaction of experience with heredity. While genetic programming determines many of the characteristics displayed by any human being, a variety of environmental influences combine to affect the development of the brain and consequently the individual (Shaffer 1999). The balance between these two key factors varies within each child, but the impact of 'nurture' on 'nature' will determine the characteristics which differentiate one child from another and make his or her development unique. Hereditary influence means that given the same set of experiences, one child's abilities will differ from another's, irrespective of the experiences they have. Equally, a child raised in a particular set of environmental circumstances can have their genetic programming nullified and their hereditary advantages diminished (Meadows 1993).

Until fairly recently, the emphasis in education has been to make up for the deficits of a poor set of hereditary circumstances (Anning 1991). In the 1960s and 1970s there was 'a naive belief that compensatory education would serve to combat the known effects of social disadvantage on children's educational achievements' (Anning 1991: 5). While many research studies have now discredited such assumptions, there is other evidence that highlights the negative effects on development of a poor set of environmental factors (e.g. Smith 1995). Mia Kellmer Pringle, the first director of the National Children's Bureau (see http://www.ncb. org.uk/), identified four human basic needs which have to be met from 'the very beginning of life and continue to require fulfillment – to a greater or lesser extent – throughout adulthood' (1992: 34). In Chapter 2 she identifies:

- the need for love and security;
- the need for new experiences;
- the need for praise and recognition;
- the need for responsibility.

Jennie Lindon in her book on child development (1993: 11–12) also identifies some basic needs of young children:

- the need to be cared for physically;
- the need to be kept safe;
- the need for emotional well-being.

Much current thinking about these universal human needs has its roots in the 'hierarchy of needs' presented back in 1943 by the American psychologist Abraham Maslow which, when presented as a pyramid – the most common representation of his theory – places the largest and most fundamental levels of needs at the bottom, supporting all the others (Fig. 1.1).

Research cited by the Carnegie Corporation of New York (1994) provides substantial evidence that *lack* of these basic human needs, and inappropriate or impoverished environments in the early stages of learning, may have long-lasting detrimental effects on development. The report, drawing on research that illuminates the workings of the nervous system, highlights the critical importance of the first three years of life and led to five key findings which are of profound significance to all those who are concerned with the development and education of young children:

Figure 1.1 Maslow's hierarchy of needs

- brain development that takes place before age 1 is more rapid and extensive than previously realized;
- brain development is much more vulnerable to environmental influence than was ever suspected;
- the influence of early environments on brain development is long lasting;
- the environment affects not only the number of brain cells and number of connections among them, but also the way these connections are 'wired';
- there is new scientific evidence for the negative impact of early stress on brain function.

(Carnegie Corporation 1994: 7–9)

These findings give a clear rationale for creating learning environments that offer experiences sensitive to the needs of young children and appropriate to their development, because the results of these experiences – good or bad – stay with children for ever. The fact that the effects of early experiences appear to be cumulative only adds to the need to safeguard the environmental influences determining the development of all young children:

> an adverse environment can compromise a young child's brain function and overall development, placing him or her at greater risk of developing a variety of cognitive, behavioral, and physical difficulties. In some cases these effects may be irreversible.
>
> (Carnegie Corporation 1994: xiii)

Recent understandings about brain development

Our increasing knowledge of the brain and its functioning is illuminating our understanding of children's development at an exponential rate. Indeed this knowledge about the brain is increasing so rapidly that information is often out of date before it is written down. We currently know that at birth, a child's brain contains around 100 billion neurons, each with the capacity to contribute to that individual's knowledge and understanding of skills and concepts that will determine their unique growth and development (Pinker 1977; Bruer 1999). Indeed, by nine months gestation, human beings have most of the neurons (nerve endings) in their brains that they are ever likely to have (Greenfield 1997). Of particular importance to those in early education is the evidence that it is not the *number* of brain cells that is important, but how they become connected to each other that makes them effective (Greenfield 1997; Diamond and Hopson 1998; Geake 2009). It is the use to which the neurons are put that determines the growth of a brain's functions (Calvin 1996; Geake 2009). Growing neurons can adapt sensitively to changing circumstances in order to make the best of a situation (Greenfield 1997; Howard-Jones 2010) but the key to growth is whether the neurons are sufficiently stimulated to make contact with other neurons and make a firm connection (Cohen 1997; Diamond and Hopson 1998; Geake 2009). Brain activity and growth go hand in hand. It is not only a question of 'use it or lose it' says Susan Greenfield (1997: 115), but 'use it as much as you can'.

In the first three years of life, the neural connections are established at a phenomenal rate. By the age of 5 or so, they begin to tail off and are virtually complete by age 10 (Gammage 1999; Howard-Jones 2010). However, this does not mean that after age 3 no worthwhile learning can take place, or that if connections are not made by age 3 then an individual has lost the opportunity for development and growth. Some writers, in their eagerness to exhort the benefits of early learning, have suggested that if a child has not been fully stimulated by age 3, then their opportunities for learning and development become closed off. Mercifully for most of us, this is not the case! The brain may not 'grow' more neurons, but it does go on making connections and these can be stimulated at any age (Bruer 1999; Geake 2009). Neuroscientists used to refer to the optimum moments for learning as 'critical' periods, but most have now altered this to speak of 'sensitive' periods – times in our lives when we are able to learn particular things most readily.

The best time to master a skill associated with a system is when that system is coming on line in the brain (Sylwester 1995; Pinker 1997; Bruer 1999). Language is a good example. It is easy for a 2- or 3-year-old to learn any language, but if that person waits until age 18 or 50, learning a new language will be more difficult because the systems governing this process may have been used for something else. However, not all sensitive periods happen in the first three years, nor do all cognitive systems show such effects (Bruer 1999). It seems that periods of increased synaptogenesis (the growth of synapses: the junction between neurons which enable connections to be made) and synaptic pruning (the getting rid of synapses that are not being used) may best explain these 'sensitive' periods when the human brain is in an optimum state for learning (Howard-Jones 2010).

Learning is chiefly associated with the birth of neurons and with the changes in the connectivity between those neurons. This capacity to change is described by neuroscientists as 'adaptive plasticity' – the capacity of the brain to adapt at a neurophysiological level in response to changes in the cognitive environment (Geake 2009; Howard-Jones 2010). John Geake's enlightened exposition of the application of neuroscience in the classroom (2009) draws on the work of the Canadian neuroscientist Donald Hebb who proposed that repeated coincident firing of particular synapses in response to a stimulus results in permanent physiological change in the brain. Hebb's thesis was that learning can be made more efficient with repetition because the biochemical processes that convey information across the synapses lead synaptic functioning to become stronger. In the early years of education, it is crucial that young learners have opportunities for the constant reinforcement of experiences, skills and understandings in order for repetition to forge secure pathways of learning in the brain. This is why early childhood educators must understand the power of a spiral curriculum (Bruner 1960) – one that gives children repeated opportunities to revisit and rehearse emerging skills and understandings but in new as well as increasingly complex contexts.

Donald Hebb's model of neural plasticity may also account for why misunderstandings are so difficult to counteract or eliminate in young children. If repetition reinforces misunderstandings as well as understandings, then young children's striving to make independent sense of their world inevitably leads to occasions when neural pathways are formed on a false premise or a half-truth. The brain must undo what has already been learned erroneously in order to learn afresh what is accurate. If we rush children through their educational experiences, if we are too busy 'covering' the curriculum (rather than 'uncovering' it as Lilian Katz advocates), if we are too concerned with 'next steps' rather than current steps, then children may be left with their misconceptions unchallenged – by an adult or in the course of their own repeated explorations – and find the foundations of their future learning are on shaky ground.

As educators, it is important that we do not make claims for any link between neuroscience and early learning that is overly expansive. Nonetheless, a realization of the critical importance of neural connections to human growth and development should challenge educators to ensure that the learning environments that are created and the support that adults give to young children as they learn, maximize their drive to make as many connections as they can with what they already know and understand.

Differences between the brains of boys and girls

Much has been written about the differences in the brains of boys and girls. While some authors seek to simplify differences in order to package some 'solution' to teaching boys and girls to suit their different brain development, the reality seems to be – as with most neuroscientific enquiry – that things are much more complicated than this. There are certainly differences between male brains and female brains both structurally and functionally. Females have a more robust corpus callosum than men. This is the thick bundle of white matter that is the main connection tract between the two brain hemispheres. In females there are more fibres which lead to more sites in each hemisphere. John Geake suggests that 'Such a structural advantage is not inconsistent with the stereotype of women having a cognitive advantage for multi-tasking, or of having an advantage in articulating emotional thoughts into speech' (2009: 86). Males, on the other hand, have greater variance in the structure of their parietal lobes, which are often denser or thicker than those of women. The main purpose of the parietal cortex seems to be spatial processing, especially navigation and tracking moving objects. Geake once more suggests that this structural advantage 'is not inconsistent with the stereotype of male fixation with sports involving a moving ball . . . spatial processing in the parietal cortex is a consistent neural correlate with all areas of mathematical thinking' (2009: 87). This does not mean, he hastens to add, that girls cannot achieve in mathematics as highly as boys do – but it does raise an interesting question as to whether the mathematical thinking of boys and girls is different.

Prenatal exposure to testosterone also seems to be significant in the development of the brain. On the internet, as well as in text books and articles, there is a significant literature suggesting that hormones within the womb start a natural development of the brain that takes it on a different trajectory (NIH/NIHM 2007) and at a different pace (Kotulak 1997) according to whether it belongs to a boy or a girl. In the three months following gestation, the womb is flooded by hormones, including testosterone. These trigger changes not only in brain development but physical growth, with boys developing heavier bones, bigger muscles, more red blood cells and male genitalia. Energy is diverted to these physical changes, at a time when, in a girl's brain, energy is given to the development of the left cortex – concerned with language, emotion and detail. So, as Featherstone and Bayley (2009) rather simplistically suggest, 'while boys are growing muscles, girls are growing brains'. In girls, the right side of the brain has developed in advance of the left side so, when the left side comes on stream, the female brain is ready to make connections, thus using both sides of the cortex to increase proficiency. In boys, when the brain cells in the right hemisphere of the brain reach out to the left side, the left hemisphere is less ready to receive the connections. So the links that are made tend to be within the same half of the brain rather than with the opposite sphere and, mainly, these will be in the right side of the brain thus giving boys the potential to be particularly skilled at mathematics, problem-solving, machines and technology (Biddulph 1997; Kotulak 1997).

Eliot's (2009) contribution to this field is that boys' brains are larger than girls' (although this doesn't necessarily lead to greater 'efficiency') and that girls' brains finish growing about one to two years earlier than boys' brains. Eliot also makes reference to the brain's plasticity and the fact that many of the differences we perceive between males and females are due to experience rather than genetics. The differences that emerge between boys and girls may have some genesis in hormones and genetic make-up but, she asserts, they are 'massively amplified' by the different practice, role models and reinforcement to which boys and girls are exposed.

There is indeed anecdotal as well as research evidence that shows, generally, that girls reach accepted 'developmental milestones' earlier than boys. Toddler girls generally talk before boys so have a head start in using language; girls' senses of hearing, touch and smell are better developed than boys'; girls tend to be better listeners than boys (Newberger 1999; Smith et al. 2010; Goddard Blythe 2011). But these can be cultural differences as much as genetic ones. Steven Pinker (1997) even suggests that culture is a third condition of brain develop-ment, with nature and nurture accounting for the other two. Certainly, in cultural terms, we only have to look around at everyday life to see the different ways in which girls and boys are treated and girls and boys are portrayed. But, for early childhood educators, there is something particularly significant about the way boys and girls are treated once they arrive at school or their early childhood setting. We have seen that the development of language and social skills are achieved earlier and with greater confidence by girls than by boys. Yet it is these very skills – being literate, being communicative and being socially adept – that are valued most highly in English educational settings, for which external targets are set and against which schools, settings and indeed local authorities have increasingly been judged. So, from their earliest days, boys are judged on aspects of learning for which many are not as developmentally ready and at which many fail *at that moment* in their developmental journey (Palmer 2006; House 2011). Tragically, from these earliest experiences of failure for many, stems the tide of underachievement which vexes successive government departments. If schools were to value the skills of spatial awareness, technological understanding and model-making, at which many boys excel, then perhaps their confidence would be boosted and they, too, would be seen as competent and capable learners as they move through their early schooling. Maybe too, there would be a context for early reading and writing that so often seems lacking in classrooms bounded by themes and topics that do not inspire boys' interest and engagement.

As early childhood educators we need to recognize that, whatever the reason, the ways in which most boys and most girls learn is different. While, of course, there is tremendous overlap, and all early years practi-tioners could give examples of girls and boys who are not 'typical', most boys thrive in an environment that accommodates their energetic and boisterous behaviour; that accepts and approves of their superhero, gun and sword play; that allows them to make noise and to run around. The role of the early childhood educator is to know their children sufficiently well to accommodate individual preferred modes of learning and to optimize the capacities of all children, whatever their gender.

Brain development in children under 2

While this book is concerned chiefly with the education of children from 3 to 5 years of age, it is incumbent upon practitioners working with this age group to be knowledgeable about the development of children from birth to age 3. In their influential text *How Babies Think* (1999) Gopnik et al. suggested that studying babies makes us think about the brain in new ways. The increased sophistication of neuroimaging techniques has given researchers the opportunity to study babies' astonishing repertoire of skills and competences, particularly as they ensure communication with and inclusion into the community into which they are born. They can mimic their mothers by pulling faces and poking out their tongues, they can discriminate human faces and voices from other sights and sounds and they can discriminate the sounds not only of their own language but of every language, including languages they have never heard. Within the first nine months, before those babies can walk or talk or even crawl, they can tell the difference between expressions of happiness and sadness and anger. This acute sensitivity, documented by a growing number of researchers (notably Trevarthan), enables us to understand why the experiences of babies in their earliest days and months impact so profoundly on their sense of well-being, self-confidence and resilience.

Two other more recent books have also alerted us to the importance of the very first year of life in laying down the foundations of children's emotional and social well-being and, in particular, the vital contribution of the interactions that take place between babies and the adults who care for them. In *From Birth to One: The Year of Opportunity* (2003), Maria Robinson demonstrates how important it is for an adult to understand the influence of their interactions, reactions and behaviour towards their child and, in turn, to understand the child's impact on themselves as an adult. All children, she says, need to feel secure, and that emotional security is learned from the ongoing relationship with their adult carer(s), based on the patterns of behaviour in the first year. Babies make secure attachments to their primary carer when they have their basic needs, such as being wet or feeling hungry, responded to promptly and appropriately (Bowlby 1969, 1975, 1981). Where a normal attachment develops, the emotions that babies show at times of stress or distress are soothed and managed by the caregiver and, over time, babies are helped to regulate their own reactions through the meaning given to their behaviour and the response of that caregiver. Where this cycle of attunement is disturbed, through separation from the primary caregiver or through neglect, then babies end up with overwhelming feelings of frustration, loneliness and panic. In her book *Why Love Matters* (2004) Sue Gerhardt explains that these earliest emotions, in turn, shape the baby's nervous system and that the neural pathways formed by these early experiences can affect the way we respond to stress and how we cope with relationships throughout our lives. Gerhardt, too, stresses the crucial impact of early interactions between babies and their primary attachment figure, emphasizing that emotions become organized through engagement with others and not in isolation. She provides evidence to suggest that 'expectations of other people and how they will behave are inscribed in the brain outside conscious awareness, in the period of infancy, and that they underpin our behaviour in relationships through life' (p. 24). It is clearly imperative that practitioners who have responsibility for the care of children under the age of 2 are aware of the immense responsibility they hold for providing the constant, reliable, loving care that all babies demand and the consequences for babies if they do not. There needs to be greater understanding that this care is not just about responding to a baby's physical needs – their wet nappy or hungry tummy – but about an openness to intimacy on the part of the carer, and a willingness to form emotional loving relationships with a child and their family if that child is to thrive and develop without emotional deprivation or undue stress.

What do young children learn?

Given an appropriate environment in which they thrive, what is it that young children are learning? Shaffer claims that 'we change in response to the environments in which we live' (1999: 5). The educators in Reggio Emilia, a town in northern Italy renowned for the quality of its preschool provision, see the environment as a 'third teacher', creating enriching situations and 'helping the children to be the direct agents and constructors of their own learning processes' (Spaggiari 1997: 10). But change and development lie particularly in our response to the actions and reactions of the people around us. We behave in new ways because of our observations of and interactions with important people in our lives and are affected by the events we experience together. Young children come to make sense of their world by observing, imitating, investigating and exploring. They learn attitudes, skills, strategies and concepts that enable them to understand and be understood.

Positive *dispositions* to learning arise from children's motivation to learn, to succeed in the face of many odds, and to master the exciting and intriguing world around them. The posing of personal problems teaches children the value of concentration and perseverance in the successful acquisition and honing of skills and understandings. Success fuels their motivation and determination to succeed and enhances their confidence and self-esteem as learners. The infinite range of new and exciting things to discover and explore stimulates young children's curiosity and engages their eagerness to be both successful and competent.

Important *skills* are learnt as a result of establishing patterns of behaviour which ultimately become automatic. Young children repeat movements or actions time after time in order to become expert and succeed at the goals which they have set themselves. Skills usually develop in the course of activities that the child sees as being worthwhile and which give him or her the motivation to continue, sometimes through failure after failure, to succeed. Children are motivated by the response of others, particularly their parent or carer, and this response sustains them through the frustrations of learning to stand unaided, throw a ball towards someone else or communicate so they are understood.

In the course of learning skills, children develop their own peculiar set of *strategies* for trying out, rehearsing or repeating what they have done. Some children prefer to look and think before they act. Some try and try again until something comes right. Some prefer to imitate, some to instigate. Some ask questions and others wait for answers. Whatever strategies are developed, they are tailor-made by each child. They are chosen because they serve the child's individual purpose and because they work. These strategies become part of the characteristics of the child as a learner and are the basis of all strategies that will be adopted if the child is left to learn alone.

The understandings or *concepts* that children learn are generally arrived at through a process of abstraction of the principles that underpin a variety of different experiences. Children come to understand about size and shape, about dogs, the past or the seasons through a range of first-hand experiences, leading them to see and understand the conceptual links between one experience and another. In this way children become able to generalize abstract principles from concrete experiences. It is almost impossible to rush this transition from concrete to abstract because, as has already been said, if children are forced to establish connections then it is likely that they will make inappropriate ones (Brierley 1994; Robinson and Beck 2000).

We know that children *do* make the wrong 'connections' and that, once made, these misunderstandings – or alternative understandings – can take a great deal of unlearning. The work of Wynne Harlen, Roger Osborne and others reveals that children have views about a variety of topics and that they are very often different from the views of 'experts'. However, to children they remain 'sensible, useful views' (Harlen 1985: 76) and can remain uninfluenced or be influenced in unanticipated ways by teaching. The views that children hold are a result of their personal endeavours to construct their own meaning for, and understanding of, the experiences they have had (Postlethwaite 1993). As we have seen earlier, these repeated patterns of behaviour result in permanent physiological changes in the brain. The child persists in developing a neural pathway – even when based on misunderstandings – because the child sees something that makes sense and which 'connects' for them. Since they work for the child and, since they serve the child's purpose reasonably well, they are not readily displaced by the explanation of someone else especially, as Postlethwaite says, as these explanations are often more complex than their own.

Readiness for learning

Inherent in beliefs about the competences of young children is an attitude towards the concept of 'readiness' for learning. If children are viewed as competent young learners, then it follows that they have predispositions to learn from their earliest days and, as such, are ready for learning from birth (and, many would say, before). The consequence of this view is that children are never *not* ready to learn and the notion of children 'emerging' into literacy (Hall 1987), numeracy (Hughes 1986), and so on, assumes engagement in concepts which at one time would have been deemed inappropriate for young minds. The work of Donaldson (1978), Bruner (1986), Hughes (1986) and others, however, has illuminated the view that children are ready for learning if learning is adapted to the intellectual proclivities of children (Watson 1998). The current government's mantra that children in the foundation stage should be made 'ready for school' (e.g. DfE 2012:4, para 1.1) should be turned on its head by such educational research to demand, instead, that all schools should be made 'ready for children'.

Once again we are drawn to the behaviours of parents and carers who appear to make these adaptations instinctively. Most parents, it seems, adapt naturally to their child's intellectual tendencies, attributing consciousness and intentionality to their child's actions from the very beginning of his or her life (Trevarthen 1980, 1992; Stern 1985). When parents talk to their child, they do so as if expecting a response, often long before the child seems capable of giving one. In this way, children's early learning is aided in spontaneous and incidental ways by older and more experienced members of their community, who give structure to the child's earliest, hesitant inclinations to explore the world (Rogoff 1990; Watson 1998).

A child is ready to learn when their cognitive disposition and what is to be taught are matched. Parents may make this match instinctively knowing, as they do, so much about the body of beliefs, expectations and assumptions that their child brings to a learning situation. Early childhood educators do not have the benefit of sharing each child's complete learning history and one of the most complex challenges of teaching is to become as knowledgeable as possible about the cognitive dispositions of a large number of children in any one group in order to plan appropriately for their individual needs.

Much of the influence of Jean Piaget stemmed from his view that children progress through various stages of development that determine their current level of skills and competence. Readiness for learning, he believed, depended on the child's developmental stage, and progress from one stage to the next could not be rushed. This view of development influenced many teachers to adopt a relatively passive role in children's progress (Darling 1994). Activities were planned that reflected the notion of readiness with titles such as 'pre-reading', 'pre-number', and so on. The role of the educator was to bring children to a state of readiness to engage fully in significant skills or concepts and children were taken through a whole range of early stages of learning in preparation for their arrival at the next stage of development. Piaget's notion of readiness was ultimately challenged by a number of researchers, notably Margaret Donaldson (1978), who believed that children should be actively encouraged to move towards the 'disembedded' thinking that characterizes learning in primary schools. The work of Lev Vygotsky (1978) also contributed to and extended this debate about readiness. Vygotsky believed that instead of matching teaching to existing development, teaching had to proceed in advance of development in order to challenge and extend children's maturing functions. He believed that learning comes in advance of development when progress is stimulated and guided by the expertise of others. This notion of readiness places the emphasis on *when* to teach, not simply *how* and *what* to teach. If practitioners adopt this principle, then it can be seen once again that it is the task of schools to be 'ready' for children – in the experiences, opportunities, environments and expectations they provide, and not the other way round.

The characteristics of successful early learning

Young children may be inexperienced learners, but their competence should not be underestimated. Loris Malaguzzi who inspired the development of the preschools in Reggio Emilia, said 'our image of the child is rich in potential, strong, powerful, competent and most of all, connected to adults and to other children' (1993). Modern technology has made it possible to investigate the very beginnings of human thinking, and researchers have documented critical development in the pre- and postnatal months of life. From the beginning, humans demonstrate intention-directed behaviour (Trevarthan 1992). They are both intellectually and interpersonally engaged, or predisposed to be so, much earlier than previous theories allowed (Watson 1998). The young child is clearly emerging cognitively, linguistically, physically, socially and emotionally and – most significantly – this critical development usually occurs when the child is receiving no formal education. Children have the capacity to draw conclusions about the world when the knowledge that they need has not been formally taught to them.

Given an environment in which they are cared for and in which they can thrive, young children display a range of competences that make their early learning dramatically successful.

- Young children display positive *attitudes* and *dispositions* to learn. The determination for mastery over their environment drives them to persist and persevere – often in the face of difficulty and initial failure – to succeed in their objectives.
- Young children develop personal *skills* and *strategies* that work for them in their quest to understand the world. These strategies are chosen instinctively and fulfil children's purposes for the particular task in hand.
- Young children have developed *understandings* and sometimes *misunderstandings*. Each piece of knowledge acquired, each small piece of sense that is made, fits into each child's personal cognitive jigsaw.

The construction of this personal cognitive jigsaw has many parallels with the construction of the traditional wooden puzzle. At first, the pieces of cognitive jigsaw are picked seemingly at random. Sometimes the piece fits straight away, sometimes it is turned round and round – with astonishing patience – before the fit is finally made. Sometimes the piece is turned round and round and a fit is made and only subsequent pieces show that piece to be in the wrong place. Sometimes the piece is turned round and round, does not quite fit but is jammed in anyway because it is more satisfying to have reached a solution than to have to start again.

It is the skill of the educator to be aware of the pieces of the jigsaw that the child already has in place and whether or not they have been fitted together appropriately. If they have not, then supporting the child to review the construction of their cognitive jigsaw is as delicate and difficult an operation as persuading the child to select an alternative piece of wooden puzzle. The practitioner needs to decide whether the child will be helped to understand by being told something quite factually – 'You *can* have a car wheel in the boot for emergencies' or whether being told would remove 'the active role of making links and puzzling over relationships' (Stewart 2011: 89). The *imposition* of connections can lead to the learner becoming confused and disaffected 'as if I had picked (the child) up from her stepping stone and placed her far away down the stream, leaving her powerless to know where she was, how she got there or how she could use that pathway again' (Stewart 2011: 89). However, the *clarification* of connections between existing understanding and new understanding can speed some children in certain situations more swiftly towards their personal learning objectives. Practitioners have to make instant decisions like these – what does this child need from me now? – every moment of their working day. Knowing children well enables practitioners to choose the right strategy at the right moment.

The expertise of the child's first educators

We have seen that young children's early learning is not only the result of their own predispositions to learn, but also the result of interactions with significant others in their family and their community at large (Rogoff 1990). It is important to appreciate the strategies that parents use which make them such successful educators, very often without realizing it. A series of influential research projects in the 1980s (e.g. Bruner 1980; Tizard and Hughes 1984; Wells 1985) investigated children's talk in the home and compared it with talk in a variety of early years settings. The projects were consistent in finding that children spoke more, expanded more and responded more in the home situations in these studies than they did in their various playgroups, nursery classes and nursery schools. The researchers came to some common conclusions that should provoke early childhood educators to reflect on what might be learned from the success of those who engage children in dialogue in the home. I have summarized some of the key findings from these projects in order to reflect on their implications:

1 Home conversations **'arise from the moment'**. They are embedded in real-life situations and events of immediate interest and relevance to the child.
2 At home, **children initiate conversations** to which parents respond and not the other way round. In turn, the parent is more likely to continue a topic from the child's previous utterance and extend the topic in conversation with the child (rather than change it).

3 The parent is frequently **part of the context** in which the child is exploring or thinking. Consequently the parent is uniquely placed to respond appropriately and genuinely to the child because they have shared the moment, the experience or the activity.
4 In the home, parents – and mothers in particular – **intuitively adjust their utterances** to the edge of their children's linguistic competence, introducing new and more challenging vocabulary and sentence structure, but keeping within the children's zone of understanding.
5 The response of parents is '**contingent' on the competence of the child**, increasing and decreasing the level of their help based on the knowledge the parent has about the confidence and capability of their child in given situations.
6 In the home, *children* **ask the questions** and the adults are there to supply the answers.

Following *his* research, Wells (1985) suggested that what is most important in the behaviour of the child's parents and other caretakers is sensitivity. Sensitivity to the child's current state – his or her level of communicative ability and immediate interests – and sensitivity to the meaning the child is endeavouring to communicate.

Studying children and their parents can offer those of us in educational settings many lessons about effective early learning. It is so important that practitioners draw on the expertise of parents and enable them to inform and to go on informing the school or setting about their child. It can be too easy to pay lip service to the notion of a partnership with parents, but early childhood educators should not forget that it is *they* who join the already established learning partnership that exists between the parent and their child.

How do young children learn?

The English Statutory Framework for the Early Years Foundation Stage (DfE 2012) reminds practitioners that while learning and development are sometimes compartmentalized artificially into discrete areas of learning, it is *how* children learn which determines their attitudes to and ultimate success as learners throughout their lives. So, while practitioners need to be expert in the progression of the different Prime and Specific Areas of Learning, they should be just as much – if not more – expert in encouraging those characteristics of effective teaching and learning that underpin every aspect of learning in the foundation stage:

• **playing and exploring**: children investigate and experience things and 'have a go';

- **active learning:** children concentrate and keep on trying if they encounter difficulties and enjoy achievements (what most early years specialists would refer to as dispositions to learning); and
- **creating and critical thinking:** children have and develop their own ideas, make links between ideas, and develop strategies for doing this (DfE 2012: 7).

These characteristics are drawn from a number of theorists who have tried over the years – with increasingly sophisticated evidence – to explain how young children learn. These are some of the most robust theories:

Young children learn by being active

Any personal study of young children reveals almost non-stop activity in the quest for skills, strategies and understandings. The work of Jean Piaget and other contemporary theorists of child development emphasizes that 'being active' does not necessarily mean 'moving around', however. Being active means that the young child *engages* with experiences, actively (as opposed to passively) bringing his or her existing knowledge and understanding to bear on what is currently under investigation. This sense of agency leads children both physically and cognitively to construct their own view of the world, to personalize their experiences and to apply their growing repertoire of skills and competences in ways that make sense to them as individuals (Piaget 1929; Bruce 2004).

Young children learn by exploring and investigating

As children strive to make sense of the world they draw on all of their senses. They touch and smell and listen and observe in order to accumulate an understanding of how the world works and the impact they and their actions have upon it (Pound 2005). These explorations and investigations help satisfy children's insatiable thirst for knowledge and understanding. They are constantly seeking solutions to problems and answers to questions. As they do so, they make mistakes and learn from these, using trial and error as a powerful strategy to make connections between their current understandings and what is new. They strive to be part of the real world – the 'grown-up' world – and are keen to learn the skills they think they need to be accepted into the culture and society of which they are a part (Rogoff 1990).

Young children learn by playing

Play is the most natural and, often, effective way in which young children learn – all over the world (Moyles 2010). It is intrinsically motivated (Hughes 2010) and, as such, is freely chosen by the child and lacks adult interference (although may well have adult support). Play allows children to gain mastery over and to be in control of their emerging skills and competences. Through play, children can make things happen – they can become another person; they can influence a situation or a story – and all of these experiences promote their confidence in and awareness of their own sense of agency. High quality play encourages children to develop their imagination, their creativity and their skills of problem-solving and, as such, is not something that merely occupies children but, in Tina Bruce's words, causes children to 'operate at their highest levels of functioning' (1991:11).

Young children learn by using language

The language development of young children is a staggering phenomenon. The increase in young children's vocabulary and their growing capacity to use language for a range of purposes are powerful evidence of an innate drive to make meaning and to communicate. The research of Gordon Wells and his team on the Bristol Language Study concluded that in the early stages children's linguistic systems are more or less in place and a basic vocabulary of several thousand words is acquired. From that point on, however, what is learned and the order in which it is learned become 'progressively more dependent on experience – on having opportunities to hear the relevant functions, meanings, and structure used appropriately and to use them oneself' (Wells 1986: 32).

Hart and Risley's research (1995) in the USA found that the spoken vocabulary of the children from professional families in their study, was larger than that recorded for the children in what they describe as 'welfare families'. By age 3, their research suggests, there is a difference as great as 20 million words between the number of words *heard* by children who come from families where they are spoken to and where they engage in talk to communicate and those where they do not. And the tragedy is that the fewer the words that are spoken to a child, the greater the percentage of those words that will be negative . . . 'Don't' . . . 'Stop' . . . 'No'.

The recent 'Hello campaign' for the national year of communication (2010) offered a harsh reminder of the implications for those children who do not have the advantage of conversation and the skills of communication from a young age:

- *Behaviour* Two-thirds of 7 to 14-year-olds with serious behaviour problems have language impairment.

- *Mental health* 40 per cent of 7 to 14-year-olds referred to child psychiatric services had a language impairment that has never been identified.
- *Criminality* 65 per cent of young people in young offender institutions have communication difficulties.

(http://www.thecommunicationtrust.org.uk/)

Language provides not only a means of acting on the world, but also for reflecting on that action in an attempt to understand it (Harlen 1985). Piaget argued that language is a *medium*, a method of representation within which thought takes place. Vygotsky, on the other hand, believed that speech transforms the way in which children learn, think and understand and is, therefore, a *tool* of thought (Wood 1998). The theories of Jerome Bruner draw and build on the work of both Piaget and Vygotsky. His assertion is that the internalization of language is an instrument of thought and that the very young child uses language 'almost as an extension of pointing'. All of these theories depend on the understanding that thought, action and language are inextricably bound together in children's development. The successful development of all three is dependent on experiences being embedded in what is meaningful for the child.

Young children learn by interacting with others

Children may well be active learners in a highly individualistic sense, but they construct their personal meanings within the framework of a social and cultural context (Vygotsky, 1978; Wood 1998). The young child is a social being, playing, talking and living alongside others, watching what they do and imitating them, questioning what is seen and responding to questioning, drawing on the knowledge and expertise of others to interpret and make meaning of experiences (Bandura 1977; Richards and Light 1986; Wells 1986; Dunn 1988; Rogoff 1990). Everything that young children learn is influenced by the culture in which they grow up and the community in which they live. The writing of Vygotsky emphasized the significance of social contexts for learning, whereby adults – or other more expert members of the community – help children to acquire skills and understandings that they might not accomplish, or accomplish less speedily, alone. Vygotsky refers to the gap between what children are able to do alone and what they can achieve with help, as the 'zone of proximal development'; in other words:

> the distance between the actual developmental level as determined by independent problem solving and the level of potential development as determined through problem solving under adult guidance or in collaboration with more capable peers.

> (Vygotsky 1978: 86)

The work of Jerome Bruner (1968, 1985, 1990) and Wood et al. (1976) extends this notion, adopting the metaphor 'scaffolding' to describe the guidance and inter-actional support given by the adult or expert until the child is able to take over tasks for themselves. In this model of learning, children are not passively absorbing the strategies of the adult, but take an active, inventive role (Smith 1993), reconstructing the tasks through their own understanding while the adult or educator provides what Bruner (1985) describes as a 'vicarious form of consciousness'.

Implications for classroom practice

What then are the implications for educational practice of the issues which this chapter has raised? What strategies do early childhood educators need to consider if they are to build on what is known about how young children learn and how children have learned successfully before starting in their setting?

Young children learn by being active

If young children learn naturally by being active and engaging in a range of exploratory experiences, then the primary responsibility of the school or early years setting is to plan opportunities that facilitate and support these instinctive strategies. Children need opportunities to engage with a range of materials and stimuli. They need time to explore, investigate and question. They need a range of play experiences and appropriate resources of good quality. They need the space to move around, to experiment, to create and to play. They need, in other words, a learning environment that offers concrete experiences that are relevant, meaningful and worthy of active involvement. If children are to continue their struggle to make sense of the world, then the world must be worth the struggle. Clearly, before children start school or playgroup or nursery or children's centre the incentive and motivation to learn have been sufficient. It is up to practitioners to make children's new learning environments equally relevant and worthwhile.

Young children learn by exploring and investigating

Young children are particularly drawn to exploring and investigating the real world. Despite the thousands of plastic resources available to purchase, children's fascinations often focus on feathers and worms and stones and pieces of wood. These natural materials are not only often beautiful in themselves, and very tactile, but have the power to be transformative – to be turned into anything that the child's imagination chooses. In the nursery or classroom, children should have the opportunity to explore and investigate both indoors and out. Outdoors, the world is waiting to be explored and, if properly landscaped and resourced, an outdoor area will provide endless experiences and raise countless questions and challenges. But the real world needs to brought far more frequently inside, or else children's experiences in the classroom will be fake and make little sense to them in relation to their real-life learning. All the materials that practitioners provide and the learning opportunities they initiate should be sufficiently provoking to engage children in worthwhile exploration and study. There should be opportunities to test things out, for trial and error and for making mistakes – and children should be utterly engrossed in such experiences as a daily part of their learning.

Young children learn by playing

The place of play in early childhood settings is crucial to successful learning (see Chapter 7). No other activity offers the richness and range of opportunities for development that well-planned and purposeful play can provide. But the planning and sense of purpose must be the child's. The moment an adult steps in with their agenda, their target, their goal, their objectives, then the child is robbed of the control that leads play to be so creative, imaginative and satisfying. Play offers children the opportunity to remain in control of their learning – as they have been since birth. To follow their own interests and preoccupations in an environment that is, all too often, planned for and dominated by adults and their agendas. But play is not only crucial for the child, it is also crucial for the practitioner. In play, practitioners see strengths in a child that they may never see in an adult-led situation. Practitioners may see children who shine when they can initiate their own learning but struggle when they have to follow an agenda determined by an adult. Practitioners see children using skills and strategies that an adult-led situation might never inspire. So, while adult-led learning has its strengths and its place, it is not sufficient. The absence of play in an early years setting impoverishes both children and practitioners.

Young children learn by using language

The work of Margaret Donaldson demonstrates the importance of young children's experiences being embedded in contexts that are meaningful to them (1978). Her work, and that of researchers studying the relationship between language development in the home and at school, emphasize the importance of the contexts in which the adult and the child have shared experiences in common from which to draw shared meanings (Anning 1991). Edwards and Mercer (1987) claim that the establishing of mutual understanding and shared meanings is something with which educators also must be concerned. They suggest that one of the points at which education commonly fails, is when 'incorrect assumptions are made about shared knowledge, meaning and interpretations' (1987: 60). Practitioners and children need to share a 'common knowledge' about the discourse that forms the basis for communication in the setting in order for the learning that comes from interaction to be most effective.

Children use language to learn and therefore learning environments must give them opportunities to use language in a variety of ways. It is language that affords young children the means of making sense of their experiences and of internalizing their actions. In order to capitalize on the power of language to influence both thought and action, experiences must encourage talk as a key process through which young children learn. It is heartening to see in recent government documentation fresh affirmation of the critical nature of speaking and listening as precursors for competence in reading and writing as well as for understanding across all curriculum areas and the development of good social relationships (DfES 2005; DfE 2012). Talking something through, either alone or with others, is an important way of grasping new ideas, understanding concepts or clarifying feelings and perceptions. Young children need opportunities for discussion, for explanation, for description, for narration and for speculation. In learning environments where talk is recognized as a powerful and natural medium for learning, young children are able to make meaning of what is new in terms of what is familiar. Through their talk, they create a context that is personal to them and one that relates to their own experiences. What they need are attentive, interested adults, ready to be a conversational partner and to model how satisfying it can be to share ideas, opinions and pleasurable experiences.

Young children learn by interacting with others

If learning is socially constructed, then early childhood educators clearly have a critical role, a role at one time devalued by misunderstandings about the nature of 'child-centredness' and 'discovery learning' (Blenkin and Kelly 1987). It is the skilled intervention of the practitioner which will move children from their present to their future potential. Interactions with children must facilitate this progress through Vygotsky's 'zone of proximal development' and practitioners must arrange things, says Athey (2007), so that knowledge is actively constructed and not simply copied. Early childhood educators need to have regular conversations with children, but these conversations must not interfere with children's thinking. When a child is busy thinking hard about what he or she is doing then they don't have the time or inclination to talk at the same time.

In child-led situations, any talk from the adult should illuminate children's thinking rather than interrogate it. In adult-led situations, however, there is sometimes a place for conversations designed to find out what children already know and understand (see Chapter 2) or to support, through questioning or answering questions, the child's current thinking. It is important in both situations that children and adults alike see themselves as co-constructors of knowledge where both parties contribute to an exchange of ideas and views and questions in order to come to new insights and fresh understandings.

Recent material from the Coram Family Research Unit on 'Listening to Children' (Lancaster and Kirby 2010) promotes adult–child relationships which uphold children's rights to be listened to as competent individuals who should have their views, concerns and aspirations taken into account and who should participate in decisions that are important to them. This influential work promotes the view that young children are competent to express their views and supports adults to increase their skills of listening so that children's voices are heard.

Other children are also part of this social construct, and practitioners have to look at 'the context in which learning takes place in schools *(sic)* as well as at the nature of specific learning tasks' (Pollard and Tann 1993). The topic of children working together and learning together is discussed fully in Chapter 6, but there is growing evidence of the importance of peer tutoring in classroom contexts – whether it is planned or not (see, for example, Forman and Cazden 1985; Galton and Williamson 1992; Rogoff and Toma 1997; Rogoff et al. 2003). Effective teaching acknowledges the role of *all* those who have knowledge and understandings to contribute to the development of individual learners.

Conclusion

When children start attending an educational setting they are already competent learners. Competence has evolved from the fusion of the child's natural predisposition to learn and the support he or she has received while learning from birth. This chapter suggests that those responsible for the more formal stages of children's education need to look to the characteristics of children's successful early learning environments in order to develop models of teaching that will lead to the continuation of effective learning throughout the child's educational journey. In the following chapter we examine how early childhood educators establish the range of competences that children bring from home and the wider world and how those educators come to find out what children already know about and can do.

Questions to Challenge your Thinking

1 How secure are your knowledge and understanding of child development? Are there ways this could be strengthened?
2 How do you – and how does your setting – keep up to date with the latest developments in scientists' understanding of the brain and its implications for early learning?
3 How do you promote the characteristics of early learning – *playing and exploring; active learning; creativity and critical thinking* – across all areas of learning?

2

OBSERVATIONS AND CONVERSATIONS

Learning about individual children

Introduction

If we acknowledge that children bring to their school or setting a wealth of skills, knowledge and understandings already established, then a key task of the early childhood educator is to identify precisely what these are in order to build on each child's existing competences and plan for their future learning. Acknowledging children's existing competences immediately defines the experiences of both adults and children. If children already know and can do a range of things, then the practitioner becomes a learner alongside the child. The practitioner must find out exactly what it is that children already know and can do in order to ensure that the learning environment and the curriculum experiences that are planned are appropriate for particular children. This leads to planning that is tailor-made for each child because the foundations of each child's learning are unique (Fisher 2000). Each child has his or her own personal history of experiences and opportunities, which will determine not only what is currently known, but what needs to be learned next, and how this will be done most effectively.

From the child's perspective, being seen as a competent learner means that practitioners have respect for what you have already achieved. Practitioners should be interested in how you view the world and how you make sense of the experiences you have. It should mean that your views and your ideas are listened to and treated with the respect they deserve. It should mean that your interests and fascinations have an important place in the learning day and that your preoccupations are given time and space to be properly pursued.

Establishing the starting points for children's educational experiences is not a task that takes place only when a child begins in their new school or setting. Practitioners need to establish the starting points for children's learning throughout their time in the setting as part of the ongoing cycle of teaching and learning. All too often in schools, in particular, the planned curriculum establishes its starting points from the learning objectives on written documentation, and considers 'previous experience' to be what has been 'covered' in previous teaching time. However, children continue to learn in and from a range of contexts that are nothing to do with educational settings, and it is always necessary to discover what knowledge and understanding children bring with them from other life experiences in order to plan a curriculum that matches their current learning needs.

The 'teacher' as learner

Placing themselves in the role of learner (*about* the child), effective early childhood practitioners make assessments of children's knowledge, skills and understandings before finalizing the planning of an appropriate curriculum. Often, assessment is seen as the end of the teaching process, undertaken to discover whether children have learnt what was planned and taught. However, an equally critical place for assessment is at the start of the cycle of teaching and learning, when practitioners find out what children already know and can do so that the next experiences planned are relevant and meaningful. Assessment is a tool that comes before and after learning. Before, it establishes what is currently known and after, it establishes what has been learnt that is new. This chapter is concerned with how practitioners establish what children already know and can do as well as how they intervene in the learning process to take children's learning forward. The first strategy is to make *observations* of the child in action as a learner. The second is to have *conversations* with the child – and others – about the child's learning.

Making observations

Children are naturally active learners (Bruce 1987; EYCG 1992; McNaughton and Williams 2009) so it is imperative that, to learn about them, early childhood educators watch them in action. It is particularly important to do this when children are in their early years of learning because no other strategy will give the practitioner sufficient evidence of children's development and progress. While teachers of older children can collect in books or set assignments, those who work with younger children know that what can be written and recorded at this stage is little or nothing in comparison to what a young child knows and understands. Therefore, if practitioners cannot – and should not – rely on written evidence, then they must rely on their eyes and their ears to gather the evidence they need.

Children should be observed while they are engaged in a wide range of activities and in a variety of learning contexts. These should involve and include children learning:

- in familiar learning contexts;
- in environments that encourage confidence and build self-esteem;
- alongside a range of peers;
- alongside an adult;
- independently;
- when an activity is initiated by an adult;
- when an activity is initiated by the child;
- at different times of the day and week;
- indoors and outdoors.

Familiar learning contexts

If educators are to observe children and to have conversations with them in contexts in which they will be at their best, then it is necessary for the environment in which these activities take place to be familiar and comfortable (Fisher 2012a). None of us perform well – or at least naturally – if we feel insecure in new surroundings and with new people. Children need to feel at ease in their environment and to feel confident in the people around them to show what they know and like and can do. This is important to remember when children have just made a transition from one setting to another (Brooker 2002; 2008; Fabian and Dunlop 2002; Dunlop and Fabian 2007; Fisher 2010). Even if it is from the preschool across the playground or the class down the corridor there will be so many strange and unfamiliar things to which children will be giving their attention that they will not necessarily have the concentration to show off their learning powers. It is easy to forget just what preoccupies children when they are uncertain. In Oxfordshire we asked our 4-year-olds what they felt about starting school (OCC 2005) and then every reception year child what they felt about moving into Year 1 (OCC 2006). The responses reminded us so powerfully that far from being concerned with the curriculum or planning and assessment procedures, the children were preoccupied with toilets, spiders (mainly in the same context), where to put their coats and lunch boxes, being knocked over in the playground, their new teacher and being with their friends. Young children need to be helped to feel secure by adults who listen to their concerns, their aspirations and their views and who understand that these must be attended to before any effective learning can take place. It is also a strong reminder that planning for transitions must take account of the voices of children and their parents and carers, every bit as much as of the practitioners involved (Fisher 2006; 2010).

There are some children for whom the new and unfamiliar poses a particular challenge. These are the children made vulnerable or traumatized by their life experiences and situations. For such children, transitions can dredge up old fears and current uncertainties. They have a low threshold of resilience to change and may not have developed the protective factors that enable them to adapt easily to what is new (Pugh 2002). As we saw in Chapter 1, there are children in almost every classroom and early years setting who may find change difficult because they did not have secure attachments to caring adults in the first two years of their lives (Robinson 2003; Gerhardt 2004; 2010); children whose parents were too ill, too busy or too neglectful to respond to their children in ways which made their babies secure and soothed. There are children who cannot cope with transitions in school or preschool because change is a painful and constant factor of their home lives: children who are taken into care and then returned to birth families; children fleeing to a refuge, and then returning home; children being sent out of the blue to family members because a parent falls ill, and then being returned without warning when that parent comes home. Not knowing where you live, to whom you belong, who will be there for you at the end of a day requires constant readjustment and vigilance. This can result in a thin veil between coping and collapsing, or an impenetrable wall to guard against future hurt (Karen 1994; Smith 1995; Cairns 2002). These multiple transitions in children's home lives can damage the capacity to attach to new people and manage new situations and will make the task of facing a transition in school or in their early years setting all the harder to deal with (O'Connor 2012). Then there are those children who are normally settled and secure and for whom a tragic experience can be suddenly undermining, leaving them vulnerable and open to uncertainty. Loss, separation or bereavement in its many forms can cause even the strongest child to find yet another transition one thing too many to bear. For vulnerable children the need to have learning environments that are secure, engaging and playful is crucial (Read 2010). Practitioners need to be reliable and expectations adaptable. Practitioners must be sensitive to what may be innocuous to a secure child but cause deep trauma to another. Everyday early childhood experiences such as bringing in photos of when you were a baby if you are adopted and you do not have any; being asked to bring in your most treasured possession when, as a refugee you had to leave everything behind when your family fled; the class making Mother's Day cards when your own mum has died a few months before, can all set back the learning of a vulnerable child and cause them unnecessary hurt and upset.

An environment that encourages confidence and builds self-esteem

Young children's attitudes and feelings are crucial to their achievement in all aspects of life. It is important that those working in the field of early childhood education fight to preserve the affective domains of the curriculum and to sustain the social and emotional aspects of children's development. It is for profoundly important reasons that personal, social and emotional development (PSED) continues to be placed at the heart of the early years curriculum. The recent Statutory Framework for the EYFS (DfE 2012) reminds us that, together with communication and language and physical development, PSED is 'particularly crucial for igniting children's curiosity and enthusiasm for learning, and for building their capacity to learn, form relationships and thrive' (DfE 2012: 4). Rosemary Roberts (1995a) examines how children's feelings affect their attitudes to school and shows how self-esteem can be the key to effective teaching and learning. As early childhood educators we can help to build self-esteem through the responses that we give to children and to their ideas, opinions and efforts. This does not mean heaping them with empty praise but supporting them in the self-assessment of their achievements and encouraging them in the development of their abilities (see Box 2.1).

Box 2.1   Example 1: Responding to children's work

A teacher of a vertically grouped class of Year 1 and Year 2 children wanted to develop the children's ability to evaluate their own work. She wanted them to move away from relying on her for decisions about whether what they had done was 'enough' or 'good enough'. She suspected that this reliance stemmed from the fact that, as she had set the tasks, the children believed that only she could judge the quality of the results. So she decided to change the entire way in which she introduced activities to the class. After the initial discussion and the introduction of the activity she would ask the children what they thought was important in completing the task. She supported the children in thinking through the processes, the skills, the knowledge and the understandings they might need to demonstrate in the course of the activity and what the outcomes might be. They then

---

decided which of these were the most important and these were recorded on a large sheet of paper and left pinned to the wall. At the end of the session the children would gather with their work and then review their own efforts against the criteria, which the class had collectively compiled. In this way the children were developing their personal responses to their own work and in the process were being challenged to use their initiative and to take responsibility for their learning and its outcomes. The teacher reported growing confidence and self-esteem as the children became involved in setting their own criteria for achievement in this way.

To have positive self-esteem children need self-confidence and this can be developed most powerfully when children are encouraged to use their initiative, to make decisions and to be responsible for sharing in the planning and the evaluation of their own work. If we want children to develop positive self-esteem, then we have to show them that they are capable, however young they are, of decisions that have an impact on their own experiences and their own lives. The United Nations Convention on the Rights of the Child (1989) recognizes all children's need for special protection because of their age and vulnerability. However, it also recognizes their competences and their right to have their views listened to and respected (Articles 12 and 13). Children whose voices are heard grow in confidence and self-esteem (Lancaster and Kirby 2010). Sometimes practitioners must listen more carefully to those whose voices are uncertain. Liz Brooker's research for *Starting School: Young Children Learning Cultures* (2002) demonstrates how disempowering it can be for children when there is a clash of culture between home and school. She writes of the experiences of Bangladeshi children making the transition from their home culture to school and how parenting practices, perspectives on childhood and beliefs about work and play all make a difference to how the children adapt to their new learning environment. As educators we must be aware of our children's histories, their cultures and their life experiences. Children who are proud of their cultural heritage, their gender, their family and themselves have been profoundly affected by the attitudes of those around them and the early years practitioner is a critical part of that network of influence (Siraj-Blatchford 1994; Lane 2008). If we are to make observations of children that reflect the best that they can do, and in which they have the confidence to share with us what they know, then we must give them an environment that encourages their confidence and builds their self-esteem.

A range of peers

Early years practitioners are also concerned with the social development of children. As with all other aspects of their development, the social experiences of children before they start at school or their early years setting will vary enormously. Some may have come from large, extended family groups, including brothers, sisters, uncles, aunts and grandparents. Some may have had significant periods of time with childminders or at a day nursery and have become used to playing and being alongside their peers. For some children, however, their new school or nursery or children's centre will be their first introduction to the competition, collaboration and cooperation that are required when you are one among a number of others, all vying for space, resources and attention. Like all skills, being sociable is something you get better at with practice. The more people you meet, the more you learn to adjust and adapt to differences in attitudes and behaviour. Some adults are better at this than others; some children are better at this than others. Home circumstances, life experiences and general dispositions will mean that certain children are ready to manage a range of social situations while others need support to increase their social skills (Dowling 2010). The more opportunities children have to learn alongside the full range of children in their group or class, the more opportunities they will have to learn those social skills that will make life in the setting, and life in general, a more positive and pleasurable experience. Children should be supported to communicate and cooperate with a range of others irrespective of their gender, race, physical attributes or ability. A profile of the social development of the child is best founded on observations of children alongside a range of peers, demonstrating a whole range of characteristics, attitudes and behaviours.

Children working with an adult

There will be many opportunities for early childhood educators to observe children while they are working and playing alongside them. By supporting a child, or facilitating their activity, the practitioner is able to observe and, if appropriate, to record what the child says and what the child does as evidence of their growing conceptual awareness or skill development. Practitioners can also observe *how* the child approaches tasks, what strategies they use for solving problems, their persistence and motivation and their dispositions in general. What has to be remembered is that the presence of the practitioner will, to a lesser or greater degree, alter the behaviour of the child; to what extent depends on the task and also on the sensitivity of the practitioner. If a child is engaged in an adult-initiated activity and that adult is close by, then the child may frequently look to the adult for affirmation that they are doing the task 'right'. Some research in a reception class (Fisher 1996) illustrated the impact of the task on children's reliance on the teacher (see Box 2.2).

Box 2.2   Example 2: Building independence

As a researcher, I spent one day a week for two years in the same Reception class, observing the interactions throughout the day between the teacher and members of her class. There was very clear evidence that the more directed the task, the more frequently the child went to the teacher for help and, particularly, affirmation. As the teacher's aim was to make the children more independent and to give herself more time to focus on her planned activities, this observation presented her with an instant strategy for achieving both aims at once. If she wanted to be less interrupted, and have time to work with particular children or do an observation, then the rest of the class had to be engaged in tasks which were less prescriptive and over which they had more control. The teacher changed the balance in the activities she planned. The activities where there was an adult present were more directed and the activities where children were working independently were more open-ended. Once this new way of planning was established, the teacher reported far fewer interruptions by children engaged in independent activities.

When an early years practitioner gives a child a task and then sits with them while they tackle it, or when they come alongside some work or play that is already in process, then the child's approach to that activity and the amount of support they look for will undoubtedly alter because of the practitioner's presence. This is not to say that a practitioner should not work and play alongside a child – far from it. The practitioner's role in supporting, challenging, guiding and extending children's learning in all situations is critical (see Chapters 1 and 4), but it is important to be sensitive to the impact the presence of a practitioner can have on the process and outcome of any activity.

Children working independently

When children play or work independently, they display different behaviours and often different strategies and skills than when they work under the direction of a practitioner. Dependent upon how much independence they are used to, an observation of children working or playing alone usually reveals fresh insights into the children as learners. Whatever the task, the conversations of children working independently usually reveal far more than is revealed when they engage in tasks where practitioners are present. A group of children or an individual child might be engaged in child-initiated learning or they might be responding to an activity initiated by a practitioner, but their own unique way of looking at the world, the connections they make with their previous understandings and their prior learning experiences will all impact on the process and the outcomes of that activity because of the child's greater levels of control. The observation of independent learning offers practitioners another view of the child as a learner – their strengths and their approaches to learning – and also offers valuable insights into how to plan for that child in a more adult-led situation.

Adult-initiated and child-initiated activity

Observations of children need to encompass activities that have been self-initiated and those that have been initiated by the practitioner. Self-initiated activity gives children opportunities to make choices and decisions of their own. It enables children to demonstrate their independence as well as their social skills in choosing to work with others. Self-initiated activity gives children control over situations, and sometimes their peers, and puts children in rare positions of learning power (Warham 1993; Claxton 2002). Appropriately resourced and supported, child-initiated activity can bring about some of the most creative and innovative learning in the classroom (Whitehead 1993).

In adult-initiated activities there are opportunities for children to work alone or with a variety of peers for a range of purposes. Adult-initiated learning is more focused (by the adult) than child-initiated learning and the practitioner plans an activity addressing specific elements of the curriculum or specific skills. However, because children are left for periods of time to work without an adult by their side, adult-initiated activities still enable children to show their own thinking, to demonstrate independence and self-management and to show how well they can persevere and maintain concentration without constant supervision. Much of this depends on the quality of the activities planned (see Chapter 4), but both kinds of experience – adult-initiated and child-initiated – are important and one without the other will not give children sufficiently broad and balanced opportunities for learning. Different children will shine in different learning contexts, and practitioners will see different strengths displayed in those different contexts. Neither adult-led learning nor child-led learning is sufficient on its own. Young child have a natural drive to learn independently and to discover things for themselves and this must be harnessed and optimized in any early learning environment. But skilled and experienced practitioners are always necessary to introduce children to what is new and what needs explanation; to describe and name and model; to support and facilitate and extend (see Chapter 4). One learning context without the other will not give the early childhood educator a sufficiently rounded picture of the child as a learner.

Different times of the day

Children are no different from adults: some are 'larks' – those who wake up bright and perky and cheerful straight away, and some are 'owls' – those who begin sluggishly, but improve as the day goes on. Observation of children at different times in the day shows us that some children take a long time to settle in the morning, while others can concentrate almost immediately. There are many children who are adversely affected by breaks in the learning day – assembly, PE, and so on – whereas others seem to take these in their stride. Many children are affected by playtimes and lunchtimes and take a long time to settle afterwards. My reception class research showed that it can be the period from break to lunchtime that is the most disrupted. After lunchtime, children are tired but usually more able to settle to their various tasks than after break when they are still wound up from rushing around, and need more intervention from adults to engage in their activities (Fisher 1996). It would benefit all primary schools in particular, to review their school timetables to see just how many interruptions to learning children experience (Fisher 2010). The great advantage of the planned provision in the best quality early years settings is that there are long periods of time for sustained experience and activity, uninterrupted by such things as playtime and assembly. Young children need time to develop their thinking and to explore what is intriguing and preoccupying them at that moment. Practitioners know well that if a child's attention has been taken by an unexpected incident or by a preoccupation with something outside the classroom or nursery, then the child will not focus on any planned activity until their curiosity and interest in the unexpected have dwindled. Likewise, being removed from a learning experience just when it becomes intriguing and just when the child has become deeply engaged, is both frustrating and counter-productive. Young children often take longer to become engrossed in something because they can take a while to make sense of new resources, experiences and situations. When much of the world is still new and maybe confusing, then finding the right pieces of the cognitive jigsaw can take time. The wise practitioner gives a child sufficient time to enquire, investigate, explore and play so that the child reaches their own satisfactory conclusions (with or without adult intervention) without being disrupted just at the most important moment of personal discovery.

Young children will be at their best at different times of the day as well as in different learning situations, and so it is important that when we observe them we take this into account. One legacy of the literacy and numeracy strategies in England (DfES http://www.standards.dfes. gov.uk/primary/) is that many primary schools have retained timetables that devote the morning session up until break time to literacy, and the session from break until lunch to numeracy (or the other way round). Despite the fact that Reception classes are supposed to follow the principles of the Early Years Foundation Stage (DfE 2012), too many schools still organize and manage the learning of the youngest children as though they were the first year of the primary school. First, as has been said, young children need sustained periods of uninterrupted learning in order to consolidate or to discover or to make the necessary connections between what is new and what is already understood. If this time is interrupted, then the threads of young children's thinking can be lost, and frustration and confusion can occur.

Second, young children's learning is not naturally compartmentalized. When children discover and explore for themselves they cross the boundaries of mathematics and science, physical skills and creative development. To segregate learning into subjects can confuse young children at times and, at others, prevent children from seeing the natural overlap and connections between their learning because of the false delineations that adults have drawn. Third, for young children, doing the same as the rest of the class is doing is not always helpful. Literacy, for example, is a very adult-dependent area of learning at this age. It is not something that children come to as naturally as most other areas – such as creative development, or scientific enquiry – and as such it usually depends on the practitioner to introduce it and explain it and teach it. If a practitioner is working with one group on an adult-led literacy activity, such as phonological awareness, then other children are frequently best engaged in something that is not so adult-dependent and which they can manage independently with greater ease.

A young child's learning day should have an ebb and flow: between what a practitioner asks them to do and what they want to do; between what requires a lot of concentration because it is new and maybe tricky and that which is familiar and affirming and can be done more easily; between what is consolidation of something already known and experienced and what is new and provoking; between what depends on adult input and what can be done better independently. When children's learning is determined by timetables rather than naturally moving on to and between different experiences then this can give children the impression that all learning is compartmentalized and chopped up in this false fashion. It also means that the child who has not finished their maths, for example, is then expected to switch to something else without the satisfaction of completion while other children are given more and more 'extension work' (far too often in the form of worksheets) in order to 'keep them going' until the clock says that lesson can finish.

Timetables frequently stop children learning (see Fisher 2010). They stop them, tidy them up, line them up, move them on, unline and unpack them again and, in among all this disruption, young children who are often not much more than 48 months old are expected to manage. It is little wonder that many children, particularly in Reception and Key Stage 1 classes, find school learning difficult and confusing. Young children need a day without unnatural breaks. They need learning experiences that flow naturally from one to the other in the course of which they are encouraged and not inhibited from seeing the links between their learning. Most of all, they need practitioners who are sufficiently knowledgeable about child development to see clearly the interference that timetables cause and to plan a learning day that enhances rather than obstructs children's learning.

Indoors and outdoors

Finally, young children need to be observed learning outside as well as inside. As with the difference between adult-led and child-led learning, the learning that takes place indoors and outdoors can offer children very different experiences (see Bilton 2002; Wellhousen 2002; White 2008) and can offer practitioners very different perspectives on the child. For a rounded profile of each child, the early childhood educator should take the time to watch how the child tackles their learning in an environment that offers more space, a different deployment of physical energy, a closer relationship with the natural world and, in the best outdoor environments, places to be where adults cannot be seen, dens, gazebos, bushes and tunnels.

This means that adults need to be where children are. It is inappropriate for the teacher or room leader to remain inside while the teaching assistant is sent to the outside area. Nothing sends signals so clearly about the status of different areas of provision than where practitioners are deployed. All practitioners, but certainly those in charge, should see all children learn in every environment. The outdoors, if it is well designed and resourced, will offer children opportunities that the indoors never can – and the early childhood educator needs to be there to see them. Only through close observation of different environments can the practitioner plan to resource, facilitate or extend children's learning further. Outdoor environments where teachers or lead practitioners do not regularly observe are those that have the same equipment, the same opportunities, day in and day out and leave children frustrated and bored. There should be no area of the environment in a good early years setting that is not observed, evaluated and improved regularly by all the practitioners who work with and on behalf of the children.

Having conversations

In order to get to know the child well; in order to have robust starting points for planning and preparing for children's learning experiences and in order to know what kind of support a child needs and wants, early childhood practitioners need to have conversations with every child as an individual. In addition, it can be valuable to have conversations with the range of people who also have knowledge of the child as a learner and will offer different perspectives.

Conversations with children

Successful conversations with children are based on relationships where practitioners listen respectfully to what children have to say (Cousins 1999; Chilvers 2006; Fisher 2012a). Conversations with children – where children do most of the talking – provide early childhood educators with evidence of children's responses to learning and to experiences. They offer the child's version of what has been experienced – not the *intended* learning outcomes, but the *actual* learning outcomes. They reveal how children have approached an activity or experience, what they found interesting, what strategies they used for making sense of the world and where any misunderstandings might be. They reveal what children are currently thinking about, rather than what they are doing, and show how learning for young children is a constant process of making sense of previous experience – with comments and questions that frequently relate not to what has just happened, but to experiences or incidents that took place a considerable time ago.

Conversations with children give practitioners hard evidence of children's development. When children have to put into words what they have experienced and learnt, then their responses give clear messages to the practitioner about what is known and understood and what needs to be planned for the future. At this age, as has been said, what the child says provides more detailed and reliable information than what the child records. Indeed, at this age, written evidence can present a very impoverished version of children's knowledge and understanding. Young children can be limited by their capacity to record, to write or draw what they have done or understood. They can be limited by their understanding of the task or the worksheet. They can be limited by the page or sheet that simply requires that boxes are filled in and leaves no space for their original thoughts or interpretations. Since the foundation stage in schools and settings has been subjected to inspection by the Office for Standards in Education (Ofsted) there has been great concern among early years practitioners that evidence of children's achievements must be in written form. It is often believed that a child's picture, model or talk does not carry the same weight as a piece of writing, and worksheets are increasingly in evidence. This is very misguided. A child is a far more complex learner than can ever be evidenced by a worksheet. If practitioners want to have evidence of what a child knows and understands, then they must collect the richest and most powerful evidence available – the child's own actions and the child's own words. Conversations with children offer the practitioner a marvellous assessment opportunity as they reveal needs *and* interests, and can be a critical moment in the cycle of teaching and learning.

It is crucial, however, that conversations are meaningful to the child and that the practitioner genuinely wants to find out about what he or she is asking about. Questions should elicit answers that the practitioner does not already know, otherwise the questioning technique is simply being used as a checking device, to discover whether children are paying attention or not (Fisher 2012d). Young children are all too aware of whether adults' questions are genuine. This is scathingly exemplified by 5-year-old Sonnyboy who responded to his teacher's meaningless questioning with a question of his own: 'Why do you keep asking the kids questions when you knows all the answers? Like . . . like . . . what colour is it then? You can see for yourself it's red . . . so why do you keep asking them?' (Cousins 1990: 30).

Skilful, open-ended questioning leads children to share their own thoughts, ideas and perceptions with the practitioner and teaches the adult something more about the child. But effective questioning is not about checking that a child has absorbed the adult's teaching points but should show that the practitioner is joining in the child's own quest for knowledge and understanding. Such questions:

- stimulate children's curiosity and thinking;
- challenge children to modify their ideas;
- generate a fresh point of view;
- take children's learning forward;
- ensure the process is given more emphasis than the outcomes.

However, even open-ended questions have their limitations. There are times when even the best questions interrupt children's thinking and Jerome Bruner suggests 'When a child is thinking hard about what he's doing, elaborating his play, he is not *talking* about it but *doing* it' (1980: 63). The research project in which I am currently engaged (Fisher and Wood 2012) has evidence to show that often practitioners talk to children when what children need more is time to think. Practitioners talk when what would help children more is a period of quiet to work things out for themselves. Practitioners talk to make themselves feel more secure and so that they feel as though they are doing 'something worthwhile'. Practitioners talk because they are trying to lead a child towards an early learning goal when maybe the child's interests lie elsewhere. Deciding whether and when to intervene is key in the effective support of children's learning and a question at the wrong time can simply interfere with, rather than enhance, children's thinking.

Evidence from this research project also shows that, in order to engage young children in conversations that illuminate and challenge their thinking, there are strategies that work more effectively than questioning. Questions often lead to quite brief answers from children, even when they are engaged in the discussion, for example:

Teacher: *(with group looking at nest in bush)* How do you know what was in there?

Boy 1 (5:1): 'Cos it's made out of feathers and sticks

Teacher: Feathers and sticks . . . is that what a nest is made from?

Boy 1: Yeh

Girl 1 (4:11): Just sticks

Teacher: Just sticks you think. Do you think they put the feathers in?

Girl 2 (5:1): No, it comes off them

Although these children are excited about the discovery of the nest and they are attending to the teacher's questions and answering them, the questions are doing little more than 'checking' what the children already know.

Questions can also interrupt children's learning when they have little relevance to what children are actually concentrating on at the time, for example:

Teacher: *(talking to children hunting for 'treasure' planted by her in sandpit)*
What did you use these for? (picking up a pair of tweezers)

Boy 1 (4:7): Umm *(keeping on searching for treasure)* . . . I think . . .

Teacher: What did they help you to do?
(no answer)

Teacher:	What did they help you to do? What did they help you to do, William?
Boy 1:	Umm . . .
Girl 1 (4:9):	I got, I got, I got lots of treasure!

The children are far too excited about 'finding the treasure' to want to talk about the tweezers, which were not the 'point' of the activity for them. Practitioners need to ensure their questions 'tune in' to what children are *thinking* about, rather than just what they are *doing*.

It seems that, when the practitioner makes a statement or offers the child information, rather than asking them a direct question, then the child's thinking flows more freely and their responses are richer and more informative:

Teacher:	*(discussing a model bus the child is making)* My dad has got a spare tyre on the roof of his car.
Child (4:9):	My dad hasn't. And I've got two dads. I've got a step dad called Phil who picks me up and I've got another dad who lives at my Nanny Brenda's. That's his mum's. That's my nanny.

Teacher:	*(commenting on a child's use of a piece of wood for changing a baby's nappy in role play)* Some people like to use a changing mat because it's softer for the baby's back.
Child (3:8):	*(still using the wood)* My mum uses them an' she puts our babies on the floor on the mat and she tickles the babies' toes.

In these two scenarios above, the child has made a choice about whether to respond or not. They have taken in what the adult has said and made their own connections in their own time rather than feeling that an adult is waiting for an 'answer'. The responses themselves may have an obvious connection to what the practitioner has said or may trigger thought processes in the child that need to be acknowledged and responded to, in turn, by the practitioner. It is as though the business of answering a question puts the child on the spot. What is the answer the practitioner wants? What does the practitioner mean by that question? How can I express what I think so s/he'll understand? All of this seems to inhibit children's responses to questions at times, whereas the response to a statement or comment is in the hands of the child, there is less pressure, and the child does not feel the need to try and work out what the 'right answer' might be.

There are, of course, a number of occasions when questions illuminate children's thinking and effectively sustain conversations without causing the child to feel they are searching for one 'right' answer. Such questions are usually used by the practitioner to clarify what the child is meaning in order to stay tuned in to their thinking. Exchanges like the one below are effective because they are built on close and respectful relationships and because the practitioner has a genuine interest in what the child is saying, in their thinking and in the connections they are making:

Teacher: So is Rover a real dog?

C (4:10):   Mmm

T: If he goes like this 'urhm' 'uhrm' – why does he do that and not 'woof woof huhuhuhu' (panting)?

C: Because he's not – because he's not really – that's how he's made. He wasn't made to go 'wof wof wof', he was made to go 'uhrm' 'uhrm'.

T: Who made Rover?

C: Ribble . . . because they both had instructions. Ribble made Rover and Ted 'cos she – she's got instructions in case they both got broken and Ribble could follow the instructions to make them again.

T: So Rover the dog is a kind of Robot dog, is he?

C: Yeah – and Ted – Ted's a Robot dog – robot, but he talks like us and doesn't have a gas mask, he doesn't breathe gas.

T: Perhaps he doesn't breathe anything at all?

C: Well, he must breathe *something*.

T: Perhaps robots don't have lungs – don't need air – don't need oxygen?

This exchange, taken from an MA dissertation by my colleague Sue Vermes (2008), shows how effective questions challenge children's thinking – *'perhaps he doesn't breathe anything at all?'* – and extend their understanding of the world – *'Perhaps robots don't have lungs – don't need air – don't need oxygen'* – without taking over the child's agenda and without interfering with the flow of their thoughts.

Effective conversations with children usually stem from an individual child's interests and observations and are sustained by the genuine, natural response of an attentive adult. When conversations flow in this relaxed way, the practitioner is able to learn far more about the child than when an exchange is dominated by the practitioner and keeps to their planned agenda.

Conversations with others

As well as conversations with the child, the child's learning journey is illuminated and informed by a number of other conversations with those whom the child lives and learns alongside – parents and/or carers as well as other adults who support the child's learning. Having a range of conversations gives practitioners a variety of perspectives on each child and these perspectives help to form a rounded and balanced profile of the child as a learner. Each perspective is valid and needs to be valued, and each contributes something fresh to the practitioner's understanding of the child and their needs. Putting together this profile is rather like undertaking a detective investigation as the practitioner gathers together the pieces of the evidence that they need in order to make hypotheses and judgements upon which to proceed in their work. Conversations with other adults will provide information about:

- what interests the child;
- what motivates the child to learn;
- how the child perceives him or herself as a learner;
- how the child goes about the business of learning;
- what the child already knows about and can do;
- what the child would like to know about or do.

Conversation with parents

Parents and carers bring knowledge of the child in a variety of contexts which the early childhood educator may never be privileged to see. A good case for home visiting is made when practitioners recount what they have learnt from seeing the child in the surroundings of their own home, and how relationships change when parents meet teachers on their own territory (see Edwards and Redfern 1988, for a very practical account of the development of partnerships with parents, and Liz Brooker 2002, who traces the learning experiences of Bangladeshi families in London through the eyes of the children and families as well as the school).

Conversations with parents should take place well before the child starts at their new school or setting, when the child starts and at regular points throughout the child's time in the setting. The conversations need to acknowledge the expertise that parents have about their own children and the understanding that parents have about their children's current needs and interests (Hutchin 2007). They should be respectful of the parents' own perspectives and not seek to mould the parents' views to coincide with those of the setting. If early years practitioners want to know about children in order to build on the children's existing abilities, then a significant part of that knowledge comes from the home, and practitioners need to acknowledge this by providing a range of opportunities to listen to and record parental knowledge, attitudes and ideas. Parents have a fresh, different and crucial perspective on their child's development, their attitudes to learning and their growing skills and competences. We all know that children can behave as two different beings – both in attitude and approach – at home and in the setting, and it is an impoverished profile of the child as a learner which only takes account of the child in the context of the school, preschool or nursery.

> It would not make sense to try to educate a child without taking account of the most significant people in his/her environment, and trying to work with them. It is through the home context that school becomes meaningful, or not, to a family.
>
> (Bruce 1991: 15)

Before children start school/setting

From the time a family first makes contact with a school or setting, or that school or setting first makes contact with a family, there are opportunities for a dynamic partnership to be established. To enable this to develop, foundation stage settings could offer some of the following:

- an invitation to use resources, a toy library and/or to borrow books;
- invitations to special events such as performances or fêtes;
- invitations to share amenities such as a hall or family room.

These informal contacts are invaluable for building confidence between parents, children and staff. From such beginnings a more formal induction process can evolve naturally.

Parental entitlement

Each setting needs to think carefully about how they help *all* parents and children to feel valued and welcomed at the beginning of their school life. Practitioners may want to consider the extent to which, in their setting, parents have an entitlement to:

- share their greater knowledge of their child, prior to entry, and throughout their time in the setting;
- enter a partnership with the setting which takes account of differences in culture, language and style;
- sufficient time and opportunity for regular formal and informal communication with staff;
- dialogue with practitioners where their opinions and ideas are listened to, valued and have influence;
- communicate their aspirations for their children;
- comment on and contribute to the records of their child's achievements in all areas of development.

Parental partnership

In order to facilitate a partnership with parents, foundation stage settings may need to initiate many or all of the following strategies:

- visit families at home (remembering that some parents may prefer to meet in the school or setting);
- design an entry profile for completion by parents and children;
- use photographs and/or a video camera to record everyday and special events;
- communicate aims and routines using visual material;
- share activities taking place in the setting by making a range of small books;
- use home/setting diaries, either audio-taped or written and using community languages where desirable;
- organize a range of times during the day and evening for meetings and appointments;
- organize a crèche for younger children;
- arrange for someone at meetings who can speak the community languages;
- enable an outreach worker/key worker/friend to attend with a family if support is required;
- adopt a flexible and imaginative response to the needs of families and the community;
- recognize the diversity of values within the wider community;
- give parents opportunities to express their own expectations of the setting;
- give parents opportunities to express their hopes for their children both inside and apart from the setting;
- give parents opportunities to express their own fears and misgivings;
- ask parents to describe:
  - their child's interests,
  - what their child can do,
  - their child's health,
  - what is special to the child,
  - what the child hopes to do at the setting,
  - their child's likes and dislikes,
  - the history of their child's experiences,
  - their child's friends,
  - people who are important to the child,
  - what the child fears about the setting;
- share the strengths and achievements of the child in the setting;
- discuss ways in which parents and the setting can work together to support the child's learning.

Conversations with parents can benefit all parties concerned. It benefits early childhood practitioners because of their increased knowledge of the child, it benefits parents by making them genuine partners in their child's learning, and it benefits children, who see home and their setting as mutually interested in their education.

Conversations with other adults

The third group of people with whom early years educators need to have conversations is those other adults who have experience of the child as a learner before or during their time in the setting. Individual children may, for different reasons, be receiving help from a speech therapist or a social worker and the experiences of these other professionals can illuminate the practitioner's understanding of difficulties the child may be having or strategies that might work better for him or her in class. Reception age children may have been diagnosed as needing additional support while in school. It is crucial that the teacher does not send these children off for this additional support without making connections with the adults involved and having conversations with them about what has been learned about the children in this different context. It is particularly important that practitioners talk to adults offering this additional support as too often children who are most in need of learning that is continuous and makes sense to them are pulled out in the middle of a lesson and do not complete their class's work, and are then catapulted back into the middle of another lesson having missed the beginning of it and never quite catch up. Schools need to be far more aware of discontinuity in the experiences of children who most need learning to have some sense of order and where connections in learning are clearly made. Conversations with other adults who spend learning time with children can strengthen the assessments of a child's key practitioner and ensure continuity and cohesion.

The purpose of observations and conversations

Early childhood educators who want to find out about children choose strategies that tell them most about the individual child. Unless those strategies leave room for the practitioner to learn from the process, then the strategies will not be informative but merely affirmative. Practitioners come to know what they already know and teaching remains rooted in *assumptions* about what children need to know next.

Having made an observation or recorded important elements of a conversation, the practitioner needs to translate these records into appropriate action. The professional skill of the early childhood educator is in knowing what it is that they have seen or heard in relation to each child's development and what to do next. They have to make decisions about whether what they have seen or heard means that something in particular needs to be planned and whether an individual child has needs that have not previously been identified. Much of what has already been planned will remain relevant, but ongoing assessments of children inform the fine tuning of short-term plans (see Chapter 3) and enable practitioners to ensure that time is spent on a curriculum that starts from the needs and interests of the child.

Conclusion

Having conversations with children and observing them in action acknowledges the competences with which children come to their new school or setting, not only at the beginning but throughout their educational careers. Observations and conversations are tools for assessment that recognize children's individual competences as the baseline against which their future learning needs should be identified. Such assessment practices define the role of the early childhood educator as being that of a learner, alongside their children, finding out about and then building on what children already know and can do. The assessment practices described in this chapter are the starting point for planning rather than the finishing point. The next chapter explores how practitioners use the information gained through initial assessments of children to plan an appropriate curriculum for the needs of each child.

Questions to Challenge your Thinking

1   Do your observations give you robust evidence of the learning needs of every child in your setting?
2   Does the organization of your setting enable you to spend the time it takes to get to know individual children well?
3   Do you observe children, and have conversations with them, when they are learning independently just as much as when they are engaged in adult-led activity?
4   In conversation with children, how do you encourage them to share their thinking and their ideas rather than merely answer the questions of adults?

3

PLANNING FOR LEARNING

Decisions about appropriate experiences to consolidate and extend learning

Introduction

Acknowledging the child as a competent learner should ensure that the starting point for planning an appropriate curriculum is the child's developing interests, skills and understandings. These are established through the initial assessment of children described in the previous chapter. What children already know and can do should determine the experiences that are planned for their development (Bruce 1987; DES 1990; EYCG 1992; Ball 1994; Fisher 2002). However, in England, the imposition of an externally imposed National Curriculum and the introduction of first the Desirable Learning Outcomes (DfEE/QCA 1998) and then the Early Learning Goals (DfES 2000) challenged the plausibility of such a notion. Many practitioners have felt torn between their early years principles, rooted in the ideals of child-centredness, and their statutory obligations to meet an agenda purporting to meet the needs of all children. The introduction of the new Statutory Framework for the Early Years Foundation Stage (EYFS) (DfE 2012) has done little to assuage such concerns. While the document exhorts practitioners to 'consider the individual needs, interests, and stage of development of each child [and] . . . use this information to plan a challenging and enjoyable experience for each child in all of the areas of learning and development' (DfE 2012: 6), such messages are undermined by the same government's requirement that:

> In the final term of the year in which the child reaches age five . . . the EYFS Profile must be completed for each child.

This national, statutory Profile assesses the attainment of children at the end of the Reception year, whether the child is 5 years and 10 months or has *not yet reached* their fifth birthday; whether they have been alive 70 months or 58 months, a colossal difference development-ally at this stage of life.

So what are practitioners to do? My belief – and experience – have always been that children learn most readily when what is being taught is relevant to them and makes sense to them. This frequently means that what is new is readily linked to what is already known and under-stood (Geake 2009; Howard-Jones 2010). So starting from children's interests and preoccupations – which are strong and deeply held at this age – makes more sense to me (and to children) than starting from outcomes that politicians want achieved at age 11, and which they mistakenly believe will be achieved more readily if practised at a younger and younger age (see House 2011).

There are many aspects of the EYFS which run contrary to its own principles. The statements that 'every child is unique' and that chil-dren 'develop and learn in different ways and at different rates' (DfE 2012: 3) are undermined by the requirement that all children are assessed at the same point in the school year, irrespective of their age within that year. No wonder so many summer-born children end up on special needs registers because when judged against the EYFS Profile statements, they are seen as 'less able' when, in fact, they have merely not yet been alive long enough to be judged fairly alongside children who are perhaps 11 months older.

The EYFS principle that 'children develop and learn in different ways' (2012: 3) is undermined by the government's recommendation that every school in England use synthetic phonics for children from the start of the Reception year. While all government initiatives concerned with literacy and phonics are 'guidance' and non-statutory, they are constantly reinforced by the requirements for teacher educa-tion and by the expectations of the inspection regime. Many of these recent initiatives have taken little account of the 'unique child' with their 'different ways' of learning and recommended a one-size-fits-all approach based on minimal evidence of effectiveness (Wyse and Styles 2007; Ellis 2009). How can one strategy meet the needs of the wide range of abilities and aptitudes, styles and approaches to reading in one class? Irrespective of the fact that by age 5 some children will have already learned to read without using phonics at all, that many will rely on a far more complex selection of strategies before making meaning from the printed word and that some – certainly at age 4, 5 or 6 – will have their attitudes to and capacity to engage with the written word hampered by poor spoken language and auditory discrimination that is still developing, the government continue to recommend a one-size-fits-all approach which makes a mockery of the notion of individualized or personalized learning.

Perhaps most contradictory of all is the statement on every page of the 'Development Matters' Guidance (Early Education 2012) accompanying the new EYFS, that 'development statements and their order should not be taken as necessary steps for individual children. They should not be used as checklists.' Yet experience shows that in almost every setting this is how they are indeed being used. While the intention of the Development Matters statements was to offer a framework for *planning*, in the absence of any national assessment tool to demonstrate the progression of children through the EYFS, settings and schools use the Development Matters statements because of the demand to quantify children's progress (see Edgington 2012). No longer are samples of children's work, collated in personal portfolios, considered sufficient. Advisers, inspectors and, therefore, headteachers are now demanding graphs and charts that facilitate the analysis not just of the progress of individual children, but the progress of groups of children such as those with English as an additional language or with special educational needs. Despite the fact that within each of these groups there is as wide a spread of needs as within any random group of children, the progress of a given group is judged as though the children within it were homogeneous. Whether assessing individual children or groups of children, it has become almost mandatory to offer evidence of progress as a number rather than as a complex individual story of one child's idiosyncratic learning journey over time. Because so many of the people who make judgements about the quality of young children's learning have little professional knowledge of early education, young children's development – in all its intriguing complexity – has been reduced to a number which can be plotted on a graph.

In the current educational climate, early years practitioners need to be aware of these conflicting messages and make professional decisions about how to manage them. First, I would suggest that it is important to remember what is statutory and what is not. For those working in the early years, the *Statutory Framework for the Early Years Foundation Stage* (DfE 2012) is statutory, but *Development Matters in the Early Years Foundation Stage* (Early Education 2012), *Letters and Sounds* (DfES 2007a) and the recommendations of the *Independent Review of the Teaching of Early Reading* (the Rose Review) (DfES 2006) are not. Second, it is crucial to be confident enough about practice that is based on knowledge of child development and the needs of individual children to be able to counter some of the more extreme and inappropriate demands made by people without the experience and expertise to realize the reductive nature of what they are demanding. Finally, it is imperative that practitioners remember that monitoring and inspection remain highly subjective processes. All those who engage in them, whether or not they use a common tool or schedule to arrive at their judgements, do so through the lens of their own experience, expertise, prejudices and expectations. The only people who give practitioners consistent, accurate feedback about what is relevant, meaningful and purposeful early education are the children. 'Starting from the child' is not an empty mantra. If early childhood educators start from children – their needs, interests and understandings – then they will be secure in knowing that their teaching is likely to lead to higher quality learning. If educators then observe and assess children meticulously, they will have evidence about what works in their classrooms and for the individuals within it, and what does not. In this way, early childhood professionals will have an evidence base that is sufficiently robust to enable them to counter the worst excesses of external demands.

So, there remains a perceptible tension between the interests of young children as learners and the interests of their educators, brought about over recent years by successive and excessive government initiatives. Early years educators, like all of the teaching profession, have goals to reach, targets to meet and standards to raise. These are the outcomes by which they are inspected and against which they will be judged. There is a pervading concern among some practitioners that to detour from the planned path, to encourage children to divert or digress, will mean that outcomes will not be achieved and that somehow this equates with failure. It is highly problematic that the standards agenda, so beloved of recent UK governments, has attainment in a narrow range of subjects, as a marker of effectiveness. High attainment has always been easy if you narrow the range of things that are to be attained. Look how many children in the 1960s and 1970s got to the 'top' of their reading scheme – but could not transfer any universal reading skills to other texts. Likewise, working constantly to arrive at goals and targets can mean rushing through the vital processes of learning and not having time to revisit experiences and opportunities over again – a necessary and crucial aspect of children's developmental needs (Bruner 1960). However, the foundation stage and, now, the Early Years Foundation Stage, are aptly named. Foundations have to go broad and deep before a building of quality can emerge. Foundations must be firm but flexible, skilfully connected to what already exists and strengthened when construction is on poor ground. If the foundations of learning are to be adequate, then it may be some time before any measurable outcomes emerge. However, once constructed, the structure should reach higher and be more adaptable than anything constructed with narrower, more hurried, less secure foundations (Fisher 2002).

The notion of child-centredness

To understand some of the current tensions in the early years between the child and adult agendas, it is important to be aware of the long tradition of early education in this country and the principles on which it is founded. Being principled has been an enduring characteristic of early years educators across the years and never has there been a greater need to be reminded of why those working in the early years hold the beliefs they do and stand up for those beliefs so strongly.

Early childhood education is rooted in a belief that children should receive an education designed to meet their own individual needs. Child-centred thinking has its roots in the work of philosophers such as Rousseau and Dewey and stemmed, as described by John Darling (1994) in his review of child-centred education, 'from radical dissatisfaction with traditional practice'. This practice was characterized by an emphasis on content over process and on the memorizing of facts rather than an understanding of concepts. Classes were taught as a single entity, with little or no account taken of individual differences in previous experiences, current understandings or rates of progress. The time-honoured metaphor that children were 'empty vessels to be filled' made the classroom roles of children and teachers very explicit. It was the duty of teachers to fill the vessels with knowledge and the duty of children to learn what was being taught, and if they did not, then the onus of blame was well and truly on *their* shoulders.

Yet long before such practice was established, there were some more enlightened thinkers who were commited to the notion of children as individual learners. As early as 1762, Jean-Jacques Rousseau declared in *Emile* that 'Nature provides for the child's growth in her own fashion, and this should never be thwarted' (Rousseau [1762] 1976). His approach to thinking about children and their development was taken forward by Pestalozzi, Froebel and Dewey, each developing and revising the work of the others until a powerful philosophy for the education of young children was formed. However, it was not until the 1960s that this philosophy really began to have any impact on practice in Britain. The main reason for the change in pedagogy was the public endorsement of a more child-friendly approach by official reports, most notably *Children and their Primary Schools* (The Plowden Report) (CACE 1967). The Plowden Report promoted a more liberal view of education, encapsulated in the celebrated quotation:

> at the heart of the education process lies the child. No advances in policy, no acquisitions of new equipment have their desired effect

unless they are in harmony with the nature of the child, unless they
are fundamentally acceptable to him [*sic*].

(CACE 1967: para 9)

Child-centred education is concerned with the *development* of children.
It is seen as a natural progression that is best aided by adults who, in
Darling's words, 'have an appreciation of and respect for the ways of
children' (1994: 3). This is an important element. Part of the criticism
of child-centred practices was that the child was able to choose and
control their own actions and that the role of the educator became
diminished for fear of being accused of 'interfering' with this natural
development (see Blenkin and Kelly 1987; Darling 1994).

Interestingly, it was the work of Jean Piaget (1896–1980) that did
much to fuel this misconception. Piaget believed that children pass
through certain stages of development and could not operate at the
later stages before passing, in their own good time, through the earlier
ones. This theory supposed that children passed through these stages
irrespective of adult support and that the best an adult could do was
interfere! The obvious assumption was that if children passed naturally
through these stages of development, then the most dangerous thing
one could do was to rush them through the process.

This theory led to the notion of 'readiness' (see Chapter 1), with
educators believing that they had to *wait* until a child was ready to learn
something rather than being in a position to move them on or extend
them beyond the stage where they were. Such a notion rendered the
teacher somewhat impotent. Knowing the next stage of development
and perceiving the learning needs of the child are of restricted use if you
believe that it is damaging to use such knowledge. Another facet of
Piaget's work which apparently diminished the role of the educator was
his emphasis on the child as an individual explorer of the world, discov-
ering and making sense of new situations through action and self-
directed problem-solving (Piaget 1953). Piaget's influence on thinking
and practice in the 1960s and 1970s caused many practitioners, as well
as critics, to believe that the role of the adult had been sidelined and
that children were to be encouraged to do as they please. The power of
these assumptions can be seen all too clearly in the series of Black Papers
written between 1969 and 1977 (see Cox and Dyson 1969a, 1969b,
1970; Cox and Boyson 1975, 1977) and the impact of the resultant
conservative backlash is, I would suggest, still being felt today.

Much of Piaget's work became challenged even by those who
acknowledged his tremendous contribution to the development of
thinking about children and their learning. One of the most influential
challenges came from his colleague Margaret Donaldson. In her book
Children's Minds (1978) she argued for a fresh interpretation of Piaget's

views based on her own research in which she replicated some of Piaget's tests but using significantly different methodology. She and her colleagues found that by setting Piaget's tasks in contexts that were familiar to the children and using language that was clear and relevant to the tasks, a significantly greater number of children were able to complete the tasks than had succeeded in Piaget's original tests (Piaget and Inhelder 1956). Donaldson's work adds powerful weight to the notion of the young child as a competent learner and the critical role of the adult in extending those competences:

> the normal child comes to school with well-established skills as a thinker. But his [sic] thinking is directed outwards on to the real, meaningful, shifting, distracting world. What is going to be required for success in our educational system is that he should learn to turn language and thought in upon themselves. He must be able to direct his own thought processes in a thoughtful manner. He must become able not just to talk but to choose what he will say, not just to interpret but to weigh interpretations. His conceptual system must expand in the direction of increasing ability to represent itself. He must become capable of manipulating symbols.
>
> (Donaldson 1978: 88–9)

It was the work of Lev Vygotsky (1986–1934) that firmly reinstated the role of the educator to a central place in the developmental journeys of children. Vygotsky saw children's cognitive development operating at two levels, the present level and the potential level. He believed that the role of more knowledgeable others was to move the child from the actual to the potential next level of understanding. The task of the adult was to encourage children to do *without* help what they can do only at present *with* help (Anning 1991). In other words, children's learning could be extended by the right intervention at the right time. 'Teachers have a highly interactive role in a Vygotskian framework. Children's development is static unless they are able to work in their zone of proximal development. Teaching does not wait upon development but propels it' (Smith 1993: 56).

This support for children's learning is what Wood et al. (1976) have called 'scaffolding', and this offers an appropriate metaphor for the notion of adult-supported child-centredness in its aim to offer experiences, opportunities and interactions that match and then challenge the level of competence and maturity of the child. The work of Jerome Bruner (1915–) is of particular relevance to early years practitioners here, because he works from an analysis of children's learning, to a model of classroom pedagogy and then to a curriculum framework. It is the very fact that the National Curriculum attainment targets and the Early Learning Goals work in precisely the opposite way that seems to set them at odds with the notion of child-centredness and its concern for the individual – and unique – child.

Comparisons between the pioneers and modern theorists

The child-centred notions of Rousseau, Dewey, Pestalozzi and others can be seen clearly in the principles and practice of the early childhood educators who followed on, such as Froebel (1782–1852), Montessori (1870–1952) and Steiner (1861–1925). Tina Bruce's book *Early Childhood Education* (1987) takes the threads of influence even further by comparing the principles of those early pioneers with the work of other modern theorists such as Piaget, Vygotsky, Bruner and Mia Kelmer Pringle, founding director of the UK National Children's Bureau. The 'ten common principles of the pioneers' (Bruce 1987) is a valuable framework for the development of good early years practice in current settings. As with so many aspects of early childhood education these principles stand the test of time because they are about the needs of children rather than the needs of some external agenda. The principles have been adopted and developed in many subsequent documents (e.g. EYCG 1992; Roberts 1995b). The Oxfordshire Early Years Team (1996) adapted them to reflect their work with children from birth to 8 years, and the adaptation in Box 3.1 offers indicators of those early years principles in practice.

Box 3.1 Principles of early childhood education

1   *Childhood is seen as valid in itself. It is a stage of life and not simply a preparation for the future.*
  - experiences and environment should be appropriate to the age and developmental stage of the child;
  - experiences should be relevant to the child's *current* needs;
  - each child should be valued for themselves, what they are, what they know and what they can do;
  - learning at this stage may improve later performance but, first and foremost, learning enables children to achieve their present potential and enriches and fulfils their present life (Moss and Penn 1996).

2   *The whole child is considered to be important; social, physical, intellectual, moral and spiritual aspects of development are related.*
  - all aspects of the child should be considered in planning resources and experiences;

- the balance between these areas needs to be sustained once children begin statutory schooling;
- *all* areas of development should be observed and assessed in order to inform future planning.

3 *There is potential in all children which will emerge powerfully under favourable conditions. Each child is unique and special, with individual ways of learning.*
- every child should be known well by at least one adult;
- children should be valued with full regard to their gender, race and ability;
- the environment should be sufficiently flexible and responsive to meet the range of children's learning styles and strategies;
- children need time and space to produce work of quality and depth (EYCG 1992).

4 *Parents are the first and continuing educators of their children. Schools should value and build on parental expertise.*
- schools and settings need to establish systems where parents can tell staff about their child;
- schools and settings should develop a partnership with parents and carers based on mutual respect and a shared interest in the child;
- parents should be involved in the process of assessment and contribute to decisions about future plans for their child.

5 *Learning is holistic and interconnected. The young child does not separate experiences into different compartments.*
- short-term planning should be sufficiently flexible to make space/allow time for the children's spontaneous interests;
- planning should identify the understanding, skills and attitudes that are important for developing learners; activities and themes should support rather than determine these objectives;
- broadly based and integrated experiences are appropriate when working within the National Curriculum.

6 *Young children learn through exploration, play and talk.*
- young children learn most effectively by doing rather than being told (EYCG 1992);
- play should occur throughout the day, alongside adult-directed activity;
- play is given status when it is valued, assessed and used to extend learning;
- children should be encouraged to initiate conversations and pose questions.

7 *Our starting points for supporting learning are what children **can do** and what they **can nearly do**.*
- children should be helped to identify their own targets and achievements;
- observation-based assessment should be the basis for planning;
- adults should sensitively support and extend children's learning to the edges of their potential.

8 *Intrinsic motivation is recognized and valued as a powerful force for learning.*
- autonomy (physical, social and intellectual) and self-discipline are emphasized;
- children should have substantial periods of uninterrupted time for sustained self-initiated activity;
- children should have a range of opportunities to make choices and decisions.

9 *The relationships that children establish with adults and other children are of central importance in their development.*
- the education of young children should be the responsibility of appropriately trained and experienced educators with a knowledge of child development;
- children need planned experiences that encourage the interpersonal and cognitive skills necessary for collaboration and cooperation;
- educators should be aware of themselves as models.

10 *Children's education is seen as the total experience of, and interaction with, their environment.*
- children's educational experiences should draw on their personal context of family, culture and community;
- there should be provision and planning for an indoor and outdoor environment of equal quality;
- the way in which we talk and respond to children throughout their time in school should create a climate that nurtures self-esteem.

The translation of early years principles into practice has been particularly influenced by the writing of Geva Blenkin, who espouses a commitment to a developmental view of education and argues cogently for a concept of education:

> not as a device for the transmission of certain bodies of agreed knowledge and values or as a process of moulding people into some

predetermined shape, it is of the enhancement of capacities, the widening of every person's horizons of appreciation and understanding, the maximization of everyone's potential, the development of everyone's powers of self-direction, autonomy, understanding and critical awareness.

(Blenkin and Kelly 1987: 11)

In Chapter 2 of *The National Curriculum and Early Learning*, Blenkin, in Blenkin and Kelly (1994: 29) draws together four broad themes of early childhood education which, based on the principles of a developmental curriculum, are peculiar to this stage of education:

1 The young child is dependent on adults and is new to institutional life. The process of learning to be a pupil is thus of great importance.
2 Rates of development and learning are at their most rapid during this stage of education, and they are highly susceptible to environmental constraints and advantages. The young child, therefore, needs to be stimulated by a wide range of experiences rather than confined to a narrow and restrictive programme.
3 Although social interaction is important at every stage of learning, it is of particular importance at this early stage, since young learners are not able to make sense of experiences which are represented in a more formal or abstract way.
4 Early education must not only provide a rich array of practical experiences but it must also nurture the playfulness of children. For secure mastery of skills or knowledge depends on play, because it is through play that the child is able to test out, informally and personally, what is newly learnt.

All those early childhood pioneers who have valued children, their competences and their individuality would echo the words of Blenkin and Kelly in saying 'what a complex and subtle matter is the learning of pupils in their early, formative years' (1994: 197).

How to manage children's needs alongside the external agenda

For the practitioner working in early education in the twenty-first century there has to be a fresh approach to child-centredness. While there remains no doubt that children learn most effectively at this age by pursuing their own interests and preoccupations about the world and how it works, there is also a necessity for skilled, supportive adults to help consolidate and extend this learning. The challenge for early childhood educators is how to introduce the statutory external agenda – what the state believes the child needs to learn and do – when it might not be what a child is choosing to think about or do right now.

My belief is that, *if handled appropriately according to the child's stage of development*, there is less of a problem with the external agenda than some people fear. From the moment babies are born, interested and attentive adults introduce them to things that they might not otherwise see or experience unaided – a squirrel in the park, a new rattle, a song or a story. Babies may be born with an innate drive to explore and discover and make sense of the world around them, but at the same time, many of things they learn to do or come to understand in their earliest days and months are as a result of the intervention and initiation of a supportive adult. We saw in Chapter 1 that there are common features of the interactions that fortunate children experience at home that stimulate communication and development very effectively. Classrooms should do the same. While children need considerable time and opportunities to explore and discover and make meaning, they also need interested and attentive adults to introduce them to new learning, skills or understandings that they might not learn if left unaided.

Nancy Stewart (2012) in her book about the characteristics of effective early learning describes the importance of the child's voyage of discovery as he or she actively engages with resources and materials in order to come to an understanding of how things are and how things work. If an adult constantly interrupts that thinking process or tries to control or manipulate it, it would 'remove from her the active role of making links and puzzling over relationships' (Stewart 2012: 89). This perspective supports the Piagetian position (1929) that the child is the major determinant of their own development as they actively construct their personal view of the world, 'assimilating' what is new and trying to map it onto what is already known. If that process of assimilation causes 'disequilibrium' – if the child has to 'think again' because what is new does not match their existing model of the world – then there follows a process of 'accommodation' as the child adjusts their existing model to make room for these fresh understandings.

But alongside this Piagetian perspective of the child as a lone explorer, there is another as we have seen, that places great emphasis on learning as a social activity. Barbara Rogoff (1990) explains how many of children's skills develop in the context of ongoing communal activities as children mimic and try to emulate older and more able members of their community 'as apprentices in thinking, active in their effort to learn from observing and participating with peers and more skilled members of their society' (Rogoff 1990: 7). At the same time Vygotsky, the great Russian psychologist, was adamant that adults (and more knowledgeable others) were vital in moving children's learning on, taking children to the very edges of their current thinking and to the potential next level of understanding.

So child-led learning and adult-led learning both have value and purpose and benefit. Children need to have opportunities to explore and discover the world for themselves, at their own pace and in their own way. They might follow their own interests alone or with peers or with the support of an attentive adult. Equally, young children need time to observe others doing and learning, to talk to others who have alternative views and ideas, and to learn through mimicking and observing skilled and knowledgeable adults. This is the complex matrix of experiences and opportunities that should characterize every early learning environment. The skill of the early years educator is in using strategies and approaches to introduce the adult agenda that are suited to the child and their stage of development. Many recent initiatives have not been introduced with the needs of the youngest children in mind but have 'trickled down' to Key Stage 1, reception and nursery classes in a form that is inappropriate for a learner of 4, 5 or 6 years of age. Guidance is given that sometimes does not sit comfortably with what is known about child development and children's optimal ways of learning. And it is not only the initiatives themselves that can be inappropriate but what the inclusion of those initiatives does to the rest of the learning day that can be so damaging. If young children are expected to be taught phonics for 'a discrete period of time – around 20 minutes on a daily basis', for example (DfES 2007c: 10), then in the hands of an inexperienced practitioner this can be interpreted as 20 minutes of whole class teaching with everyone on the carpet. This may not be the best strategy and may interrupt other valuable learning that is taking place. Good practitioners will plan for systematic daily teaching of phonics but may find it more effective if it happens in the context of other activities where letters and sounds arise naturally and spontaneously or in small groups where differentiation is more easily achieved. It is not the expectation of daily phonics (or any other initiative) that is the problem, but the way in which it is introduced to children that can be problematic. Teaching should always be relevant and appropriate to the children in the class and initiatives have to be made child-friendly so that learning makes sense to children and so that it is contingent upon their current competence.

The skill of the early years educator is in planning appropriately for both adult-led and child-led learning to take place alongside each other in the learning day. Chapter 4 considers the role of the adult and how time for child-led and adult-led learning is managed. For now, this chapter considers how observations of children and conversations with children can lead to effective planning for their needs – in both adult-led and child-led situations.

Stages of planning

Deciding whether an aspect of the curriculum will be successfully learned through an adult-led activity or a child-led activity comes towards the end of the planning process. Practitioners need to know their children well before such decisions can be made. Indeed, one way of making the planning process relevant and meaningful is to decide what can be planned in advance of knowing children and what must wait until the child or the group or the class are well known. Broadly speaking, the long and medium stages of planning can be undertaken in advance of knowing a class while short-term planning *cannot*. It may be helpful to think that while long- and medium-term plans are about the *curriculum*, short-term planning is about the *child*.

In summary, *long-term planning* is concerned with children's entitlement to a *broad and balanced* curriculum and is achieved through the appropriate allocation of time to the Areas of Learning and Development in the Early Years Foundation Stage, the National Curriculum (where appropriate), religious education and other curriculum aspects required, particularly, in the Reception year.

Medium-term planning addresses *continuity and progression* from one stage in each area of learning/subject to the next, and from one setting or class to the next. It draws on schemes of work and the long-term plan and identifies the concepts, skills, knowledge and attitudes to which children will be introduced over a specified time. It is at this stage that the curriculum may be most effectively organized by linking together different areas of learning/subjects possibly through themes or topics. Medium-term planning should also record the ongoing learning that will take place outside of any planned topic or theme, and which simply does not fit in with a focus on 'People Who Help Us' or 'Journeys'– e.g. certain elements of mathematical development or physical development.

Short-term planning is concerned not with the curriculum but with the needs of specific children. It is concerned with *differentiation* and planning for the needs of specific groups and individuals. It provides the detail of activities, experiences, resources, groupings, adult support and teaching strategies which are identified through ongoing observation and assessment of children in action.

Long-term planning

Long-term planning usually takes place well before the start of the new academic year. In many schools and settings this stage of planning is formalized in planning cycles that identify the elements of the areas of learning or subjects to be addressed by topics in different terms and over different years. Many schools and settings I know use a planning sheet which has on it the 'Development Matters' aspects of the EYFS which might be appropriate for the age and stage of the children for whom they are responsible, and highlight in different colour pens those that will be the focused on each term. Long-term planning should show that the statutory requirements of the curriculum are being addressed over the course of the children's time in the setting. This stage of planning is about children's entitlement to the curriculum and practitioners need to demonstrate that what is being planned covers the breadth of the curriculum and that there is an appropriate balance between the different Areas of Learning and Development.

While it may be attributed to overall 'effectiveness' (Ofsted 1994), long-term planning cannot purport to be concerned with the developmental needs of individual children because practitioners have frequently not yet met the children to whom the planning relates. Even if the children are known, their needs will have changed in many ways between the time when the planning is undertaken and the experiences take place. So the long-term plan cannot have activities or experiences earmarked but should be seen as a framework for ensuring curriculum coverage.

Medium-term planning

It is at the medium-term planning stage that I feel most difficulties lie. Medium-term plans are usually written at the start of a new term or half-term, or at the beginning of a theme or topic for younger children. Although the children may now be known to their practitioners, their future developmental needs will not. Children's needs change rapidly at this stage in their development – too rapidly to be predicted, with accuracy, even several weeks in advance. So it is important that medium-term planning also addresses subjects and areas of learning, rather than children. The most important feature of medium-term planning is that it should identify the concepts, skills, knowledge and attitudes that constitute the planned learning for that period of time, and it should show how the children's learning will build on and progress from that which has gone before. It may also show how the teaching of potential skills or knowledge, for example, will be integrated and linked together. However, all too often, on carefully produced planning sheets, there is a column for the activity or task which will be the vehicle for the intended learning outcomes. If a decision is made that this activity or that task will be appropriate for children before their actual needs are known, then the decision may be the wrong one. There is a lot of sense in pencilling in possible activities and accumulating a bank of ideas on which to draw, but activities are only the vehicles for learning, and planning must be sufficiently flexible to change ideas and to accommodate the needs and interests of individual children, once they are known.

Topic work

Topic work acknowledges the fact that children do not naturally compartmentalize their learning into subject areas or areas of learning. It seeks to capitalize on the notion of cross-curricular learning, with its intention of mirroring the real-life learning of children in a range of contexts. However, cross-curricular learning and topic work are not necessarily the same thing and the one may not be a useful vehicle for delivering the other. Cross-curricular learning emphasizes the opportunities for children to cross the boundaries between traditional subjects and see the application of skills and the consolidation of concepts in experiences and activities that enable such cross-fertilization to occur. In an effective early learning environment most activities and experiences offer learning potential across most areas of the curriculum all at the same time and it is only in adult-led learning that the outcomes are limited to one particular curriculum element.

Topic work, however, while rooted in this notion, has been hijacked over time by the agenda of teachers and other early years practitioners. Increasingly, as topics become planned by whole staff teams together, the links that are made between areas of learning are not seen by the child but engineered by adults. They sometimes involve excruciating contortions to involve all areas of learning and early years practitioners must guard against making topics as incomprehensible to children as subject divisions are.

A particular concern for early childhood educators – particularly teachers – is the expectation that they fit in with the school's cycle of topics. Very often the topic titles are inappropriate for young children and do not meet their current needs and interests. Equally, topics and themes may not last as long for younger children as they do for older pupils and yet early years teachers feel locked into the cycle and compelled to continue with a topic even when it is not bringing about effective learning. Either way, practitioners in the early years should have the flexibility to select topics for the length of time they are relevant and meaningful to the children – or to choose not to use topics at all – or to plan for different themes for different groups of children according to their interests. Topics should be as expendable and exchangeable as activities and experiences. They are the vehicles for learning, not the purpose of it. If one topic, theme or activity better suits one class or group than another, and either can bring about the intended learning, then any planning system should be sufficiently flexible to accommodate the alternatives.

Short-term planning

It is at this stage that planning moves from concern with the curriculum and areas of learning, to concern for the child. It is at this stage that the practitioner has the opportunity to incorporate the developmental approach to learning, by making first-hand observations of children engaged in active learning and through having conversations with children about what they have experienced and what they are thinking. Through observations and conversations, practitioners can gain information about children's knowledge and understanding as well as their skills and strategies. All of this information is necessary if practitioners are to plan experiences that have relevance and purpose for each child. Some intentions or objectives may come from the medium-term plans or from more recent analysis of learning needs, but the actual activity or experience or the resources that are to be provided, will be planned in light of what the child already knows and can do, and what the practitioner judges he or she needs to know or do next.

What to include in short-term plans

While short-term plans may vary in format, there are certain features that should be included in order to ensure that the individual needs of children have been considered adequately.

1 The observation(s) from which this planning comes

It is crucial that the observation, assessment and planning cycle is visible. Planning should never appear as though in a vacuum. All planning in the early years should arise from observations of a child in action and from assessment of their current needs. The identification of specific needs should be seen either in the profiles of children – where an assessment of a significant step in learning has been recorded – or on the planning sheet as a prompt for the intended outcome of the next activity or experience.

2 The previous experiences that have led to this planning

It may be that a particular experience – the child's or the class's – may have led to something specific being planned as a follow-up. A child's visit to hospital in order to have a plaster put on or a class visit to a wildlife park may both trigger further activities to clarify, consolidate, or extend that experience purposefully. Recording that previous experience on the short-term plan makes the purpose of the follow-up activity transparent.

3 The concepts or skills it is intended children should experience or practise or extend

These concepts or skills may well be in the medium-term stage of planning and that may be sufficient. However, some practitioners choose to repeat these on their short-term plans as prompts about the purpose of the planned activity, particularly if a session is to be taken by a teaching assistant or supply teacher it can be important to understand what it is intended that children should *learn* rather than simply what they are to *do*.

4 The activities or opportunities planned to bring the intended learning about

This is where the needs and interests of individuals and groups of children should be most apparent. Even if there are two or three classes with the same age children within a school, the activities taking place in them may be quite different. Activities and experiences should reflect the interests of the children within a class, so that it is clear that the practitioner has found a meaningful 'hook' on which to hang the learning outcomes in order to capture the involvement of particular children or the class.

5 Children's own ideas about what to learn

An increasing number of classrooms I visit have a space where children can say what they would like to learn – somewhere to write or to put a sticky note or to hang a sign, so that the teacher can accommodate these ideas into his or her short-term plans. Likewise, there can be places for parents to write what they think might be of interest so that their ideas can also be included in the planning process.

6 What differentiation is necessary for activities/experiences/support?

It is crucial that short-term plans identify any differences in provision for individual children or for groups. Even though practitioners may have identified and planned activities that are pertinent to the children in their class, there will still be differences between the children in that class in the work and the support that they need. If these differences are not thought through and planned at this short-term stage, then opportunities to give children the support they need in practice may be missed.

7 Whether this learning will take place inside or out

It is necessary to plan for learning to take place indoors and out and for those decisions to be reflected on short-term plans. The outdoor environment should not just be a place where child-led learning takes place but should be the chosen environment for adult-led and adult-initiated activity as well (see Chapter 4). The outdoors is rich in opportunities to learn skills and concepts that may traditionally be thought of as 'indoor learning'. When outdoor learning is a planned part of the learning day, then it is easy to monitor whether there is an appropriate balance between outdoor and indoor learning and whether every member of staff takes their turn to support (not merely supervise) learning out of doors.

8 Whether learning will be adult-led or adult-initiated

Chapter 4 will unravel the differences between adult-led and adult-initiated learning, but suffice to say here that practitioners need to decide when they plan how much support a child or a group needs for the intended learning to be achieved. Sometimes the practitioner needs to be with children all the time to achieve the intended outcome (adult-led), sometimes the practitioner can instigate an activity or an idea but leave the children to get on with learning independently (adult-initiated). As will be seen in the following chapter, the nature of these two kinds of activity can be quite different, so planning needs to identify the level of support necessary *before the activity itself can be chosen.*

9 Whether resources for child-led learning need changing or extending

It is not possible to plan for play. As we will see in Chapter 7, play that is planned becomes an adult-initiated activity. Play is freely chosen by the child and is in the control of the child, so any attempt to plan for it removes that choice and control. Nevertheless, practitioners can and should enhance the environment for play. Through careful observation it will become apparent whether a scenario needs further resources to extend or revitalize the play taking place, whether fresh materials need to be introduced and whether the play needs sensitive adult support.

10 Observations made in the course of the activity

Sometimes practitioners will plan for specific assessments to be undertaken while an activity is in progress. Sometimes an observation will be quite spontaneous but equally significant. In both cases, if the practitioner learns something new about the child that they did not know before, then this needs to be recorded so that the child's learning trajectory can be scrutinized and so that planning for the next day or days can be adjusted to address what has been learned by the practitioner.

11 Action to be taken as a result of these observations

This section completes the cycle. As a result of the observations the practitioner has made, what will be done about:

- *the child:* does an activity or an experience need to be planned that will support this child's learning in different ways?
- *the environment:* are any additional resources required to extend or rejuvenate play and exploration?
- *myself (the practitioner):* was I in the right place at the right time for this child? Does the child need me to support their learning more at this stage or does the child need me to back off so they can learn or consolidate their learning more independently?

12 Scribbles!

I have added this heading following an INSET day when a practitioner quite rightly said that good planning is covered in scribbles! If short-term plans are to be altered in the light of practitioners' observations and assessments of children, then they must be adaptable and change-able. This means that they are 'work in progress', and will be scribbled on, altered and amended according to the practitioner's new-found knowledge about the needs of the children in his or her class. So, good quality short-term planning inevitably looks messy.

Differentiation

Differentiation is a key feature of good quality short-term plans, but is more complex to explain than the brief sentences above allow.

While long- and medium-term plans are the concern of the staff as a whole and may well be similar in format, short-term planning should be more responsive to the requirements of individual practitioners. Educators need to adopt strategies that allow for these short-term plans to address the issue of *differentiation*. Differentiation is the key to matching experiences to the developmental needs of children.

In the foundation stage, differentiation can be addressed in two ways. First, a practitioner can plan to differentiate a learning experi-ence by knowing the stage of development of the children for whom she is responsible and then planning an activity or experience that will take that individual or that group to the 'next steps' in their learning.

This is called *differentiation by input*. Alongside this more adult-focused learning, early years practitioners also plan activities and provide resources that are very open-ended, and what children learn will be differentiated by the knowledge and understanding that they bring to the experience. *This is called differentiation by outcome.*

The recent emphasis on the value of whole class teaching in schools has challenged this notion of planning to meet individual needs. While both the national literacy and numeracy strategies (DfEE 1998; 1999) emphasized the importance of differentiated questioning and some teachers have become highly skilled at this, it remains the case that more whole class teaching has resulted in many children receiving the same undifferentiated diet. Whole class teaching is not appropriate for foundation stage children. Apart from the joy of a large group singing together, there are few early learning experiences that are not preferential in a smaller group, where individual young voices can be heard. Sitting still and engaging in relatively passive, adult-dominated learning takes a level of physical control and concentration that is simply too much for most 3-, 4- and 5-year-olds to manage (Goddard Blythe 2005; 2011). Indeed, Goddard Blythe suggests 'The most advanced level of movement is the ability to sit still' (2005: 137). Consultation with children in the foundation stage reveals time and again a desire to be active and a dread of being 'on the carpet' for long periods of time (Ofsted 2004; Sanders et al. 2005; OCC 2005; 2006). Observation of classroom practice shows all too frequently how often 4- and 5-year-olds sit for registration, followed by assembly, followed by explanations of the day's activities, followed by adult-led introductory input. Each valid in its own right perhaps but, placed one after another, a numbing experience in more senses than one. While whole class/group experiences can sometimes have a meaningful place in early education, they must not take the place of experiences that specialist educators know would be more effective in smaller, more intimate circumstances.

As differentiation is so critical to children's development and progress, however, it is important that educators clarify what elements of their planning can be matched more closely to children's differing needs. Differentiation may be concerned with:

- the *concepts, skills, knowledge and attitudes* that are the intended outcomes of an activity/experience;
- whether these concepts are to be introduced/developed/consolidated (the *spiral curriculum*);
- the *activity or experience* itself – different activities and experiences can be vehicles for the same outcomes and differ according to the interests of the children;

- the *introduction* of an activity – more or less detailed, verbal or written etc.;
- the *process* of an activity, determined by the importance of the outcome, not necessarily uniform, but open to the most effective strategy for the child/group;
- the *outcome* of an activity (if indeed there is one at all), determined by the importance of the process; it may be open to interpretation by the child/group;
- the *support* given to an activity by an adult or other children, which may be minimal or substantial;
- the *resources* planned – different levels and different kinds;
- the *evidence* of learning, which varies according to the intended outcomes;
- the *collection* of evidence – which technique, by whom, when;
- the *assessment* of work – by the adult, child or both;
- by whose *criteria* the assessment takes place – adult, child or both;
- follow-up *action* – what, for whom, how, when.

There is no need for every element of this process to be addressed on every occasion, but it is important that all of these elements are open to change and adaptation in order to make learning experiences relevant, meaningful and effective for children. A prompt sheet for supporting the planning of differentiated activities is given below. Rather than offering a format for short-term planning, I think a prompt sheet is more helpful so that, irrespective of the format that suits the individual practitioner, plans can be checked against certain indicators of differentiation. Box 3.2 is offered as a starting point. You may find it helpful to formulate your own list with colleagues from your setting.

Box 3.2   Differentiation in short-term plans

Differentiation by input
- Why are the children doing this activity?; Why have we set up these resources?
- What do I intend that they should learn?
- Is this activity relevant for all children or just some?

Activity/experience
- What activity/experiences will meet the intended learning outcomes?
- Do the children all need the same activity/experiences?
- Do I need to differentiate the introduction/the process/the outcome?

- Who will give the support or will children work independently?
- What grouping is most appropriate?
- What resources are needed? Are they the same for all children?
- Does the activity/experience meet the learning requirements of children with special needs?
- Will this activity work best indoors or out?

Assessment
- What evidence do I need to gather?
- Will this enable me to assess the intended learning outcomes of the activity/experience?
- Will this be done during or after the activity/experience?
- If evidence is to be recorded by an adult, what vocabulary, actions, behaviours are we looking for? How will the adult record this?
- If evidence is to be recorded by children, will they be able to select their own method of recording and then explain it to an adult or their peers?
- Should samples of work be saved or photographs or tape recordings taken?
- In what way might children be involved in assessing their own work?
- Were the intended learning outcomes achieved?
- If not, why not? What do I need to change?
- If the learning was not what I expected, what *did* I learn about the children from the outcomes of the activity?

NB be prepared to note spontaneous and unexpected assessments too!

Action
- Do I need to change my short-term planning?
- Does a child/group/the class need to revisit a concept or have further practice of a skill?
- Should a child/the children have experience of working with a different child/children?
- Does a child/group need more support at the next stage of development?
- Does the child/group need different resources to support their learning?

The need for observation and assessment to inform planning

Having looked in detail at the planning process it is timely to review the importance of observation and assessment in ensuring that what is planned is appropriate, relevant and meaningful to the child. As we saw in Chapter 2, assessment activities are often seen as a check against the effectiveness of teaching, a measure of whether children have learnt what it was intended that they should learn. As such, assessment is thought of frequently as coming at the end of the learning process and often gets tagged on to the seemingly more important stages of planning and teaching. However, if assessment is only ever seen as completing the cycle, then educators lose the powerful and necessary potential of using assessment to inform future planning. It leaves them either predicting or guessing what knowledge or understanding children bring to the introduction of a new concept or the learning of a new skill. Practitioners often make elaborate introductions to new ideas and then use the discussion time following the introduction to elicit a range of understandings from children. However, this knowledge is not always used to inform or to alter planning. If practitioners always begin by teaching, then there is an implicit assumption that what has been planned is appropriate and that, apart from the necessity for differentiated follow-up, the needs of children will be met.

We have seen, however, that children bring with them a whole range of knowledge, understanding and skills which are nothing to do with formal education. Peers, different adults, the television, books, outings and homes all give children a vast array of insights which educators ignore at their peril. Assessment should *begin* the cycle of teaching and learning and plans should remain flexible until precise knowledge of each individual learner is gleaned. There is always a danger that when planning, educators draw on records from previous years or terms and, if an aspect of the curriculum has not been covered, then the assumption is made that an individual child knows nothing about it. All the children then receive the same starting point according to their *presumed* lack of knowledge. As professional educators we must make it our business to find out what individual children already know and can do and ensure that we do not underestimate their existing skills, knowledge and understandings. Children bring so much knowledge with them from the lives that they lead away from our settings that it is essential that we establish their individual starting points for learning rather than assuming that they all need the same starting points or the same learning experiences.

Conclusion

This chapter has been concerned with planning a curriculum that acknowledges the developmental needs of children within the constraints of an externally imposed framework. It suggests that this is most easily achieved when long-term and medium-term planning are seen as meeting the development of the *curriculum* and short-term planning is seen as meeting the development of the *child*. An early years curriculum is concerned with process above product. An appropriate curriculum is one that meets the needs and interests of children and also introduces children to a range of skills and concepts that are deemed, by adults, to be relevant and desirable for their development. The task of the early childhood educator is to fuse together these dual interests and to ensure that children's experiences do not lead them to believe that education is something that is imposed by somebody else. Education should be a dynamic and liberating experience. If children are to be lifelong learners, then their independence and motivation to learn must be cultivated at every stage of their educational journey. The next chapter examines how educators achieve a balance in the activities and experiences they provide and explores the role that adults play in supporting the development of competent young learners.

Questions to Challenge your Thinking

1 What theories of early learning have influenced your practice? What are the principles of early childhood education that give your setting its values and vision?
2 Is everyone in your setting sufficiently clear about the purposes of long-, medium- and short-term planning?
3 Is your short-term planning sufficiently flexible to be altered daily (if necessary) following the observation of children? Does this planning clearly identify individual children's needs?

4

THE ROLE OF THE ADULT

Optimizing practitioners' time with children

Introduction

The role of the adult, as educator, is inextricably bound up with how children are viewed as learners. Once it is acknowledged that children are competent (albeit inexperienced) learners, then this shifts the way in which practitioners respond to them and their varied and various abilities. Whatever it is intended that children should learn and however it is intended that they should learn it, the most effective learning is rooted in previous experience (Donaldson 1978; Wood 1988; Meadows 1993; McNaughton and Williams 2009). Children are active learners, constantly constructing their own internal model of the world (Wells 1986; Wood 1988; Kuhn 2000; Smith et al. 2010). By acknowledging this, the educator rejects a 'transmission' approach to teaching where the adult is seen as having, or having access to, knowledge and skills which it is their responsibility to transmit to the learner. Instead, the adult adopts what Rowland (1984: 4) describes as an 'interpretive' model of teaching, and which involves 'not only the child's attempt to interpret and assimilate the knowledge and skills offered by the teacher, but also the teacher's attempt to understand the child's growing understandings of the world'. This symbiotic relationship (Pascal et al. 1997) is identifiable by its reciprocity – with the adult's style of engagement affecting the child's level of involvement and the child's involvement impacting on the adult's style of engagement with them and their learning.

If we ignore what children already know and can do, then their learning will not be embedded in what is already secure and what already makes sense to them. Effective learning comes about when what is new becomes connected to what is already known and under-stood. The brain functions most efficiently when consolidation enables neural pathways to be strengthened and new experiences cause new connections to be created. Embedding learning in what is already known and understood also sends messages to children that their competencies and contributions are valued which, in turn, can have a positive impact on their self-esteem and motivation.

The educator as observer

We saw in Chapter 2 that, in order to incorporate what children already know and can do, educators need to spend a considerable amount of time finding out what that is. Time for observation and conversation needs to be found not just at the beginning of the year or term, but throughout the day, so that planning is constantly informed by observations of children in action as learners. The problem for many practitioners is that sitting still, not obviously engaged in inter-action with a child or group of children, seems to be a dereliction of their duty. Early childhood educators are so used to orchestrating a myriad of different activities and experiences all at the same time and being immersed in the action, that sitting back and simply watching children go against the grain. However, time for observation is critical. If practitioners do not watch children as they go about the business of learning, then many important moments in their development may be missed. Of course practitioners can and do make observations of children when they are playing or working alongside them, but the nature of these observations is different. Children react and respond in different ways when adults are alongside them, and if practitioners want to see how children approach activities independently or along-side their peers, then they need to remove themselves from the action and not be distracted by having more than one role at that particular time.

Making time for observation may seem daunting, but without time being set aside for focused observation of children involved in their learning, practitioners will not collect sufficient information about children as learners and planning will not be rooted in strong enough evidence of what children know and can do and where their interests lie. Early childhood educators who spend a significant amount of their time observing children say that the knowledge they gain enables them to plan far more appropriately for the individual child, group or class the next day or week. Time is not wasted in planning activities and experiences that are too easy or too difficult and time is not wasted in repeating or revisiting activities unnecessarily. Time is actually *saved*, because the practitioner is able to differentiate his or her planning on the basis of an improved knowledge of the children's needs.

Practitioners need to make time to observe children during the teaching day. As with so many things in the early learning environment it is a question of prioritizing time, but if time spent on observation saves time in planning and teaching and makes these more effective, then it is time well spent. Practitioners are all too aware of how short the learning day can seem and the planning of their own time needs to be undertaken carefully. It also needs to be realistic. Time for observation should be planned rather than it being fitted into snatched moments between other adult tasks. One way of achieving this is to identify on daily plans first what/who is to be *taught*, and second, what/who is to be *observed*. In this way, the practitioner can see how, given the time available, these two kinds of activity can be realistically achieved. Planning for observation in this deliberate way may mean that time is taken from time that was previously set aside for direct involvement with children. However, observation is part of the role of the early childhood educator and can only be done when children are at work or play and it should regularly be done when children are working independently, not just when they are working alongside the adult. In a letter to all reception practitioners, the National Assessment Agency (NAA, July 2006) stated quite explicitly that 'When making a judgement for the FSP (the Foundation Stage Profile), practitioners should draw on at least 80 per cent of evidence from knowledge of the child, observations and anecdotal assessments, and no more than 20 per cent of evidence from adult-directed or focused assessments.' This guidance suggested, albeit implicitly, that the balance between child-led and adult-led learning in reception classes should be heavily weighted towards the former.

Learning alongside an adult and learning independently

Making good use of time does not, of course, only apply to observation. An early childhood educator has many roles to fulfil. When looking to make the best use of teaching time, it is necessary to be realistic. In preschools and nursery settings the problem is less acute. A team of early years educators can work together to identify those who will support the play and learning of the children and those who will observe their activity. But in schools where there is one teacher and possibly 30 children, then the teacher has one of two choices. The easiest option is to teach the class as though it were a single unit, delivering the same curriculum to all children at the same time. This means that the class size is relatively immaterial because the onus is on the children to receive and inwardly digest the curriculum, with the teacher differentiating where possible through questioning during whole class sessions and some differentiated follow-up activities. Any teacher knows, however, that such strategies may guarantee curriculum coverage, but will not guarantee *learning*. The same diet of experiences can be delivered to a class of children and their digestion of those experiences will be different. Some children will go hungry, some will end up feeling sick, some will turn up their noses because they don't like what's on offer and some will eat the bits they enjoy and leave the rest on the plate. It is the very fact that children cannot be neatly fitted into a curriculum but need a curriculum that fits *them* that makes teaching so challenging.

There are times when effective teaching and learning happen in a large group. The sharing of a big book, planning for a visitor or singing number rhymes all can be effective as a large group/whole class experience. However, whatever the adult:child ratio in a setting, for the majority of their time, young children need to work and play – individually, in pairs or in small groups. This is first because young children do not yet possess the powers of concentration to listen successfully to an adult as part of a large group where their individuality is often subdued. They may 'sit quietly', but concentration – and learning – are definitely not guaranteed. But children also need to spend most of their time individually or in small groups because, from the practitioner's point of view, teaching any other way cannot possibly meet the learning needs of the diverse range of children in one class. It may be possible to keep children entertained, or even interested as one of a large group. But that is not sufficient. Once learning objectives are concerned with skills and understandings, then children need to be in small enough groups to match the planning of experiences and activities to their specific learning needs. Young children need to be able to say what they think and blurt out the ideas they are formulating. They need to feel a personal interaction with the practitioner through his or her eye contact, attentive listening and responses. This is the egocentricity of childhood: to have *your* say, to express *your* ideas, to ask *your* questions. Some people will say that children need to learn to listen to others because that is a skill that they will need as they grow older, but this will only distract many children from learning. Many young children find sitting and listening very physically demanding (Goddard Blythe 2011). So much so that the concentration required by this physical activity distracts their minds and their thinking away from any planned learning and onto the demands of managing their bodies in the ways that are expected.

If a practitioner manages children by teaching individuals or small groups, then the next question is – what are the rest of the class doing?

If one group (of, say, six children) is with the practitioner, then that leaves potentially 24 other children learning independently. It is crucial, therefore, to ask that question – what are the rest of the class doing? Because if, for most of their day, children are learning independently, then what they are learning has to be every bit as valuable as what is learned when alongside an adult. It is a mistake to think that learning without an adult alongside is somehow less important or less worthwhile than learning when an adult is there. Children will learn differently and learn different things according to whether they are learning alongside an adult or not, but both have value.

Learning alongside an adult, the child is often helped to focus. Their questions are answered more directly. They have a conversational partner. They are supported and encouraged to arrive at outcomes because the learning is usually planned by the practitioner. *Learning independently*, the child has to draw more on their own resources. They may rely on and collaborate more with their peers. They may test out a number of strategies to find what works for them. They may pursue their own thinking and draw on their own ideas to arrive at outcomes that satisfy their personal needs.

So both learning alongside an adult and independent learning have a purpose and have beneficial outcomes. If children only ever experience independent learning, then they might miss many opportunities to learn something new, to see things from different perspectives, to have their thinking challenged and extended. If children only ever learn alongside an adult, then they may lose their capacity to think for themselves, to use their initiative, to draw on their own resources. Children, young people and adults need both sets of skills. The ability to focus and think one thing through alongside others; the capacity to think independently and to get on unaided. So a good early learning environment should offer the opportunity for both kinds of learning to take place.

If independent learning is to be seen as equally valuable as learning alongside an adult, then it must be of the highest quality and the quality of independent learning is heavily dependent on the quality of the learning environment. The learning environment needs to provoke, to consolidate, to question, to challenge children in just the same ways as an effective practitioner.

An effective environment for independent learning

An effective environment for independent learning should be:

1 *Indoors and out*: there can be few people now who do not realize that an effective early learning environment needs to have an indoors

and an outdoors. Indeed, when there is a choice between the two I would always choose 'out'. Learning opportunities for children are totally different outdoors and learning out-of-doors is not simply a matter of putting what is indoors out when the weather is fine. Children in every foundation stage setting should be entitled to free access to the outdoors throughout the learning day, for without it a child's capacity to learn is inhibited by the constraints of an indoor learning environment that lacks the natural and spontaneous potential of the living, breathing world.

2 *Natural and not fake:* it must be full of natural resources and real-life experiences. It must pose questions that are meaningful and relevant to the children and not manipulated and drawn for someone else's book of ideas. It must draw on what is happening in the children's world – the builders down the street, the fair in town, the violent wind. It must be full of intrigue, surprises and real-life problems to solve as well as plenty of opportunities to consolidate emerging theories, ideas and skills.

3 *New and familiar:* children need opportunities and experiences that are familiar. They need to revisit what is known and to rehearse and repeat newly acquired skills and understandings. At this age, so much that is concerned with progress is, in point of fact, the consolidation of emerging concepts. Children need time to put down the foundations of learning (Fisher 2002) before they can confidently take 'next steps'. But children also need what is new and novel and intriguing. They need to be surprised and to be amazed. They need to be challenged to think about and to try and explain things they haven't met before and do not yet understand. They need to assimilate what is new by accommodating it alongside what they currently think they know, sometimes finding that adjustments have to be made to do so.

4 *Flexible and responsive:* space and resources need to be sufficiently flexible to meet the changing needs of large groups of individual children. Space that is cluttered by tables and chairs cannot make way for models that expand across the floor. Rigid demarcated areas can inhibit the child's desire to take resources from one area and use them creatively in role play or model making. Resources should be as adaptable as possible. Boxes, crates and swathes of materials can be used more imaginatively than games and resources that are designed for only one purpose. Most plastic resources are less responsive and less inspiring to children's ideas than those that are natural and can be transformed on the spot to become what the child wants them to be.

5 *Positive and respectful:* how the practitioner responds to individual children will establish whether this is an environment in which

each child's ideas are valued and respected. It will tell the children whether they can explore and experiment in the certain knowledge that their efforts will be respected and appreciated. It will tell them whether they can make mistakes and take risks because they have been shown that this can help their learning. It will be shown in a myriad of ways such as whether the practitioner stops to have a conversation about something of importance to the child, or whether the child's conversation is ignored in favour of the practitioner's agenda. Treating children as capable of learning independently gives children a sense of self-worth and self-awareness and can only contribute positively to their growing social and emotional development.

The early childhood educator creates the learning environment and the ethos of their setting way before the day begins. These become adapted and refined as children live and work and play in the different learning spaces. The environment is developed effectively by establishing, to begin with, the reciprocal relationships that will underpin successful independent learning; then by making best use of the available space for active learning; then by trying and refining activities, opportunities and experiences that maximize children's capacity to be independent in their learning and the strategies that support their reliance on each other as learning partners.

The balance of classroom experiences

Once the learning environment is established, then the practitioner can concentrate on the different ways in which children will learn – both alongside an adult and independently. There are three kinds of learning scenarios that can be planned to offer children a balance of experiences. These are:

- *adult-led* activities
- *adult-initiated* activities
- *child-initiated* activities

Adult-led activities

It is clearly part of the early childhood educator's repertoire to work directly with children to support their learning and extend their thinking. Once practitioners have carried out observations of children and found out about their interests and preoccupations, then they will want to draw some children together to teach a new skill or introduce a new concept. They may also want to revisit some activity or learning outcome if there have been misunderstandings or if they notice that some children need greater support than others to reach the next stage of learning. They may need to challenge some children whose thinking and understanding are in advance of their peers or work with children who are particularly vulnerable and need to have more adult support than usual. Then, as has been said already, practitioners need to plan time for their focused observations and this comes during their adult-focused time. Practitioners are often very skilled at identifying learning intentions, planning an activity for a group of children and supporting them to learn what has been identified for their learning needs. However, planning for and ensuring the quality of the activities of the rest of the class are often more challenging.

Adult-initiated activities

Adult-initiated activities are activities that are planned by the practitioner but which – once introduced – will be undertaken independently by the children. This will be the case because the practitioner has gone to teach their adult-led activity or to undertake an observation. The first step towards planning for adult-initiated activities is realizing that the nature of what children do when they are working independently is significantly different from the nature of an activity when children work with the teacher. *Activities that children will be doing independently are not simply the same as adult-focused activities but without the teacher there.*

Adult-initiated activities differ from adult-led activities in various ways. They need to be:

- sufficiently *clear* for children to be able to work without constantly checking that what they are doing is 'right';
- sufficiently *motivating* that they will sustain the interest and involvement of the children so that they do not interrupt the practitioner;
- sufficiently *open-ended* for children to be able to extend them in ways that interest and engage them until the practitioner comes alongside again.

These activities are often, though not exclusively, at either end of the cycle of learning. They are either repeating or rehearsing what is familiar – giving children the opportunity to try independently that which previously they might have done with support from the practitioner; or they are introducing something new – so that children are left to discover the properties of materials or resources, or to test out ideas or solve problems before meeting up with the practitioner again to share and discuss what they have found out.

The key to successful adult-initiated activities is open-endedness. If an activity is so tightly prescribed by the practitioner that there is clearly only one way of doing it – and that's the practitioner's way – then children will repeatedly come to check that what they are doing is 'right'. If practitioners want uninterrupted time during adult-led activities, then a great deal of consideration needs to be given to these activities which children are to undertake independently.

This does not mean of course that the practitioner will not go near the children working on adult-initiated activities once they have begun. Far from it. At the appropriate time, the practitioner will observe the learning that has been taking place, have conversations with the children about their ideas and solutions and answer any questions they may have. But this will be done *when the practitioner is ready*. The practitioner should be in control of his or her own time. This support for independent activities – 'spinning the plates' as it is sometimes called – will occur after the practitioner has finished one adult-led activity and before starting the next. There is a world of difference between practitioners being in control of when they move from one role to the next and being at the mercy of the children, doing little more than servicing their needs, because the planned activities all need adult input at much the same level at much the same time.

Most of the children in an early years setting will, most of the time, be learning independently, so it is crucial that the activities in which they are engaged are worthwhile and bring about effective learning. Most children spend far too much of their day on independent activities for these to be mere time-fillers. It is necessary to challenge the notion that the only worthwhile learning occurs when a practitioner is there. Children are learning all the time . . . and only a small amount of that time is spent anywhere near a 'teacher'!

Child-initiated activity

There is a third kind of activity that is central to high quality early years provision and that is activity that is initiated by the child. Child-initiated activity is vital to the acknowledgement of children as competent learners. It is through such activity that young children make sense of their world, and are able to explore, experiment and take risks. The place of play is fully explored in Chapter 7, but suffice to say in this context that child-initiated activities encourage children to make their own choices and decisions about what they will do, the resources and equipment they will use and the processes and outcomes of the experience. Child-initiated learning is at the cornerstone of good foundation stage practice for it allows the child to try new skills, to play alongside other children and develop socially, to use their imagination and creativity and try out things that are fascinating and preoccupying them at the time. Child-initiated activity is not the same as a child being given play resources and then being directed by the adult in how to use them. So, for example, if the adult tells the child to build a castle for Rapunzel from the wooden blocks, or if the adult puts outfits from the three bears story into the home corner and asks a group to act out the story – this is not child-initiated learning. The moment that an adult gives a child an outcome to achieve, then the activity ceases to be child-initiated. There are many times when an adult legitimately uses play resources and initiates what children will do with them, but this makes the activity adult-initiated and not child-initiated and it is important to distinguish between the two.

No early learning environment can be effective without high quality child-initiated learning, but this is the learning that is most often a challenge particularly for inexperienced practitioners or for those not trained to work with young children. Because children can become so easily involved in play, it is often child-initiated learning that is most easily abandoned. Children are 'occupied' so the adult leaves them to it. Supporting and extending learning through play is a highly skilled business and all early childhood educators need to understand that, for play to be of high quality, it needs to be supported in just the same way as adult-initiated learning (see Chapter 7). So, within the learning situation, practitioners must interact with children at play where and when this is appropriate. They must observe the learning that is taking place in play situations and review and revisit this with children if this is appropriate. In this way, play develops and it is given the same status as all the other learning that is taking place. Neither adult-initiated learning nor child-initiated learning will survive or thrive without adult support at key moments in the process. Without adult support and interest, both these activities can rapidly become abandoned learning rather than independent learning.

In foundation stage settings then, there should be a balance between these three types of activity – adult-led, adult-initiated and child-initiated. I find it helpful to see these three types of activity as the three corners of a triangle (see Fig. 4.1). The differences between the three activities can be summarized as follows:

- *child-initiated:* activity that children control in terms of experience, time and resources;
- *adult-initiated:* activities that arise from adult planning; sufficiently open-ended for children to work on independently until the adult is ready to interact;
- *adult-led:* individual, pair or group work, usually differentiated by input; the focus of adult time.

How the balance is maintained between these three types of experience will rest with the practitioner and will change from day to day and

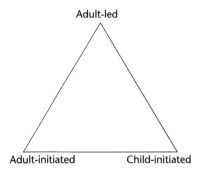

Figure 4.1 The balance of learning experiences 1

sometimes session to session. It will certainly change according to the age of the children, because the younger the children, the more the emphasis needs to be on child-initiated learning. What is powerful about this triangle model is that it works for whatever kind of learning situation is planned. It makes no difference whether children are engaged in an integrated day – experiencing different areas of learning simultaneously – or in a session where all the children are engaged in mathematical experiences at the same time (except of course the child-initiated experiences which cannot be prescribed). The principle of needing a balance of experiences within an early learning environment still applies. When there are a number of adults in the setting – as in a nursery school or day nursery – then this too will change the balance of the experiences. It may be that with two adults constantly available, one engages in adult-led learning while the other undertakes observations or supports more independent learning. It may be that one leads an adult-led activity indoors, while another leads one outdoors. The permutations are many and varied. However, for the lone teacher in the school classroom, the movement between these activities can be summarized as follows:

1 The teacher works with an individual or small group on an *adult-led* task.
2 The rest of the children are engaged on either *adult-initiated* or *child-initiated* activities.
3 These activities must enable children to be independent of the teacher so that they do not need to interrupt the *adult-led* task.
4 The teacher completes the *adult-led* task and moves to both the *adult-initiated* and *child-initiated* activities in order to support and extend these experiences as appropriate.
5 Independent learning should not be abandoned learning. Adult involvement in all activities is crucial if they are to have status and purpose.

6 Once children working independently have been adequately supported, the teacher returns to the next *adult-led* activity.

7 The rest of the children move independently between *adult-initiated* and *child-initiated* activities until/unless the teacher draws them to a *adult-led task*. (How children move from one activity to the next is the subject of Chapter 9.)

8 *All* classroom activities are shared at a review time at some point during the day if that is appropriate (see Chapter 9) – but not necessarily with the whole class.

One interesting feature of the triangle of learning experiences in practice is that different activities sit at different points of the triangle on different occasions. For example, the practitioner may introduce a mathematical game to a group one day as an adult-led activity and then once children have become familiar with the rules of play, it can become an adult-initiated activity. Equally, the practitioner may lead a discussion with a group of children as an adult-led session before leaving children to follow up the discussion by designing a lay-out for the outdoor climbing equipment independently as an adult-initiated task. Sometimes, children will have heard a story in an adult-led session that – several days later – appears in the role play area as spontaneous play (very different from the adult directing children to play out the story of The Three Bears). Conversely, children may engage in block play or water play that reveals to the adult who is observing them, that they would benefit from an adult-led input – either more support or different resources – to extend or consolidate children's learning.

Figure 4.2 summarizes these points and demonstrates the vital interaction between assessment, planning and teaching.

Once a practitioner uses the triangle to plan for the balance of learning experiences within the foundation stage, then it can be seen that this gives rise to different learning opportunities. Figure 4.3 shows how:

- *Adult-led* activities are concerned with **intended learning** – the practitioner plans an activity and, by and large, that is what the children learn.
- *Adult-initiated* activities are concerned with **potential learning** – the practitioner has specific learning intentions in mind when selecting resources and tasks, but when left to work or play independently the children may take the learning a different way and end up with different learning outcomes.
- *Child-initiated* activities are concerned with **spontaneous learning** – the practitioner may have acquired the resources or set up some experiences to begin with, but children approach these in varied and individual ways and follow their own lines of enquiry, making their learning spontaneous and unpredictable.

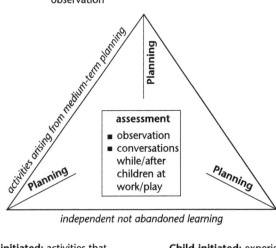

Adult-led: (adult-led teaching or observation) individual, pair or group work, usually differentiated by input; the focus of adult time. Can be used for observation

independent not abandoned learning

Adult-initiated: activities that arise from adult planning; sufficiently open-ended for children to work on independently until the adult is ready to support

Child-initiated: experiences that children control in terms of experience, time and resources

Figure 4.2 The balance of learning experiences 2

From this explanation it can be seen even more clearly how important it is that practitioners observe and evaluate all of the learning experiences that are taking place in their setting. If the practitioner only observes children engaged in adult-led activity, they are gathering evidence of the most predictable kind. While it will be possible to see that some children grasp a new concept or skill more readily than others, the range of what the children are learning is fairly limited to what the practitioner has introduced. However, when observing adult-initiated activities the practitioner can see whether or not the children take the activity or resources where intended or change the learning outcomes and become interested in something quite different. This lets the practitioner know whether she picked a good enough challenge for the children to follow independently, or whether the children's minds and imaginations diverted her plans down a more interesting and intriguing (for them) path. Either way, observations can be used to instigate a learning conversation or to plan what experiences

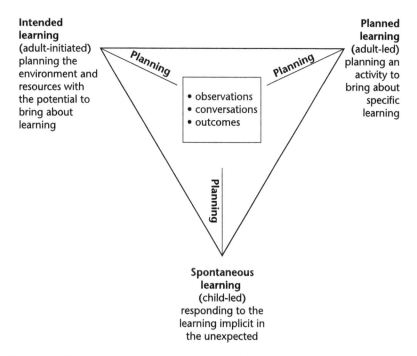

Figure 4.3 The balance of learning opportunities

and opportunities to provide next for that group or individual. Finally, when observing child-initiated learning, the practitioner has no idea what children will be doing or learning. Children at play provide the richest source of observational evidence. Because of the divergent thinking that takes place when children are at play, the practitioner will find out a whole variety of things about what children know, what they are interested in and what they can do . . . and none of it can be predetermined.

Differentiation

Adult-led, adult-initiated and child-initiated learning all have different purposes and different outcomes. When planning, the practitioner draws on observations and conversations with children and then plans:

(a) activities and/or experiences that will be adult-led and adult-initiated;
(b) resources to extend or refresh child-initiated learning.

One of the greatest challenges of planning is the identification of the differences within those experiences, opportunities, activities and support according to the needs of the children. Differentiation is a challenge both in planning but also in practice, and the quality of teaching is often an indicator of how well known children are within a setting. So, how should practitioners consider differentiation for the three kinds of learning experiences?

Child-initiated activities will be, by their very nature, differentiated by outcome. Children's own decisions about activities are a reflection of their ability, their knowledge, their understanding and their skill. Observation of these activities will inform the practitioner about these, and about the child's attitudes and motivations. They show the child's confidence and self-esteem, their perseverance and persistence and their willingness to try new things or their need to repeat what is familiar.

Adult-initiated activities are best planned so that differentiation will be by outcome. Sometimes it is appropriate that an activity is planned for a group of children of certain ability and that this activity is targeted exclusively at them. But more often than not, the very nature of an open-ended, problem-solving task is that children will tackle the task at their own level. As long as there is no 'right answer' and children know that their own solution will be valued, then they will differentiate these activities in their own way. Differentiation by outcome places an emphasis on the practitioner learning *about* children through the selected activity, as much as children learning *from* the activity.

Adult-led activities are most likely to be differentiated by input. In other words, the practitioner has planned to work with a group of children who have reached the same stage at the same time and will benefit from being introduced to, or consolidating, or revisiting an activity, task or experience together. The practitioner's knowledge of the needs of these children will have come directly from his or her first-hand observations of them at work or play independently and as they work with adults.

Use of practitioner time

Adult-led, adult-initiated and child-initiated learning each give the practitioner a clear and purposeful role in supporting the learning that occurs in the different contexts. Each role is planned but each role demands something different from the practitioner.

Adult-led learning is learning that is planned by an adult with the learning outcomes already determined. As the practitioner stays with the child or children as they are learning, **the role of the practitioner in adult-led learning** is to:

- introduce the child/ren to learning they may not have otherwise met or which needs additional adult support;
- focus exploration, discussion and learning on a certain set of objectives;
- establish what is already known/familiar to the group;
- steer and guide the child/ren towards the planned objectives;
- explain, inform, introduce skills and knowledge that will help the child/ren achieve the objectives.

Adult-initiated learning is also planned by the practitioner and has predetermined objectives but, because the activity will be carried out largely independently, the child/ren's interpretation of the task and the ideas and thinking they bring to the task may lead to different outcomes and different learning than the practitioner intended. When the practitioner returns to such an activity, to find out what children have learned, **the role of the practitioner in adult-initiated learning** is to:

- observe: What direction has this activity taken? Can I tune in to the child/ren's current thinking?
- be intrigued: What is this child trying to achieve? Why has this activity taken the course it has?
- enquire: What have you been finding out? What has interested you?
- suggest: Maybe you could try? I wonder what would happen if?
- see if there is a way back to the original objectives – *if* child/ren have strayed away: Can I sensibly bring the child/ren back to the planned objectives or have they pursued something far more interesting from which I can learn more about their thinking?

In *child-initiated* learning, the role of the practitioner is to be what the children need you to be. In other words, **the role of the practitioner in child-initiated learning** is to:

- watch: What is this child doing? What are they trying to achieve?
- wait: Is the child getting on alright on their own? Are they getting stuck and frustrated? Can I be of help?
- wonder: I wonder what they are thinking right now? I wonder how they arrived at this line of enquiry from where they started? I wonder if I can support their learning now or whether they are better left alone? I wonder whether there is something I can provide tomorrow that will extend this play further?

Yet, while there are differences in the ways in which practitioners offer support to children in these different learning situations, there are also similarities in the role of the adult that underpins every effective interaction, whatever the context.

In research conducted in Oxfordshire schools and settings with children from 6 months to 6 years, (Fisher 2012 a/b/c/d; Fisher and Wood 2012), practitioners have analysed the following characteristics of effective interactions:

About children Effective interactions –

- involve and engage children;
- are meaningful and relevant to children;
- always support and frequently extend children's thinking or understanding;
- leave the child with something positive from the adult they did not have before.

About relationships Effective interactions –

- require high levels of respect and reciprocity;
- are built on strong, safe relationships where children feel special and are listened to;
- benefit from high levels of warm attentiveness[1] from an adult (this does not necessarily involve speaking).

About prerequisites Effective interactions –

- rely on the adult's flexibility and adaptability to provide whatever support is appropriate and desirable;
- show the adult to be sufficiently responsive to the child's interests and ideas;
- are more readily established when the adult knows the child well and tunes in swiftly to their current needs and interests.

About characteristics Effective interactions –

- are characterized by adult responsiveness over and above adult direction;
- are characterized by questions that clarify the adult's understanding of the child's intentions over and above checking the child's current understanding;
- are clearly rewarding for the adult as well as the child.

The significance of these characteristics is that they are constant, no matter what the age of the child and no matter what the context for

---

[1] 'Warm attentiveness' – where an adult shows through their body language and facial expression and focus that they are deeply interested in the child and what they are doing.

learning. In other words, there are features of effective adult–child interactions that remain identifiable in every classroom encounter, no matter what its purpose.

Encouraging independent learning

In determining the role of the adult it is essential to be clear about the purposes of learning in its different contexts. Independent learning is not second-rate learning. It is not what some children have to do while practitioners are busy with an adult-led group. A key purpose of education is to prepare children to be lifelong learners and key skills that make this possible are the abilities to work, think, experiment and persist independently. As we have seen, children learn different things in an adult-led session than they learn in one where they are expected and encouraged to be independent. Both situations have value and both draw on different styles of learning and reveal different learning strengths. There are children who thrive in one situation and not the other. Those children who like to be at the front of the class with their hand up, who like to answer questions and who respond positively to adult input and direction, may flounder when left to think and act for themselves. Likewise, children who struggle to focus and concentrate on an adult's agenda may be just the children who thrive and shine when left to problem-solve, to lead and to organize their own learning. Every practitioner should see children in both learning situations and, in that way, they are more likely to get to know the 'whole' child as a learner.

When the practitioner plans an adult-led session, it should be because the practitioner believes the child/ren will not learn that set of objectives on their own. When the practitioner plans an adult-initiated activity, it should be because the practitioner believes the child/ren will learn something of value by engaging with resources, the environment and/or their peers independently. If the practitioner plans for child-initiated learning, it should be because the practitioner wants children to have the opportunity to control their own learning and its outcomes (se Chapter 7) and believes this to be an enriching and invaluable source of early education. Each situation teaches the child something different and teaches the practitioner something different in return.

The aim, within the busy classroom, is to make independent learning of such high quality that the adult is released to focus on their own planned activities and not be sidetracked by unnecessary or uncalled for demands. When children are encouraged to be independent learners they are far less likely to come and bother the practitioner with questions about 'what do I do next?'; 'is this what you wanted?'; 'can I do something else now?'. I am not suggesting that, by encouraging independence, children will *never* interrupt. Some children – for justifiable reasons – will need help or reassurance. But by planning independent learning with care, the number of interruptions will be minimized.

The recorded interactions between a teacher and her reception class (Fisher 1996) provide fascinating data that chronicles the growing independence of children and the changes in their attitudes and behaviour towards their teacher. At the beginning of the school year, in the autumn term, the children related to the teacher in ways that revealed their dependence on her:

Child: Do you want me to do any more?
Child: Can I stop this now please?
Child: Where are the pencils?

As the children became more independent they seemed to revise their concept of what 'being a pupil' meant, started to revel in their new-found independence and ignored the teacher almost completely. During the spring term the teacher was often left alone for 15–25 minutes without interruption, allowing her to get on with her adult-led activities. Then, towards the end of the spring term the relationship changed once again and the children began to refer back to the teacher, but the nature of the exchanges had altered. The children were no longer seeking reassurance, but were coming to their teacher simply to share the pleasure of a discovery or an achievement or specifically to request her support:

Child: Do you want to see the model I've made?

Child: I can't do my 'a's.
Teacher: Do you want me to help?
Child: Yes.

Child: Can you help me finish the story I'm writing?

The children's perceptions of the role of the teacher had changed. Because they had independence and a considerable degree of autonomy in the classroom, it seemed as though they came to see the teacher as yet another valuable resource to enable them to achieve what they wanted to achieve.

Worksheets

We cannot leave the subject of independent learning without addressing, head on, the issue of worksheets. Sometimes practitioners feel they need written evidence that something has been learnt, and I hope that Chapter 2 has dispelled that particular myth. More than any other reason, worksheets are given to children to keep them occupied while the practitioner does other things. The emphasis in this chapter on high quality independent learning should have shown that learning away from the practitioner should be every bit as demanding and interesting and thought-provoking as learning when the practitioner is alongside . . . and worksheets rarely offer this. When tempted to offer a worksheet to a young child, consider the following issues:

1 The difference between many children's literacy skills and their conceptual understanding is great. It is possible for children to have a relatively sophisticated understanding of a concept and yet be unable to record this because the worksheet uses language that they cannot read or don't understand or their own written language is not sufficiently developed to record what they know.

2 Worksheet answers can be copied or guessed at. Since so many of them require gaps to be filled in, the chances of doing either or both are quite high. All this may give evidence of is how able another child is on the same table.

3 A worksheet restricts what a young child can tell you about what they know and understand. If children devise their own ways of recording knowledge and understanding, then they will select ways that make sense to them and that give all the information they want to share.

4 Children frequently spend more time colouring in worksheets than they do engaging with the concepts behind them. By the time the worksheet is finished, most young children are hard pushed to tell you what it was about.

5 Young children spend far *less* time completing most worksheets than adults spend laboriously drawing – or photocopying – them.

It is unreasonable to criticize things without offering viable alternatives, so:

- if *evidence of learning* is needed, *watch* and *listen* to the child and record what they do and say;
- if *recorded evidence* is needed, let the child devise their own ways of recording – pictures, diagrams and maps, or take photographs of models or activity or mark-making;
- if *time-fillers* are needed, think again; address the issue of independent learning positively and initiate activities that are valuable and valid.

Every activity in every classroom should be purposeful, meaningful and worthwhile. Independent learning should be stimulated and facilitated by a high quality environment and high quality resources (see Chapter 5) and be as effective, in its own way, as learning with an adult alongside.

Status and quality

Some practitioners are concerned that giving children too much independence will result in outcomes of inferior quality, especially if these require recording. There are a number of ways of ensuring that this is not the case and most of these hinge on the practitioner's own attitudes to the activities that are going on. In order for children to value their own work, whether it is adult-led, adult-initiated or child-initiated, it has to have status. Status can be conferred by the child and their own involvement and pride in their efforts and ideas. Status is also conferred by the practitioner, however, who confirms or denies the importance of different activities through a myriad of different messages – given both explicitly and implicitly. All foundation stage activities should be worthwhile. If they are not, then they should not be given house room. The three kinds of activity will be given equal status if they are:

- *happening at the same time* as each other, not one always preceding the others ('finish your work and then you can have some time to play') because it is seen by the practitioner as being more important;
- *observed, monitored and assessed* by the practitioner when children are in action;
- *the subject of conversations* in order to find out what children have done and discovered, and to show interest in their efforts and achievements where observation has not been possible;
- *used to inform future planning.*

In this way, the activities and experiences all have a clear purpose and the use of precious practitioner time is maximized.

Conclusion

The role the adult adopts in the foundation stage learning environment is the key to the quality of learning experienced by the child. If early childhood practitioners are to emulate the success of children's earliest educators, then their role will be most successful when they facilitate and support children's learning and respond to what children initiate (Sharp 2000). While foundation stage practitioners are responsible for transmitting the values of society and introducing children to areas of learning and experience that they might not otherwise discover for themselves, learning is most successful when the strategies that adults use enable children to own the experiences as much as possible and to see the relevance of those experiences to their daily lives. Early childhood educators manage a complex orchestration of activities and experiences within the foundation stage environment. What is crucial to the success of the enterprise is to remember that when involved in early years education, practitioners will not be directly teaching all of the children all of the time. Indeed the reality of the situation is that more children will spend more of their day working and playing independently than they will working with an adult. It is vital then for practitioners to focus their attention on those activities that encourage independence and autonomy. They should be demanding and challenging and not planned in order to fill in time until the adult is free. By looking at the balance between adult-led, adult-initiated and child-initiated activities, early childhood practitioners can make their role both responsive to the children's needs for independence and realistic in terms of their own need to spend targeted time with individuals and groups. The next chapter explores a variety of ways of encouraging children to be independent learners and considers how the learning environment can be organized to facilitate this.

Questions to Challenge your Thinking

1 What is the value and benefit *to children* of whole class/ whole group teaching?
2 Are you sufficiently clear about the differing purposes, and benefits, of adult-led, adult-initiated and child-initiated learning?
3 Do you observe and support children's learning equally in adult-led and child-led situations?

5

ENCOURAGING INDEPENDENCE

Environments that develop children's learning autonomy

Introduction

As we saw in the previous chapter, while adult-led learning is crucial for young children's development, much of the time children spend in their different learning environments is independent of direct adult support. But young children who are learning independently are not just 'waiting for the adult to get there'. Early childhood educators know that what – and how – children learn when they are learning independently is qualitatively different from, but just as important as, what and how they learn directly from an adult. Learning from adults enables learning to be focused and directed. It is often highly specific and has a narrow focus and set of objectives. It requires the child to concentrate on someone else's agenda and to learn within someone else's parameters. Learning independently, on the other hand, puts greater demands on the child to find and choose their own resources, to problem solve and make decisions on their own, to use their initiative and collaborate with others if necessary, all without adult intervention and guidance. So, while on the one hand independent learning puts greater responsibility onto the child and expects more of the individual or the group, it is also more liberating in that it is not as tightly prescribed as adult-led learning. The child is free to follow their own threads of thinking and to take an activity or experience down unexpected pathways, making links between what has been suggested to them and what ignites their interest.

Independent learning can be provoked by the adult or it can be entirely child-led. If it has been provoked by an adult it is adult-initiated learning, in a situation where an adult has put out certain resources or set a challenge to be completed by an individual or group (see Chapter

4). If it is child-initiated learning, then the activity or experience is: 'freely chosen by the child, and is under the control of the child. The child decides how to play, how long to sustain the play, what the play is about, and who to play with' (DCSF 2009: 10). In both contexts, the onus is on the child to follow their own thinking, to come to their own decisions and to use a variety of skills such as problem-solving, prioritizing and negotiating, that will be invaluable to them as lifelong learners and that will never be experienced or rehearsed if the child's learning diet is entirely adult-led. For all its strengths, adult-led learning has its limitations. Children who find it easy to follow an adult's instructions and intentions are usually those who shine. Those who prefer to follow their own lines of enquiry and get on with their own investigations often struggle. Those who can explain their thinking and like to talk about their ideas usually do well. Those for whom language and communication are a challenge and who prefer 'doing' to 'talking about it', often struggle. Not only is a diet solely of adult-led learning disadvantageous for many children but it is disadvantageous for the practitioner, as it shows only one side of the child as a learner. The child who can sit still, listen, concentrate and offer answers may be seen as 'successful' and the child who is itching to go and be more hands on and interactive with their learning may be seen as difficult or less able. The child who is at their most creative and dynamic in less prescribed learning situations may never get the chance to show what they can do and to shine.

Independent learning is a necessary and desirable element of early education. It shouldn't just happen because there isn't an adult to be alongside every group. Indeed, an adult alongside every group would be inappropriate and undesirable. It would inhibit all those skills that can only be learned when children are free to try their own ideas, to express their own thoughts and to learn from their own mistakes.

An environment for independent learning

Although an adult is not close by at the time, they will have a profound influence over the quality of the learning that children experience when they learn independently. The quality of early learning is stimulated, supported and provoked by the quality of the environment in which young children are being educated. The educators in Reggio Emilia refer to the environment as the 'third educator' (alongside the adult and a child's peers) and, indeed, the environment should be as good as another adult in the stimulation, support and provocation it provides. A high quality early learning environment will be constantly evaluated for the impact it has on children's learning experiences and opportunities in just the same way as, or indeed as part of, the evaluation of the impact of the quality of teaching on children's learning and development. This reiterates the point made in Chapter 4, that independent learning is not abandoned learning. While children may be, and should be, left for periods of time to get on with things uninterrupted, this does not mean that independent learning is abandoned. Children learning independently need to be observed, talked to and supported at key moments to ensure the quality of that learning is sustained. If children believe that independent learning is of no interest to the practitioner, then they, in turn, may lose interest and will almost certainly come to believe that independent learning is of less importance than learning that takes place alongside an adult. Furthermore, if independent learning is abandoned, then some really important moments for both learning and teaching may be lost. Children are often at their most receptive to talk about and think about their learning when, after a period of independence, an adult comes alongside an activity and acts as a sounding board, listening to theories and ideas and offering attentive and expert support.

When the learning environment engages and involves children at the highest level, then there is also an immense and immediate benefit to the quality of adult-led learning. As children become increasingly able to learn without constant adult guidance, then the adult is left free, if they choose, to get on with teaching an adult-led group without interruption. A sign that a classroom is one where independent learning is operating effectively, is when the practitioner can lead an adult-led activity without a queue of children forming to ask 'what do I do next?' or to tell the practitioner 'I've finished'. Independent learners know what to do next, they know how to sustain their own learning, they know where to put things when they are finished and what to do if there is an accident or spillage. They take pride in being able to 'get on' with their learning and have a sense of purpose – their own purpose – rather than being reliant on an adult for every move they make.

Replicating children's early experiences

Independent learning is not something that children have to be taught. Exploring and investigating the world around them are instinctive responses that children demonstrate from the moment they are born (Goddard Blythe 2011). But experience – usually in the form of adults – can cause these natural instincts to become blunt over time. Adult fears over health and safety, lack of time or the inclination to respond, expectations and constraints, can all diminish the inbuilt inquisitiveness that make children such natural and spontaneous learners. Yet, in these first years of life, children learn more than at any comparable period of time in their lives. Long before they are of school age, long before many have even been to a nursery or childminder, young children learn many of the most important lessons they will ever learn: to communicate, to recognize a whole range of different objects and sights, to walk, to talk. This means that the world clearly presents children with sufficient stimulation to keep their inquisitive juices flowing and offers sufficient answers and solutions to the questions children pose about the world to maintain their interest in being active and interactive learners. So, what experiences does the real world offer children that enable them to be such successful early learners? For most, fortunate children:

1 their world is full of *interesting objects*: some of these are toys and playthings but many are the objects of everyday living – saucepans, telephones, plants, spoons, pens, baskets. These objects stimulate young children's senses. They smell and touch and taste them to come to understand their properties and what they can do.
2 their world is full of *interesting experiences*: going to the shops, to the park, watching mum put the washing on; seeing adults playing football. These experiences stimulate children to be part of their community; to do the things that older people can do; to want to join in the activities they see as an equal participant.
3 their world is full of *interested people*: people who communicate with them and people to whom they relate; people who smile back; who reply to their noises and burbles and first words; who tell them stories; who answer their questions and tell them things they didn't know before.

The world is so interesting to young children that it raises numerous questions as they try to make sense of what is all around them and, if they are fortunate, the objects, experiences and people they come across provide answers to those questions and in turn provoke new questions to be answered.

These natural and inquisitive learners are those who come to our nurseries and classrooms and yet, so quickly, many become anxious and reluctant to learn because they are confronted by objects, experiences and people that do not support their view of themselves as confident and competent learners. For many, if they are unfortunate:

1 their world is full of *replica objects*: plastic, fake resources that are there for an educational rather than a real-life purpose; that represent things rather than being the real thing; that are unappealing to look at or touch (plastic again) rather than being natural (stones, feathers) and very tactile;

2 their world is full of *fake experiences*: planned by adults for an educational purpose rather than a real-life one; that seem to bear little relationship to experiences that have any point to them; that take them away from what they are actually interested in and which seem of little relevance to them as individuals;
3 their world is full of *unresponsive people*: people who ask them endless questions rather than answering the ones that they are interested in; who seem to spend more time checking and testing their knowledge and understanding of the world rather than extending and enhancing it; who expect them to do what is planned rather than encouraging them to follow their own ideas.

It is little wonder that some children find this kind of learning environment alien and excluding. Early childhood educators need to work hard to make the transition from real-life learning to school learning as seamless as possible and to replicate, where they are able, the real-world contexts that made early learning so very successful (Fisher 2010).

Learning out of doors

> The best classroom and the richest cupboard are roofed only by the sky.
>
> (Margaret McMillan 1919)

The most natural learning environment for young children is the outdoors. The outdoor environment can no longer be thought of as an added extra but should be an entitlement for all children learning in the early years foundation stage. If we believe that children thrive and learn best in environments that stimulate their curiosity and open up their imagination, then we see this most naturally when children are out of doors. Most children are naturally drawn to the outdoors. There, they have greater freedom to explore and to investigate; to be adventurous and messy; to observe living things and to pose questions about them; to learn quite naturally through all their senses; to use their whole body which both stimulates the brain and is good for the body itself; to feel free and uninhibited and, as Jan White says in her book about playing and learning outdoors 'to be their natural, exuberant, physical and noisy selves' (2008: 2). The outside environment offers a rich world of learning possibilities – usually so much richer than the fake and fabricated world indoors. How much better to use acorns than plastic bears for counting, to investigate a bird or a worm in its natural habitat rather than looking at pictures, to feel the wind in your hair rather than get eye strain from artificial lighting.

The outdoor learning environment is 'a complete learning environment which can cater for all children's needs – cognitive, emotional, social and physical' (Bilton 2002: ix). Sometimes the outdoor environment mirrors what takes place indoors and sometimes it offers something quite unique. What makes an outdoor area effective, however, is that it is seen as an integral part of the teaching and learning space to be planned for and assessed in exactly the same way as spaces indoors. It should provide for the flow of learning between the two environments. The highly informative ILEA document *A Curriculum for Young Children: Outdoor Play* (1990: 6) identifies three different ways of linking the indoor and outdoor environments:

1 the inside can be *transferred* outside – that is elements from the inside are physically moved outside – like rebuilding the home corner outdoors;
2 the provision is *linked* or *paralleled* – for instance, inside water play using tubes and bottles to move water can be paralleled outside using guttering, drainpipes and buckets;
3 an outside activity can be *contrasted* with an activity indoors – small-scale painting inside can be contrasted with the use of large sheets of paper and decorating brushes outside.

However, there are things that happen outside that simply cannot happen adequately anywhere else. Experiencing weather and the seasons is rich and real outdoors and secondhand if children are inside; the thrill of growing and cultivating living things has so many more possibilities outside than in the indoor environment; opportunities for being away from adults and finding spaces to be alone and secret are so much greater in a good outdoor area than inside. Most of all, there is a sense of size and scale about being out of doors that cannot be replicated inside. The chance to run, to leap, to feel free and to use the whole body, so often too cramped and constrained inside, is a compelling reason for most children to be outside for much of the time. And in today's world, of course, there are many reasons why this matters. Too many children, as we know, are having too little exercise. They are constrained by adult fears for their safety, or by having no garden or green space near their homes to play in, or by having no adult with the time to take them swimming or to play football. Children in our society need outdoor spaces more than ever to offer all the rich and tantalizing possibilities of outdoor learning but within a safe and secure environment. That does not mean, however, an environment without risk. Risk is a valuable part of children's learning experience. If they do not learn how to approach and manage risk then, in White's words, they become 'either timid or reckless, or unable to cope with consequences' (2008: 10). Risk enables children to learn to make judgements about the world and their own capabilities. It gives them opportunities to extend themselves and to try something challenging, exhilarating and satisfying. It is up to staff within a setting to have assessed the environment so that the risks are reasonable and in keeping with the principles of early childhood education which promote challenge, experimentation and error as features of high quality learning.

The role of the adult

The role of the adult outdoors should mirror precisely the role of the adult indoors. It does not suddenly become supervisory because the space is larger and some of the children are involved in physically challenging activity. The role of the adult remains to facilitate adult-led tasks with individuals or groups; to be moving between individuals and groups to support and extend children's independent and spontaneous learning as and when required; to observe children at work and play. Managing an outdoor environment in this way is, of course, far harder when there is no second adult. All foundation stage settings should have at least two adults, qualified to teach young children and knowledgeable about their learning needs. To expect one adult to manage an indoor and outdoor learning environment is entirely unreasonable and, as has already been said, the UK government should make a far stronger stand about ratios in reception classes being reduced.

The weather

The British weather is not as bad as we sometimes imagine (just think how relatively few playtimes are lost to bad weather). The provision of a covered veranda should protect the children from both extremes of temperature – the sun in this country is a far greater threat to children's health than rain. So good quality provision places sails, canopies and gazebos in strategic places to protect children from the harmful rays of the sun. It ensures there is shade and cool places to relax even in the warmest weather. Then, at the other end of the continuum, practitioners need to protect children from adverse weather. This does not mean keeping them indoors! The Danish early childhood educators say there is no such thing as bad weather – only bad clothing. Good quality provision offers children macs and boots to change into when going outside. Practitioners role model pleasure at being outside in different conditions rather than looking fed-up while clutching a mug of coffee. Bad weather offers a wealth of learning opportunities that simply cannot be experienced if the weather is always fine. Just think what can be learnt through playing in puddles!

Space outdoors

Clearly the design of an outdoor learning environment will be dependent on whether or not there is direct access to the outdoors and what opportunities lie outside. Having said that, most classrooms could make better use of the available space – such as it is – than they currently do. It is important to explore the possibilities and to take on board whatever is feasible while lobbying for extended provision.

A high quality outdoor learning environment should have a landscape with:

- grassed areas and hard surface areas;
- tracks using different surfaces, e.g. bricks, cobblestones;
- shaded areas and sunlit areas;
- places to run and places to sit;
- places to hide;
- places to dig;
- places to perform;
- areas to cultivate and areas in which to encourage natural habitats;
- trees, shrubs, bushes, flowers and vegetables;
- animals and birds to care for.

Resources outdoors

The outdoor learning environment should be organized and planned with the same attention to detail, accessibility and independence as the indoors. A large shed will be necessary to store some resources overnight, but all resources should have their place and children should be taught to find and return what they want and need just as they do indoors.

A high quality outdoor area for learning needs the following resources:

- those that encourage the development of gross motor skills:
  - swings and ropes,
  - slides,
  - climbing frames,
  - mats to jump on or over,
  - structures for balancing and jumping between – all sited on appropriate safe surfaces,
  - bicycles and tricycles,
  - wagons and wheelbarrows to push and pull,

- scooters,
- bouncing and rocking equipment – and pathways to travel on without interrupting the activities of other children;
- those that encourage fine motor development:
  - balls and bean bags,
  - hoops,
  - quoits,
  - woodwork table,
  - creative area,
  - small sand and water play area;
- those that encourage exploration and discovery:
  - construction materials,
  - sand pit/tray(s) (think big ... I now talk to headteachers and architects about golf bunkers so they get the idea of scale!),
  - water features/tray(s) (again, think big, children want to dam water, to move it from one place to another, to pour it, to fill containers with it. A water tray alone just won't do!),
  - role play props,
  - roadways and playmats,
  - design and creative materials,
  - unstructured materials (large cardboard boxes; guttering; crates; cones; bits of material),
  - music and rhythm materials; some teachers acquire large carpets that can be put on concrete outside the classroom to enable children to sit and work;
- those that encourage imagination and expression:
  - drapes for hideaways,
  - an outdoor 'house',
  - boxes and crates,
  - masks, cloaks, hats and shoes,
  - bits of material to represent costumes,
  - puppets,
  - an old boat,
  - an amphitheatre or performance space,
  - large blocks,
  - long ropes and pulleys,
  - logs and branches.

Some of the elements of an outdoor learning environment may need long-term planning because they are costly (climbing equipment or surfaces, for example), but most are feasible with little or no expense and practitioners find that once the outdoors is established as part of the continuous learning provision, then all sorts of things improve about the quality of learning and teaching in their nursery or classroom.

Independence

Because a good outdoor area has space, children need to be independent as learners and know how to manage themselves, their resources and their own safety. Practitioners who teach children about how to manage all of these find that children manage very well, excited by the opportunities that being out of doors offers them. They become adept at organizing themselves and their activity and do not demand time and attention from adults. Nevertheless, just as with all other contexts for early learning, children's independent learning out of doors still needs to be observed, supported and extended by well-timed adult intervention to maintain the highest quality.

Behaviour

Practitioners who introduce free flow outdoor provision as part of children's daily learning entitlement consistently report an improvement in children's behaviour. It is as though the space and opportunity to have greater physical freedom release some of the pent-up feelings that being constantly inside can exacerbate. Sitting still on the carpet, sitting in assembly, sitting listening to an adult's instructions – all these impose a strain on active children who need to move to learn most effectively (Goddard Blythe 2005). Children who arrive at school tired, without a proper breakfast, from a home situation where there are arguments or unhappiness often benefit from being able to go straight outside to a space where they can relieve some of their tensions, thus allowing them to face the rest of the day with a greater sense of equilibrium. Outdoor learning improves behaviour too, simply because when a large number of children are outside, it increases the space for those inside which, in turn, improves behaviour there also.

Curiosity and involvement

The natural materials that young children should find in a good quality outdoor area for learning have a very high play value. They are, of course, entirely open-ended and can be used by children in a myriad different ways. As children explore and play with these versatile resources their curiosity is stimulated and their levels of involvement are high. They are constantly asking 'what is this?' and 'what does this do?' Observation of children in well-resourced outdoor areas shows they can spend 'long periods of time lost in their own worlds as they handle, manipulate, explore and imagine' (White 2008: 16). As White's book so powerfully reminds us, children have a natural affinity with the outside world and they enjoy the aesthetic qualities of natural things. This spontaneous interest in all things natural leads to learning that encompasses pattern, shape, size and position as well as the use of natural materials to represent a whole variety of objects in both solitary and shared play.

Learning indoors

Space indoors

Although learning out of doors is critical for young children, many of their learning experiences will still take place indoors. The problem for many practitioners is that there simply isn't enough space to do all that they want to do inside. Having a high quality outdoor area is one way of instantly relieving space inside, but it is still necessary to prioritize how space will be used indoors to optimize learning opportunities. The following is a list of those areas that most practitioners say they would like to have in their indoor environment:

- carpeted area(s) for:
  - sharing work,
  - games,
  - construction,
  - grouping together;
- home/imaginative/role play area;
- sand tray(s) – wet and dry;
- water tray;
- interest/discovery/exploratory area;
- bed for children to rest;
- quiet area;
- writing/mark-making area;
- reading area;
- listening area;
- music area;
- table tops;
- creative area:
  - gluing,
  - painting,
  - cutting,
  - dough,
  - clay,
  - plasticine,
  - modelling;
- computer area.

It might be useful to draw up your own list of what you believe young children need in their indoor learning environment. The most important questions to ask are: how do young children learn most effectively? (see Chapter 1); is my classroom offering them those learning opportunities? In some early years classrooms, in particular, too much space is taken up by tables and chairs. A class of young children need never to sit down at a table all at the same time. By eliminating unnecessary tables and chairs, space is instantly created that can be used more flexibly. Floor space is flexible space, children have room to build and create imaginary worlds – but also somewhere to go to read and listen to stories; they have space for small-world play and space to build models; they have space to create train tracks and draw pictures on huge pieces of paper. They need floor space to take their learning where it wants to go and not be inhibited by tables and chairs that block their way. Children learn most effectively through first-hand, active and interactive experiences and opportunities and need space inside to make that kind of learning a daily entitlement.

Box 5.1   Making decisions about the use of space

- Draw up a list of those areas that are valuable for young learners.
- Prioritize them in order to make adjustments for the available space.
- Eliminate those that are of little value or seldom used.
- Create space by getting rid of unnecessary tables and chairs.
- Plan the remaining areas within the space available.
- Be able to justify decisions on sound educational grounds.

In order to support children in being as independent in their learning as possible, it is necessary for the space indoors to be planned so that everyone knows that certain resources belong in certain areas. Classrooms need areas for:

- mathematical equipment
- resources for writing
- scientific equipment
- books
- home play and role play
- art, craft and creative materials
- construction materials
- resources for imaginary play
- sand and water play.

These areas can be labelled and children and adults should all be aware that this is where resources are kept and where resources need to be returned. The naming and labelling give a sense of order to what can otherwise be a very confusing environment. It might help to imagine going into an unfamiliar supermarket and looking for the washing powders or the cereals without signs identifying where these are to be found. Clearly identified areas for learning make the organization and the management of resources so much more straight-forward for both practitioners and children.

It does not mean, of course, that children must learn only in those designated areas. To undertake a maths activity a child does not have to sit in the maths area; to write, a child does not have to sit by the writing resources; to build a model, the child does not need to stop when the carpet area runs out. Areas are there to make independent learning easier; to make finding, fetching and returning resources more efficient, not to constrain the child in what he or she can or cannot do there. I was in a classroom recently where a child involved in small world play said he couldn't go to the construction kits to get a model television set which he wanted for his story because 'I am not on construction'. This is to misunderstand the point of organizing spaces for learning – they are to contain the resources, not the children.

Box 5.2   Principles about using space

- Some areas will be determined by fixtures such as sinks and floor surfaces (indoors) and resilient surfaces and sand pits (outdoors) and these need allocating first.
- Each area needs sufficient space for children to move around comfortably and safely.
- Some learning experiences naturally benefit from being placed alongside others, for example, the home corner can extend to a café which can benefit from being near the block play area for interrelated play.
- Some areas benefit from *not* being near others, for example, the listening area or book corner will probably be disturbed by the activity in the construction area; bikes and trikes must not be a hazard for other play taking place outside.
- There need to be areas where children can work independently, in small groups and as a large group.

Resources indoors

Once space has been allocated, then all the resources that will be needed in any one area should be made available. Children who are going to be independent in their learning need to know where to find resources and where to return them once they have been used.

The choice of equipment should once again be determined by the needs of the young learner. If we want children to continue to explore, investigate and discover, then we should select resources and equipment that encourage this to go on. Sometimes the resources that offer some of the greatest learning potential are the most expensive. Wooden blocks, for example, may seem expensive to those operating on a slim budget, but they provide children with a wealth of experiences in aesthetics, mathematics, the processes of science and problem-solving (see Gura 1992 and http://www.communityplaythings.co.uk/products/blocks/index.html) and, as such, they offer good value for money. Very often, however, the best and most appealing resources are those that cost nothing at all. As we have already seen, the use of natural resources for a whole range of learning is not only aesthetically appealing but means that resources change with the seasons and with children's interests rather than being made of materials which fade, tarnish and deteriorate in quality – but which are not thrown away because their initial cost was so high. Money can be wasted on resources that might preferably be replaced by natural resources that take time rather than money to collect. A Sunday afternoon walk, a visit to relatives or an outing to certain shops can result in a whole host of wonderful resources for sorting, printing, selling, describing or investigating. A high quality outdoor learning environment as we have seen, often has these resources in abundance . . . and on the 'doorstep'.

The first task in organizing most learning environments is to *gather together* what already exists – and then be quite ruthless with anything that is out of date, inappropriate, chewed or has pieces missing. If space is at a premium, then everything that is in it should be relevant, necessary and in one piece! It can sometimes be very difficult for early years practitioners to get rid of things, especially if they have been accumulating them 'just in case'. If there is unlimited space and these resources are not making the place look too untidy, then, of course, they can be kept. But if keeping some things means there is no space for others, or it is difficult to find or reach others, then the needs of the learners in the classroom should be prioritized. *Throw out* the least useful resources, and those kept 'just in case'. One rule of thumb can be that if something has not been used in the course of a full academic year, it will either be thrown away or given to someone for whom it *is* appropriate and who *will* use it.

Once all unnecessary clutter has been disposed of, it is possible to *identify the gaps* in the available resources and decisions can be made about what needs to be added or ordered. There are many resources that can be found or scrounged rather than bought, but however resources are gathered, there are certain principles to bear in mind (see Box 5.3).

Box 5.3   Principles about gathering resources

- Resources should be appropriate for both the girls and the boys in your class.
- Resources should encourage girls to play in areas that are traditionally the domain of boys and vice versa, for example, clothes in the dressing up area that will attract boys to role play; writing equipment outside.
- Resources should reflect a wide range of cultures whether they are represented by the ethnic mix in the class or not; these might include jigsaws, cooking utensils in the home corner or books.
- Resources should be appropriate for a range of special needs, interests and circumstances. No child should feel excluded from an activity or experience because the resources available reflect a cultural, gender, social or ability bias.

Having selected and gathered new resources together, these need to be sorted and *allocated* to the areas in the learning environment in which they are most appropriate. It is particularly important that the children see the significance of this sorting process. As with many other stages of this organization of space and resources, the children can be valuably involved in the process – it is real-life problem-solving – and this will be explored later. At this point, it is sufficient to suggest that adults should not make assumptions about what is 'logical' to children. There are a number of resources that can be of use for more than one curriculum area. Therefore, will the allocation be made on the basis of most frequent use or most logical use? Will there be a resource area for each area of learning or is this unrealistic?

There are no hard and fast rules about organization. What *is* important, is that the decisions that are made make sense to the children who will use them, as well as the adults, and that the organization is consistently applied. In this way, resources are more likely to be found, used and replaced without confusion.

Once the resources have been allocated to a certain area they can be labelled for further ease of finding and returning. Some adults label both the resource and the location so that even the youngest children can match the item to its correct home. The labelling can be appropriate to the age and ability of the children using them. The label may be a picture that a child has drawn; it may be a catalogue picture that has been cut out; it may be a word describing the resource; it may be a coloured symbol denoting a certain category of resource. Alternatively, a headteacher colleague I know and respect feels that it is better that children come to learn where things go *without* such prompts. As with all things, this is a decision for individual practitioners and their children. It is also a decision, along with others to do with the management of the learning environment, that a whole staff team might want to discuss. As with most aspects of an effective early years setting, the shared discussion and decision-making within a staffroom can have a very positive impact on children's learning experiences. If children are to be encouraged to be independent, then it is highly beneficial to them – and to their early childhood educators – that there is a consistent approach throughout the setting. Nothing could be more frustrating than being given independence and autonomy in one situation only to have it taken away in the next. So, do raise these issues collaboratively with colleagues. If foundation stage children can manage the levels of independence visible in any good quality early years environment, then just imagine what 7- and 11-year-olds can achieve.

In order to facilitate independence, resources need to be located in *accessible* places. This has implications for the amount of resources in a given space and is the reason for suggesting that cluttered resource areas are not helpful. If resources are cluttered, muddled, piled too high or too deep, then a child or adult may not be able to see a resource, let alone realize that it might be useful. They may know the resource is there somewhere, but be unable to find it and consequently might use something less helpful. Equally, they may not find a space to return it to or may feel that the space is in such a mess they can put it anywhere, and the space remains cluttered.

Resources are best placed on uncluttered surfaces that make them easy to be seen and easy to reach. This means that it is better not to have resources in cupboards with doors (except the outdoor storage sheds that will need doors for security purposes). Doors can hide a multitude of clutter and they also take up a lot of space. Cupboard doors have to have space in order to be opened and that space could be so much more effectively used if the doors (indoors) are removed.

Finally, children and other adults using the environment need to be *taught* to find and replace resources properly. Children are not necessarily neat and tidy by nature! They may need to be reminded repeatedly to begin with about how to treat resources so that, in time, this becomes habit. Such strategies are best made into part of the daily routine, particularly for younger children, so that at some point in each day they watch while someone finds/replaces a certain piece of equipment or resource. This can serve two useful purposes. First, it reinforces the importance of 'a place for everything and everything in its place' and how necessary that is for a space that is being used by a lot of people. Second, it is valuable to remind children of what resources *are* available, so that they can include them in their activities as appropriate. Young children need to develop an awareness of their role in the care of the environment, not just within the setting but outside in the community also. They will learn the basic tenets of respect and value for the world around them if there is an expectation that they care for and be responsible for their own learning environment.

Box 5.4 Planning and arranging resources

- *Collect* all existing resources together.
- *Throw out* all those that are incomplete and/or inappropriate.
- *Gather together* new/necessary resources.
- *Sort* into categories that fit the arrangement of the learning space.
- *Label* by object, catalogue picture, word (possibly label resource *and* location).
- *Locate* resources on accessible, open shelving.
- *Teach* children to locate and return all resources themselves.

Finally, children need to be given *time* at the end of sessions to be responsible for *sorting and tidying* their own areas and activities so that they learn to be responsible for their own learning environment and appreciate the necessity, for everyone's sake, to keep it an organized and efficient working environment. One very helpful strategy is to give children a five-minute warning. If children are told that they have five minutes before they will be asked to stop what they are doing, then it not only gives them the opportunity to start clearing away, but it also gives them time to finish off or to stop an activity at a point that is more appropriate to *them* rather than instantly. Having said that, there may be some activities that should not be cleared away just because it is the end of a session. Some models or a painting or children's self-initiated play may be in full flow and children may want to return to their activity later. Whatever children are in the middle of should be treated with respect and not tidied away just because it suits the adult. High levels of involvement and commitment to work or play are not achieved by either being interrupted and curtailed before the child has finished to their satisfaction.

Eliminating the little things

One effective strategy to begin developing children's independence is to keep a log of the interruptions that you get as a practitioner or as a staff team. Interruptions from the children – 'I don't know what to do next'; 'Can I have some more paper'; 'I've spilt some paint'. Interruptions from elsewhere – the school secretary wanting dinner numbers; the preschool supervisor asking to borrow some children for a task; being asked to show a parent around your setting. All of these interruptions take a practitioner away from valuable teaching time. Many or most of these interruptions can be eliminated. Children need to be taught the skills of independence. They can be shown how to mix paints, how to find new paper, how to mop up spillages. It may not be perfect at first, but with encouragement and good role modelling children can manage perfectly well and enjoy doing so. As far as the adult interruptions are concerned, very often the adult who has sent the message or the instruction has simply not thought through the ramifications of their request. By raising this at a staff meeting or speaking to the person concerned individually, the level of interruptions can be reduced overnight. The task of early childhood educators is to be educating children. Now of course there are a wealth of social skills to be taught as part of clearing up mess, tidying away resources and so on, but the time for teaching these should not be in the middle of an adult-led task when other children are waiting for the practitioner to return to them and the task in hand. Anything that takes the practitioner away from their planned activity – be it observation or teaching – needs to be addressed and all those involved in a setting should understand this and be supportive.

If children learn to manage the little things in the learning environment, then it can save them, and staff in the setting, valuable time. But creating time for children to learn these skills can require a change of attitude for some practitioners. To begin with, it means providing the resources to enable children to manipulate them easily – appropriately sized and shaped pencil sharpeners, for example, or a readily accessible dust-pan and brush and mop. It also means allowing children the time and opportunity to find out for themselves that too much water means their pictures look wishy-washy, that using a mop without squeezing out water can make something more slippery not less, that turning the sharpener too often breaks a lead rather than sharpens it. It also means setting time aside when new children arrive to establish this level of independence before focusing on other curriculum areas or focused tasks. To become independent, children need to be taught certain skills and then given time to practise them. It is up to the practitioner to set time aside in order to show children how to tie each other's aprons, cut paper, or find a new book. Showing children once is, of course, never enough. Experiences like these need repetition, building into the day – perhaps at whole group time – so that children are constantly reminded of the expectations within the learning environment and how to go about looking after themselves. As with many other class-room issues, time invested here will save time later on. In this instance, the time it will save is practitioner time that can then be spent on the valuable business of *teaching* rather than *servicing*. Children feel a great sense of pride and personal achievement when they manage them-selves and do not feel they have to go to an adult. It is important that the children's efforts are seen as valuable parts of the learning process.

Involving children in making decisions

I suggested earlier that it can be beneficial for children to be involved in decisions about space and resources as much as is possible. We know as adults that, given a sense of ownership and a feeling of responsi-bility, we are likely to take more interest in something and make more effort to maintain it. There are other important reasons why involving children can be of value to them and their educators. Involving children:

- gives opportunities for real-life problem-solving;
- encourages children to maintain something that they have planned;
- enables children to have an element of control over their own learning environment;
- leads to the development of organization as a life skill;
- gives children a sense of responsibility/self-esteem;
- encourages cooperation and collaboration between children and with adults;
- enables the practitioner to see things from the children's perspectives.

Children can be involved in planning and arranging:

- the use of space;
- the naming of areas within the learning environment;
- the selection of resources;
- the categorizing of resources;
- the sorting of resources;
- the labelling of resources;
- the location of resources.

In one class I was in recently, a 4-year-old saw that his teacher's class lists were not up to date (new children had arrived and two children had left since the start of the year). With the teacher's skilled and sensitive help the boy took the lists, reorganized the groups (including keeping two 'very chatty' girls apart), changed the group charts on the wall to match his new organization, and typed up the new lists. He then explained to the class what he had done and how they were to be organized from now on. Real-life problem-solving often presents itself in settings and classrooms, but practitioners can be so busy getting to their planned agenda that they miss these genuine learning and teaching moments.

Reviewing the use of space and resources

The design and management of a learning environment are always 'work in progress'. It requires both children and practitioners to review their teaching and learning spaces and to be given the opportunity to suggest ways in which improvements can be made. The following are useful questions that practitioners can ask children – and themselves:

Space

- Do children have room to move about the learning environment – both indoors and out – without interfering in other children's activities?
- Is there space for children to engage in active learning, both indoors and out?
- Is there sufficient floor space for children's play to be left untouched until they have finished with it . . . and for a story to be read somewhere else?
- Is there space for a child to sit alone or with a friend as well as in a small group or in a large group, both indoors and out?
- Is there space for a child to be quiet as well as to be interactive and boisterous both indoors and out?

Resources

- Can children access resources both indoors and out without interfering with the activities of other children?
- Are resources clearly visible both indoors and out?
- Do resources get put back in the right place both indoors and out?
- Are there enough resources for everyone's needs both indoors and out?
- Do resources reflect the real and natural world or are they dominated by plastic?

- Do resources adequately support the consolidation of learning (the familiar) as well as the provocation of learning (the new)?

Management

- How often are adults interrupted with queries that are not to do with teaching and learning?
- Do children know what to do if resources – paint/paper/glue/pencils – run out?
- Do children know what to do if they need aprons/shoes tied?
- Do children know what to do if things are spilt?
- Do children know what to do with finished work?
- Do children know what to do when they have finished an activity?
- Do children remain engrossed in their independent learning until the adult is ready to come and interact with them?

Establishing independence

Encouraging children to be independent can take time, but it is time wisely spent. It is very hard to plan a teaching day where practitioners spend quality time with individuals or groups of children if the rest of the class is not able to operate independently. It may well be that, rather than begin teaching the curriculum from day one, that practitioners spend the early days of a term or year encouraging independence. Time can be put aside so that children are taught to find and replace resources, to mix paint, to mop up and tidy away, to move from one activity to the next without recourse to an adult (see Chapter 9 for further details of this). The role of the adult during this time is to watch, to guide and to support this growing independence. Practitioners need to have the time to show a child how to do something or to remind them where to find something. This is best achieved if the practitioner has not planned to spend this time teaching the curriculum. Any attempt to teach individuals or groups while children do not have independence is likely to lead to frustration all round. Children will not know how to manage their time and will become bored or frustrated. Practitioners will be interrupted from the teaching role by low-level requests for attention. Establishing independence, and seeing this as valuable teaching and learning in its own right, will be of long-term benefit to subsequent teaching and learning of the curriculum and to the focused use of high quality time.

In order to establish independent learning and to make it the cornerstone of the balance of learning experiences and opportunities (see Chapter 4), then it is best to start with *child-initiated* activities, then introduce *adult-initiated* activities and then finally introduce *adult-led* activities. If the practitioner begins with child-initiated activities – that is, activities that children can sustain without recourse to an adult – this leaves the adult free to concentrate on supporting independence rather than anything else. Once children are independent, adult-initiated activities can be gradually introduced so that the teacher can see if children can sustain their independence. Even though practitioners need to begin to interact with children's learning at this point, time must still be left to remind and support children when they interrupt unnecessarily. When independence is really established and children can manage themselves and their learning with confidence, then the adult-led activities can be introduced in the knowledge that the rest of the class will be working and playing purposefully without needing adult support for a while. This does not mean that children will never again interrupt an adult, but it does mean that the times when this happens should be dramatically reduced, that children can feel responsible for their own learning and that the adult is able to get on with the business of teaching.

Conclusion

Independent learners are a necessary and valuable part of classroom life. While children are innately independent and resourceful about learning, there is a difference in a classroom situation where there are expectations and boundaries that may not be the same as those they are used to at home. Children need to be helped to readjust to this communal learning environment and to understand that while there are freedoms to be enjoyed, there are also the expectations that come from playing and working alongside a number of other children using the same space. Children working and playing together, without adult intervention, is an important part of learning and development, for when children are alongside their peers they develop many different skills and understandings. Learning to collaborate and cooperate is a lifelong process and it is crucial that children have the opportunity to rehearse these skills when they are young. Chapter 6 is concerned with the importance of children learning with others; it examines the place of talk in the early years and challenges some established notions about group work.

Questions to Challenge your Thinking

1   How does your setting support and encourage children to become independent (but not abandoned) learners?
2   Does the use of space and resources enable children to pursue their own learning without interrupting adults unnecessarily?
3   How closely does learning in your setting mirror real-life experiences and opportunities?
4   Does your setting make every possible use of outdoor opportunities for learning?

6

COLLABORATION AND COOPERATION

The importance of talking and learning with others

Introduction

One of the most important elements of an environment appropriate for young learners is the provision of opportunities for children to talk together, and with adults, as they learn. There is now a powerful consensus about the centrality of talk to learning, a consensus brought about by the powerful findings of studies of language in the home and at school (significantly the Bristol study 'Language at home and at school' directed by Gordon Wells (1981, 1986), the research studies of Barbara Tizard and Martin Hughes (1984) and the work of the National Oracy Project). These comparative studies have been strengthened over time by studies of children learning through talk in classrooms – chiefly primary and secondary school classrooms – which have increased our understanding that 'amongst all living things [humans] are uniquely equipped to pool our mental resources and . . . to create knowledge – through joint mental effort' (Mercer 1995: 1). Talking things through is an essential method by which we all make sense of our experience. Vygotsky (1962) saw how young children solve practical tasks with the help of their speech as well as their eyes and hands and use language as a way of sorting out their thoughts. At first, language and action are fused together in this way, and that is why young children are often heard talking to themselves when they are engaged in an activity. Eventually, language and action become separated and the activity can be represented in the medium of words (Bruner 1985).

The realization of the impact of language on thought and learning has had two significant influences on early years practice. The first concerns talk between the children and the adult:

> to be most helpful, the child's experience of conversation should be in a one-to-one situation in which the adult is talking about matters that are of interest and concern to the child . . . or about activities in which the child and adult engage together.

(Wells 1985: 44)

The second influence concerns children and their peers and a response to the assertion that 'collaborative talk not only facilitates the task, it also empowers the learner. Indeed . . . it has the potential for promoting learning that exceeds that of almost any other type of talk' (Chang and Wells 1988: 97).

Communication with adults

In the preschool years, talking and learning go hand in hand. Children communicate with adults and their siblings and peers about things that are of interest and concern to them. The strategies that children have developed for actively making sense of their experiences have, as we have seen, been highly effective. Yet once children go to school this model of active learning through talk is not always emulated. Instead, children very often meet the vestiges of the learning-by-listening model of teaching with few opportunities to engage in the kinds of dynamic interaction that might bring about the quality of learning described above (Mercer and Littleton 2007). Tizard and Hughes (1984: 14) point out that comparisons between conversations at home and in the nursery reveal how differently children can behave in two settings, and that in some cases 'it is hard to believe it is the same child who is talking'.

Adults talking to a large group

One of the dilemmas for children – and for educators – in encouraging talk for learning, is that there are so many children with something to say, and too few adults to be able to listen. Over the years teachers, in particular, have struggled to find ways of managing the talk of large numbers of children while trying to listen and respond to the individual. One strategy that has remained popular – and indeed found great currency in English classrooms after the introduction of the two national Strategies for Literacy and Numeracy (DfEE 1998; 1999) – is whole class teaching. It is perceived by some that there is no surer way of passing on a message or introducing a theme or teaching something new, than talking to the whole class all at the same time. The problem is, as countless teachers have found, that teaching something to a whole class never guarantees that the whole class will have learned something. Teaching, in this guise, is merely the transmission of knowledge or understanding and, certainly for very young children, one of the least effective strategies for *learning* that there is. Let's examine why.

First, young children are known to be egocentric (Piaget 1929). That means that they see the world from their own perspective and struggle to accommodate the views or perspectives of others. Actually, if you listen to many adult 'talk' shows on the radio, it seems to me that many adults never move beyond that stage themselves. However, we know that young children enjoy talking about what is uppermost in their minds and find it hard to focus on what someone else introduces by way of subject matter (Bredekamp 1987; Tassoni 2007; Robinson 2008), very quickly passing over it with a shrug or a nod in order to get back to their own agenda. Sitting on a carpet amongst possibly 30 other children makes it hard for your voice to be heard.

Second, in a whole class situation it is the norm that to participate, you have to 'sit still'. Indeed in many classrooms children are reminded constantly that 'good behaviour' involves 'good sitting' and 'good listening'. So the onus in a large group is not, in fact, on participating, not on having an extended exchange with the teacher about your thoughts and ideas, but on having to listen to others, to wait your turn, to share the teacher's time. This often results in young children either forgetting about or losing interest in what they have to say because they are just not able to wait that long.

Third, sitting in a whole group and being expected to sit still means that you may be uncomfortable. We know that young children find sitting still extremely hard (Goddard-Blythe 2005; 2011; Featherstone and Bayley 2010). Every text book on child development reminds us that children are active explorers of the world (Shaffer 1999; Smith et al. 2010) and, capitalizing on their instinctive, innate behaviour, learn best on the move. So to have to sit still – and learn – is not a natural milieu. Learning in a whole class situation is frequently passive and almost always abstract. The child is expected to learn through listening to, interpreting and responding to the thinking of the adult rather than through their own first-hand experience.

Then there is the problem of physically staying still. Boys in particular struggle to control their gross motor movement sufficiently well to be able to free their minds to listen and learn at the same time. The younger the child, the harder it is to sit still for long periods of time and Goddard Blythe reminds us that a child who is unable to sit still and maintain attention 'needs *more* frequent opportunities to move around and to exercise the body in order to concentrate again' (2005: 137). When a child finds it difficult – even painful – to cross their legs and keep their back straight as they sit, then learning is made so much more difficult.

Next, there is the disappointment for young children of not getting an immediate response to what they say or for being able to continue or complete an exchange once it begins. Talk, in real-life contexts, is reciprocal. Someone says something and someone else responds, and this continues until the subject is exhausted. It is how conversations work. Yet in a whole class situation, you have to have permission to speak, it is down to the adult whether they respond to you or not, and then you rarely get a chance to continue the exchange because it is someone else's turn. For young children who are often struggling to sustain the threads of their own thinking, this constant change of focus and ideas and people means that thinking becomes muddled and interest may be lost.

Finally, in a whole class situation, if you want to talk, you have to be brave. So often, in a whole class situation, the practitioner has a clear idea about where the talk should lead and what they want children to know or understand by the end of the session. This means that children are frequently left to work out what is in the practitioner's head and what the 'right' answer should be. If a child is slightly nervous or anxious, if they are not sure and want to be tentative with a suggestion, the whole class session can feel a very public place in which it is easy to lose face. It only takes a 'Good try but no' kind of an answer or worse a 'No, no, that's not it' or 'Do you *really* think so?' or 'Come on now, don't be silly' – all of which I have heard and recorded over recent months in researching classroom practice – for the less confident child to decide not to contribute in the future for fear of being wrong or being made to look silly.

Whole class teaching is valuable for many things. For enthusing a class with a new theme or topic; for sharing information about outings or visits or visitors; for sharing poetry, story, rhymes and songs; for quick fun games consolidating maths, phonics or other skills; for reviewing and sharing work, experiences and ideas (Fisher 2010). However, when it comes to learning; when it comes to getting your head round something new or tricky; when it comes to talking things through and testing out emergent thinking, then, for young children, whole class teaching will rarely do. The range of children in any one class is too great for one practitioner to respond to, understand, elucidate and follow through the thinking of each child. For young children to learn through talk, they need lots of opportunities to have their own voice heard; to have an adult who has the time and opportunity to follow their thinking and to clear up misunderstandings or to answer questions; they need to learn the art of conversation which only comes about when an adult models active listening and has the time to respond naturally and with genuine interest. Effective practitioners not only respond to but build on what children say, so that they come to understand that speaking and listening really do go hand in hand. For this to happen successfully, adults need to talk to children in small groups, in pairs and as individuals.

Talking to individuals

Conversations with individual children are a critical part of the early childhood educator's repertoire of teaching strategies. In *Researching Effective Pedagogy in the Early Years* (2002), Iram Siraj-Blatchford and her colleagues note that 'when children are engaged in one-to-one and child paired groups, the highest incidence of "sustained shared thinking" is recorded' (2002: 59). The authors define 'sustained shared thinking' as 'an effective pedagogic interaction where two or more individuals "work together" in an intellectual way to solve a problem, to clarify a concept, evaluate activities, or extend a narrative' (2002: 59).

For talk to be effective in early childhood settings it needs to have this notion of 'shared' endeavour. The skilled practitioner listens to, responds and, where appropriate, extends children's thinking. This comes about when the practitioner takes the time to tune in to the activity of a child or a group decides whether a conversation at that moment will enhance or interrupt their thinking (Fisher 2012d). However, it is important that such conversations are not one-sided – that is, on the practitioner's side. If practitioners do most of the talking or ask most of the questions, then they still run the risk of leaving the child with too few opportunities to express their own ideas or raise their own questions. Louis Malaguzzi, the founder of the preschools in Reggio Emilia, Italy, explains that the interactions between adults and children are seen as a reciprocal activity where 'the ball is passed always along. At times the children throw it, at times we do' (Malaguzzi video, 1992).

This delightful analogy emphasizes the synergy between the child's contribution and the adult's, where both are essential and neither can be effective without the other. The child's energy and ideas, thoughts and feelings are as important as the adult's, and the adult has ideas, thoughts and feelings that can enhance the child's contributions and extend them further.

As we saw in Chapter 2, studies of conversations in the home environment reveal that they are spontaneous and arise from activities in which both the child and often the adult are engaged. The conversations are, therefore, given meaning by the context in which they occur and both adult and child have a vested interest in talking about and putting forward their views about the experience. In early childhood settings it can seem harder to achieve this kind of reciprocity, especially when the adult's agenda predominates. As we have seen in earlier chapters, there is a place for adult-led learning every bit as much as for child-led learning. The secret seems to be to clarify the different purposes of, and the difference in the role of the adult between, these two learning contexts. Research into effective adult-child interactions (Fisher 2012c; Fisher and Wood 2012) shows that effective practitioners make a clear distinction between the role of the adult when supporting child-led learning as opposed to supporting adult-led learning. While there are many strategies for introducing and sustaining a conversation that are common to both learning situations (see later in this chapter and Fisher 2012c), it seems that in order for a practitioner to ensure that they allow themselves time to *follow* the child's thinking in a child-led situation, then they must be prepared to *focus* children's thinking more effectively in adult-led situations. Adults are more inclined to be relaxed and responsive to the talk of children when they are not trying to tick off a learning objective or learning goal of their own. Likewise, children are more likely to focus on an adult's agenda when they know that they will be able to follow their own interests for a substantial part of the learning day without an adult coming over and hijacking that learning for their own purposes.

The research cited above highlights several crucial elements of practice that appear to underpin the most effective interactions between adults and an individual child. While this research was carried out with practitioners working with children from 6 months to 6 years, this brief summary below draws on the findings of those working with the 3–7 age range.

1 Talking to someone and not everyone

As the REPEY research has indicated (DfES 2002), the most sustained interactions with children take place in a one-to-one situation. Some practitioners found it hard to move away from the egalitarian notion that 'every child should have a voice'. But while it is true that every child's voice should be respected and heard over time, the reality is that it is not possible to follow the complex and convoluting threads of thinking of even a small group of young children and respond in a way that is necessary to sustain, let alone extend, their thinking. While on some occasions it is desirable and appropriate to have joint discussion *amongst* a group of children, listening to and building on each other's ideas, there are also times when practitioners need to give themselves permission to focus on one child, to follow their thinking and to become their conversational partner. Mercer and Littleton (2007) suggest that practitioners should do more than just 'interact' with children, they should 'interthink' – 'combining their intellects in creative ways that may achieve more than the sum of the parts' (2007: 4). For interthinking to have a deep and meaningful quality, it is necessary at times for a practitioner to talk to someone and not everyone.

2 Creating an environment conducive to conversation

There are some places in a nursery or a classroom that appear to be more conducive to talk than others. These are not necessarily the same places in all settings. Some practitioners will say – 'it's in the outside area'; some say – 'it's in the role play area'; others say – 'it's in the sand-pit'. While areas seem to differ according to the setting, all the areas have one feature in common – they are places where children feel relaxed. Often, this is anywhere where children have greater freedom and where they are engaged in their own self-chosen activity. Often it is where adults are not leading the learning and where there is a no pre-determined adult agenda.

Interestingly, the research shows that it is not only children who need to feel relaxed. It is equally vital that adults feel relaxed too. High quality interactions do not take place when adults feel under pressure or when they have outcomes to achieve that dominate a conversation. Practitioners, just like children, need to be in the right frame of mind to have an extended conversation that follows the meandering pathway of interthinking. If practitioners are trying to get their own point across, or if they are trying to speed a child towards an early learning goal, or if they are uncomfortable because they feel they shouldn't be spending so much time with one child, then the tension inhibits the flow of thinking and the flow of conversation.

To support an individual child's thinking an adult must be in a relaxed frame of mind. But they must also be alert and attentive to what the child is saying and may be thinking, in order to say the right thing at the right time to move their thinking on.

3 Knowing the child well

It is clear that it is easier to have an effective interaction with an individual child if the practitioner knows that child well. There are obvious parallels with the conversations we have as adults. When we meet someone new we spend considerable time and energy touching superficially on subjects where we might discover a common interest. Yet, if we go out with a good friend, then we can immediately pick up the threads of our last conversation and draw on shared experiences and previous encounters to have a conversation of depth and meaning. So it is with children. If a practitioner does not know a child well, they are hampered in all sorts of ways. They may not know the child's likes and dislikes; they may not know the child's family or their community; they may not know about something special that took place at home or in the setting the previous day or week; they may not know of particular sensitivities or anxieties, interests and fascinations that are unique to the child. All of these can inhibit an interaction, can waste time as the practitioner tries to find a conversational starting point and can cause interthinking to flounder as adult – and child – try to find common ground.

A strong feature of the Early Years Foundation Stage (EYFS) is that all children in England now have an entitlement to a Key Person – someone who is 'to ensure that every child's care is tailored to meet their individual needs, to help the child become familiar with the setting, offer a settled relationship for the child and build a relationship with their parents' (DfE 2012: 18: para 3.26). The child's Key Person is often the one with whom they have the deepest and most meaningful conversations because there is mutual trust and a shared personal as well as learning history. However, in larger settings where children have access to and talk to a range of practitioners, it is a reminder that all staff need to take responsibility for knowing all children as well as they can, so that they have valuable and effective starting points for talk and for learning.

4 Tuning in to the child

Tuning in to each child's unique thinking and development is one of the greatest challenges of early childhood education. No human being can ever truly know what is going on in the mind of another, and yet early years practitioners are trying to do this every moment of the day as they seek to understand what a young child is trying to do and whether they need help and support. Older children are able to articulate their thoughts and feelings more clearly and with greater accuracy, but with young children, the practitioner is left to work out through close and careful observation and listening, what it is that the child is trying to achieve. Observation is important but not sufficient. In the Oxfordshire project we saw how often a child might be doing something, such as making a model, but was in fact thinking of something quite different. So, if a practitioner only watches what a child is doing, it may be that they will completely misinterpret the child's thinking and try to start a conversation about the 'wrong' thing. This leads to those moments when a child gives you The Look – the look that says 'what are you talking about?'; 'what's that got to do with anything?' In order to ensure that we tune in to a child's thinking and don't talk about something that is completely irrelevant to them at that moment, then practitioners need to be active listeners as well, spending time listening to conversations to see what children are talking about and thinking about.

As we have seen, tuning in to children is easier to achieve when practitioners know children well. When a practitioner has been along-side a child day after day then they are familiar with their patterns of learning and where current thinking may have originated. Mercer suggests that effective conversation is 'built on a shared history and working towards a joint future' (1995: 61). When we are closely involved in a child's learning journey, then it is easier to tune in to their current interests and fascinations.

Over-riding all of these strategies, however, it seems that what is most needed in order to tune in to children is a deep and abiding fasci-nation for each young child as a learner. Working out what a young child is thinking, making decisions about when and whether to interact with them, choosing which strategy to use, persevering in our attempts to understand their activity or their needs are challenging and demanding. It is not the easy option, but it is the most rewarding. Those who are fascinated by young children and their learning and development will take the time it takes to understand them, to tune in to their thinking and to support them appropriately.

5 Choosing the appropriate strategy when interacting

As the Oxfordshire Adult-Child Interaction Project DVD material was analysed, it became apparent that certain ways of introducing or sustaining conversations with young children were particularly effec-tive. The following are just some of those strategies:

Pondering
> I wonder if . . .
> I wonder why . . .
> I wonder whether . . .

Imagining
> I can just imagine . . .
> Perhaps . . .
> Let's pretend that we are . . .

Commentating
> I can see that you're trying to . . .
> I noticed that you've . . .
> You managed to put both of those . . .

Clarifying
> So what you are trying to say is . . .
> So what you want to tell me is . . .
> So what you've been thinking is . . .

Thinking aloud
   I'm going to try . . .
   I'm thinking really hard to remember . . .
   I did something like this before . . .
Offering an alternative viewpoint
   Maybe the little boy didn't want to be so naughty.
   I wonder if Harry had the same idea in his mind?
   Some people think/believe that . . .
Talking about feelings
   I think Sophia might be upset because she's missing her mummy . . .
   I wonder if you're cross because your hamster is ill?
   I am so happy because I passed my driving test!
Connecting
   Do you remember when/how . . .
   It's just like when we/you . . .
   If you can manage this today perhaps you can try this tomorrow . . .
Supporting the child to make decisions and choices
   Would you like the red ones or the blue ones?
   Do you think baby bear would rather have eaten his porridge or
   gone for that walk?
   What can you do to make Nadia feel better about hurting her?
Explaining/informing
   If you turn the saw like this, you'll be able to cut right through.
   They're called broad beans and they grow in a pod rather like the
   peas in our nursery garden.
   I think your ball is getting stuck because that bit of track isn't fixed
   together properly.

It was interesting to note how these strategies were effective in both adult-led and child-led conversations. Used at the right time in an appropriate way, the strategies seemed to help children consolidate existing understanding or to see the world in a new and a different way. What was notable, however, is that supporting and consolidating children's thinking seemed much easier than challenging and extending it. There were many examples of practitioners being interested in and sustaining the child's threads of thinking, but far fewer examples of a practitioner's contribution making a child stop in their tracks and have to think hard to accommodate something new, something that they had not thought of before. At the commencement of the Project, the strategy used most frequently to provoke children's thinking in this way was asking questions. However, our DVD material showed time and time again that questions very often stumped children. They interrupted what the child was doing or thinking about and caused them to try and adjust to the adult's thinking instead. Most frequently of all they put the child 'on the spot'. Even very young children seemed to sense that there was something expected of them, something the adult knew that they did not, something that they might get 'wrong'. As questions were increasingly seen to interrupt children's learning, the project participants experimented with other ways of sustaining a conversation without relying on questioning. One solution seems to be to make statements rather than ask questions; to say something in relation to what the child has said, rather than interrogating them about it. It is as though a statement plants an idea in the child's head but does not require them to respond or answer right at that moment. Examples of practitioner statements might be:

Commenting
'I can see you've used a different shape brick this time.'
Offering an alternative view of the world:
'Sometimes mums do feed their babies with milk from a bottle.'
Making a suggestion
'I don't have any clothes with animals on. Perhaps they make those more for children.'
Adding something personal
'My dad's car has got a spare tyre in the boot not on the roof of his car.'
Giving a fact
'Copyright means no one else can make a T-shirt that looks just like that because that would be copying – and that's not allowed.'
Addressing misconceptions
'Actually you *can* sleep in a loft. A builder needs to come and make the floor strong and make proper walls but then you can use it as an extra bedroom or an office.'
Saying something unexpected!
(on being offered a toffee cake) 'Sorry . . . I can't eat toffee, my dentist says it's bad for my teeth, it might make my fillings come out!' (So the child had to 'think again'.)

When a practitioner initiates a learning situation, then it is easy for them to dominate the conversation and for questions – that check what children know – to be the favoured strategy. While practitioners are leading the learning rather than following it, it is still possible and desirable to use many of the strategies above. Even though the practitioner may have very clear ideas about what learning is intended, it is little use ploughing on with the adult objectives if children's thinking is elsewhere. Skilled practitioners use children's current thinking and their current understanding as a starting point to lead them to new ways of understanding rather than ignoring where the child is and failing to make links in their learning.

6 Choosing the appropriate time to interact

Whichever strategy a practitioner chooses to use, it must be used with sensitivity. It must be appropriate to the situation and it must be timed so it does not interrupt or interfere with a child's thinking. Choosing when (and whether) to intervene in children's learning can be the difference between interacting and interfering. Jerome Bruner reminds us that 'When a child is thinking hard about what he is doing, elaborating his play, he is not *talking* about it, but *doing* it' (1980: 63). Our DVD footage showed many times when children were stopped from what they were doing by an enthusiastic adult wanting to talk. Our awareness about the importance of the timing of an interaction made practitioners far more sensitive to instigating a conversation when the time was right. One strategy that was used to great effect was 'don't speak until you're spoken to'. This was naturally most relevant in child-led situations. Practitioners went and sat or knelt alongside an activity and found that children would do one of two things: either turn and engage the adult in conversation – 'I'm building a robot with wings here' or 'Can you be the mummy cat?', or ignore the adult completely because, at that moment, they are not necessary. If practitioners wait for children to talk to *them*, then there is far more certainty that the conversation that ensues will be relevant and appropriate to the child.

The Project practitioners also learned to watch and listen more carefully to the child's level of engagement. If a child was intensely involved, then he or she was usually 'too busy to talk' and any intervention on the part of the practitioner would have been a distraction. Instead the practitioners tried to talk to the child when they 'came up for air', when the intensity had diminished and the child was in a more reflective stage of their thinking. The child then was often excited about telling their attentive adult what they had been thinking about and trying to do. Sometimes, of course, it is perfectly possible for children to engage in activity and to engage in conversation simultaneously, but in every scenario – whether role play, block play, sand or water play, or just when watching a snail crawl across the path – sustained shared thinking seems to work so much better when the adult responds to and extends a child's own thinking rather than imposing thinking on them.

7 Personal beliefs, value and attributes

While the Oxfordshire Adult-Child Interaction Project investigated and analysed a range of practitioner strategies used in effective interactions with young children, there emerged also from the analysis certain personal beliefs, values and attributes that impacted quite clearly on this effectiveness.

The decisions that practitioners make about what to say, when to say it and how to say it, all happen in a split second. Responses are frequently instinctive and usually habitual. How a practitioner speaks to a child speaks volumes about their attitude to children and to learning. Those who are fascinated by children and intrigued by their thinking, those who think that children have something worth saying and want to hear more, those who believe that children are powerful, competent learners and want to support and facilitate these competencies, talk to children *differently* than those who believe that their role is the transmission of knowledge, that children will learn most from what they, as adults, say and who see children's talk as often being irrelevant or off task. What we believe as individual practitioners impacts on every interaction we have with children every day in our classrooms.

When practitioners respect children as competent learners and are intrigued by that learning and development, then certain attributes are apparent in the way that they talk to their children. There is a high level of *sensitivity* to the child, their interest and their level of involvement. The practitioner takes a *pleasurable interest* in the child's company and conversation. The practitioner's *body language* is attentive and shows that they have all the time in the world for the child and what they have to say and their *tone of voice* does not patronize the child nor is there any hint of sarcasm. The practitioner is *alert to conversations* the child wants to have and to the ideas and thoughts that a child expresses whether in adult-led or child-led situations. The practitioner *empowers* the child, there is a strong sense of agency as the child and their thinking receive respect and support. Finally, the practitioner is *willing to de-centre*, to take themselves away from the centre of proceedings and to place the child firmly at the heart of all that happens in the classroom. These attributes are seen over and over again in the interactions of effective practitioners and they come from a deep belief in children's competence and their rights as competent young learners.

Communicating with other children

Children talking with each other to learn is a relatively new phenomenon – in educational terms. The term 'oracy' was coined in the 1960s by Andrew Wilkinson to stress the importance of the language skills of listening and talking. These separate functions were enshrined in the National Curriculum as 'speaking and listening' and given emphasis in the Area of Learning named 'Communication, Language and Literacy' within the foundation stage (QCA/DfEE 2000; DfES 2007). More recently, for early years educators in England, 'Communication and Language' have been separated from 'Literacy' and made a 'Prime' Area of Learning in the Early Years Foundation Stage (DfE 2012).

Whatever nomenclature is used, communication now has a distinctive place in the curriculum not only as a medium of learning in all subjects, but as a 'subject' in its own right – as a critical aspect of language competence which is taught alongside the traditionally recognized skills of reading and writing. It is of particular significance for young children for whom 'language plays a part not only in learning self-control but in the formation of conscience' (Pringle 1992: 47). But of course, like most life skills, those of speaking, listening and communicating develop way before children meet the early years 'curriculum'. Learning to communicate emerges as soon as a baby is born. Babies and young children learn to express their needs and feelings through facial expression, sounds and gestures (Shaffer 1999; Smith et al. 2010). If the baby is fortunate, their early attempts at making themselves noticed will receive an immediate response from a loving and attentive parent. In this way the synergy of interaction begins, first between the baby and their significant adult carer, and then between the baby and others in their family and community.

The ability to communicate gives children the capacity to participate with increasing confidence in the social world into which they are born and in which they grow up. In almost all situations in our society, there are demands on people to get on with others in order to participate successfully in whatever their current role or task may be. We all need to learn to appreciate another's point of view; to wait and take our turn when there are others to consider; to negotiate and to be prepared to compromise when a joint decision has to be taken; to be respectful of others' opinions and beliefs and to be tolerant when they do not match our own. All of these skills – which many adults struggle to acquire – are those which our children need when they negotiate the sociable worlds of childcare and early education. From a very early age many children need to learn to play and explore alongside other children who may not be members of their own family. They need the skills of turn-taking, sharing, discussing and negotiating – very often at a time when they are still striving to put their own individual stamp on the world. It is an aspect of development that needs sensitive and repeated support from adults.

But the importance of speaking and listening is not confined to children's social development, important though that is. The skills of speaking and listening also underpin those of reading and writing, skills without which children will also struggle to make their way in the world. Without rich oral language children will not have the vocabulary to transfer to the more challenging realms of the written word. Through verbal communication children share ideas and feelings and stories that can later be captured on the page. When they recite rhymes and songs and poetry they experience the different uses of language and how words can be manipulated to create different meanings and emotions. When linking language with physical movement in action songs and rhymes they not only use language for a certain purpose but can refine their gross and fine motor skills, so essential for manipulating the instruments that will help them make meaningful marks on paper.

It is crucial that we give children time to develop their spontaneous skills of speaking and listening before we force them toward the less natural skills of reading and writing. Young children are natural talkers. In her delightful book *Young Children Talking: The Art of Conversation and Why Children Need to Chatter* (2006), Diane Chilvers reminds us that children have a 'built-in urge to tell you, in some way, what they are thinking, feeling, seeing, hearing, smelling, touching. They are powerful communicators' (2006: 5). This vital and powerful urge to communicate is in stark contrast to the fears and apprehension felt by many children when they are introduced to the formal aspects of literacy too soon.

In the foundation stage, talk arises spontaneously in playful situations. In the role play area, the home corner, during block play and at the water tray, talk occurs as part of the social process of learning. Children talk to exchange ideas, to ask for help, to commentate on what they are doing and feeling and thinking. However, in more adult-led situations it is easy for conversation *between* children to be over-ridden by talk between the adult and the children as individuals. It takes great skill for an adult to lead dialogue between a small group of children where children's thinking builds incrementally on what others have said. It is a feature of the work in the preschools in Reggio Emilia where learning is based on a theory of knowledge that defines thinking and learning as social and communicative events, as coconstructive experiences for both children and adults (Edwards et al. 1994: 85).

In England, children are often placed in groups to achieve an adult-initiated activity but then given tasks to do which are individual and do not draw on this cooperative and reciprocal learning. Grouping children is such a common feature of early years and classrooms that it is important to scrutinize the reasons for children being grouped in certain ways and whether these groupings deliver the learning that is intended.

Grouping children

Grouping as an organizational strategy

Managing large classes calls for creative thinking on the part of the practitioner. Even at the level of moving children around the classroom and the school or setting it can be helpful to have children organized in small units. If children are in groups with a collective label such as 'red' group, 'starling' group or 'Pluto' group, some potentially challenging times such as lining up, getting to the hall and going out to play can be managed in a calm and orderly way.

Grouping as an educational strategy

Many educators feel that children benefit from the sense of belonging to a group. That it gives children security and offers them opportunities to respond collectively and cooperatively. This rationale is essentially social and emotional and does not necessarily fulfil the wider learning needs that a group may have. There is an important difference between children sitting together *in* groups and working together *as* a group. Because research shows that many children sit in groups but work as individuals it suggests that some teachers may group children for the purposes of their own planning rather than the purposes of children's learning. Rather than plan for the individual needs of a class of 30 or more, the teacher plans work for each of, say, four groups and the children are given tasks that are planned for the whole group to do, but which basically require each child to work as an individual.

To maximize the potential of children being grouped together, and to enhance their skills of speaking and listening with all that this entails, effective tasks require children to collaborate and cooperate. Children who sit together but do not share a common purpose for communication are likely to be distracted by sitting close together (Hastings and Schweiso 1995). This is when talk veers on to topics such as television and pet rabbits. Group tasks need to be planned so that children share, discuss, argue, rationalize, find solutions and come to decisions together, just as they did in their earlier years when playing together was a more fluid and spontaneous affair. If children benefit from speaking when formulating concepts, then it is also vital that they talk with peers who will listen to and respond to their ideas. Only if both speaking and listening are a planned part of the curriculum will the social, linguistic and cognitive benefits of group work give an educational rationale for children sitting and working in this context.

The appropriateness of grouping young children

Putting children in groups in order that they should collaborate is certainly not appropriate across the full early years age range or in all early years situations. Younger children will not cooperate simply because it is in the practitioner's plans. We have seen that young children will cooperate and collaborate with commitment when they see a purpose for doing so. Observations of young children working on construction or in the home corner reveal just how collaborative they can be, if there is a need. There is a big difference between being 'put in a group' and working collaboratively alongside other children. To encourage cooperation between young children, early childhood educators should plan activities and experiences that encourage spontaneous interactive learning opportunities in which children see a purpose for talking together, working together and learning together.

Planned grouping

If the educator decides that it is in the interests of the children to be brought together in a specific group in order to experience or to learn something, then the criteria for grouping the children need to reflect the purpose of the task in which the group is to be engaged. There are times when it is beneficial for children with similar interests to work together to inspire and motivate each other. There are times when younger children can beneficially work or play alongside older children who act as models for behaviour and skills. There are times when children of similar ability will benefit from targeted input from an adult at a certain point in their development. If the choice of group is to reflect the nature and purpose of the task, then the implication of this is that groupings will *change* in order for that match to be achieved.

Fixed grouping

Because children have different needs at different times, the adult has to plan for those needs to be met, not only through the selection of an activity or experience, but through the social context in which the learning takes place. Grouping that remains fixed and inflexible does not acknowledge the needs of the developing and individual child. Children develop in highly individualistic ways and although patterns of development can be similar, children make spurts and reach plateaux in ways that are highly idiosyncratic. Their development cannot be catered for by decisions about their ability that remain the same for any period of time, particularly if that decision is held as constant across all subject areas or areas of learning. The needs of any small group of children, however similar their ability at any given time, will not be constant from day to day. Because four children are ready to learn about the concept of 'more than' at the same time, it does not necessarily follow that they will come to understand 'the difference between' at the same time. If different rates of learning mean that children have different learning needs *within* one subject, how much more will those needs vary *across* subjects and areas of learning.

Yet sometimes, particularly in schools, children are grouped with the same children for *all* their learning experiences. Their needs may originally have been assessed in one aspect, such as mathematics, and then presumed to be similar in everything else. How rarely this is the case. Children have a range of skills, talents and understandings and to suppose that one child can be 'above average' in all curriculum areas while another is consistently 'below average' is to make inaccurate not to mention improbable assessments of children's abilities. Children usually perform according to the expectations of those who influence them. Tell them they're a 'leek' ('one of my bright ones') and they'll perform like a leek. Tell them they're a 'cabbage' ('my slow learners') and they'll perform like a cabbage, even though some children know that given half a chance they could perform like a leek in PE or art or scientific investigation.

Labelling children in fixed ability groups can inhibit all manner of opportunities for development. It can restrict the opportunity to shine, gain confidence from and develop in those areas in which the child has strengths. It can also restrict the opportunity to work with a range of peers from whom the child can learn and to whom the child can teach a variety of things. Bringing together children who have the same learning needs at a given time is a constructive use of time. Constraining children to work with the same group of children consistently might, at best, inhibit development and at worst can destroy a child's belief in themselves and their ability in anything.

Flexible grouping

Effective grouping recognizes the ever-changing needs of children and the necessity to be flexible in planning the curriculum and the context in which that curriculum takes place. It means that children are brought together because they have similar needs at that moment in time. Knowledge of those needs comes from observations and conversations that identify every child's stage of development and provide clear evidence on which to base diagnostic assessments and future plans. Early childhood educators need to be flexible in their short-term planning so that whatever they discover about children and their development can be incorporated into weekly and daily reviews of every child's needs.

There are times when children *need to* work alone or want to learn alone, and when it is appropriate that they do so. If, however, one of the purposes of an activity or experience is that children will learn with and from each other, then it is necessary for the practitioner to make a decision. Will children collaborate and cooperate spontaneously because the activity will naturally lead to them doing so? Or is there a need to manipulate the collaborative aspect by bringing certain children together for the purpose of the activity? Children may be set a task to work at as a group, independent of the practitioner, or they may be working with an adult, addressing a specific learning need. The important point is that the activity or experience is relevant at that time to those children who have been grouped together.

The child's choice of grouping

What social contexts would the child choose? Unaware of the myriad of learning opportunities presented by their friends, young children tend to play and learn alongside other children for different reasons. Young children learn best in contexts in which they feel secure. Security comes from being familiar with and trusting those who share the learning space. When given the opportunity to work alongside whomever they choose, children do not always work with a special friend. Often their own interest in an activity will determine where they choose to be. Young children do tend to gravitate towards those with whom they are comfortable and confident, however. Being secure enables children to relax, to experiment, to take risks and to stimulate their own learning. Alongside other children they may ask questions or sound out ideas which, in the company of an adult – however supportive – they may feel inhibited to do. The work of many people who have studied how small groups of primary age children work (Barnes and Todd 1977; Jones 1988; Phillips 1988; Reid et al. 1989) shows that children are more likely to generate exploratory questions, hypotheses and explanations on their own than when an adult is present. Working alongside someone with whom you feel secure is a powerful motivating factor. Just think how many adults do not go along to evening classes or join a sports club unless they go with a friend for moral support. Being with someone we like and trust adds to our feelings of enjoyment and security and this affects our application to the task in hand. So, on those occasions when it is possible to enable children to play and learn alongside children of their own choosing, then early childhood educators will find that this is likely to be beneficial both to the children and to the organization and management of the learning environment.

Conclusion

Young children talk to learn and need to have a range of opportunities to talk purposefully to their peers and to adults. Early childhood educators need to ensure that conversations are not one-sided and that children have genuine opportunities to say what they know and what they think and what they feel. When adults group children for educational reasons, these groupings should be flexible and responsive to the changing needs of children. Young children naturally collaborate and cooperate when they see the need to do so, and they do so particularly when they are engaged in self-initiated activities. The following chapter is concerned with child-initiated learning. It explores the place of play in the early years setting and asks why some practitioners can still find it hard to justify time for play at the heart of their learning environments.

Questions to Challenge your Thinking

1 Does everyone in your setting understand the value of talk for learning?
2 What are the differing benefits of talking to children in a group and talking to children as individuals?
3 Has your setting evaluated its effectiveness as a place for talk between adults and children? Could this chapter help?
4 Are children in your setting given opportunities to talk together *about* their learning (rather than just sitting together)?

7

THE PLACE OF PLAY

The status of child-initiated experiences

Introduction

No book about early childhood education would be complete without a discussion of the place of play. The Statutory Framework for the Early Years Foundation Stage (DfE 2012) says that 'Play is essential for children's development, building their confidence as they learn to explore, to think about problems, and relate to others' (p. 6: para 1.9). While messages such as this are loud and clear in all recent early years documentation (see both *Birth to Three Matters* (DfES 2003a) and *The Early Years Foundation Stage* (DfES 2000 and 2007), it remains the case that not all play in all settings is of the quality that promotes effective learning, and not all foundation stage settings give play the place and status it warrants. This chapter explores why, when so much is said and written about the subject, play across the Early Years Foundation Stage still fails to be the bedrock of high quality practice in all settings.

Theories surrounding play

Part of the dilemma surrounding play is that when we speak of it we do not always mean the same thing as the next person. There is no single definition of play and, therefore, playful activities in one form or another have been open to interpretation in different ways. There is, however, a plethora of theories as to what play is and what it accomplishes. For a detailed synopsis of the main theories I can do no better than to refer you to Tina Bruce's book *Time to Play in Early Childhood Education* (1991). In addition, the PlayEngland/NCB literature review of play entitled *Free Play in Early Childhood* (Santer et al. 2007) offers an excellent summary of different perspectives on play and how play influences children's development and learning.

The classical theories of play explain the *reason* that play exists, and view play as physically very purposeful. For example:

- *Recreation theory* This theory proposes that play somehow redresses the balance of time spent on work. That play is acknowledged as an appropriate activity for young children but not the same as, and certainly not as important as, work. In this way, play is sometimes used as a reward, as a 'carrot' at the end of a period of work when the child has the opportunity to engage in something of their own choosing once the work for the teacher is finished.
- *Excess energy theory* Here, play is seen as an acceptable way for children to let off steam and this separates 'work-time' from 'playtime'. This theory has given a framework to the primary and secondary school day that has changed little over the years. 'Playtime' is given value in that it is seen as releasing pent-up energies and preparing children to knuckle down to the more static learning experiences to which they will return.
- *Recapitulation theory* This theory suggests that play reflects the cultural environment in which the child grows up. Play is seen as being deeply embedded in children's personal experiences and a reflection of the influences of children's environments and the significant people within them.
- *Practice or preparation theory* Play helps children to prepare for adult life by letting them practise and explore what they need to be able to do as adults. Young children engage in role play that mimics – often with devastating accuracy – the behaviours of adults who are significant in their lives.

There is another school of thought, commonly termed the modern dynamic perspective, which seeks to explain the *content* of play. Here, the theorists often come from a psychodynamic perspective:

- *Play as pleasure theory* Play is seen as a source of pleasure, and in no way dependent upon end results or outcomes. This theory emphasizes the importance of play as process, a view strongly held by Bruner (1977: v) who, while not subscribing to the play as pleasure theory, nonetheless asserts that 'Play is an approach to action, not a form of activity.'
- *Play as catharsis theory* Children are believed to communicate and eliminate anxieties and fears by bringing them to a level of consciousness that can then be articulated through play (Santer et al. 2007).
- *Affective theories of play* Children are seen to gain control of their lives and to take this competence into adulthood.

Finally, there are theories of play that accentuate children's cognitive development.

- *Piaget (1951)* Piaget saw play as the means by which children unify their experiences, their knowledge and their understanding. He believed that children build up a repertoire of expertise through active engagement with the environment to which they must continuously adapt. He viewed the child's development as leading learning, with play having a strong influence on development.
- *Vygotsky (1966)* Vygotsky, on the other hand, believed that learning led development. His writing emphasized how much children learn in social contexts and how significant language is in children's construction of knowledge and understanding. Because of this, he saw adults, and other children, as having a key role in moving children from their current to their potential understandings. Unlike those theorists from the psychodynamic perspective, Vygotsky did not believe that children's play arises from unsatisfied desires, but rather that children create play that has purpose and, which, in turn, determines their affective states.

Different types of play

As well as there being many different theories of play, there are also different *types* of play in which children engage. Hughes (1996) has identified 15 types of play in childhood, but I have chosen to focus on just nine as being of most relevance to early childhood educators.

- *Exploratory play* This offers children the opportunity to use their physical skills and their senses to learn more about materials and objects – what they feel like and what they can do.
- *Symbolic play* Children use objects and materials to represent (symbolize) something else, e.g. a piece of wood can symbolize a wand.
- *Dramatic play* In dramatic play children either take on the actions and activities of others who are often most important to them in their daily lives, e.g. their mum, the shopkeeper, their babysitter.
- *Socio-dramatic play* Here children re-enact actual or potential experiences of intense personal meaning to them often becoming another character in order to lay on them the fears or anxieties that these play scenarios express.
- *Pretend play* Children create characters and situations that take them into imaginary and alternative worlds, rich in fantasy and unlikely to happen to the child in real life.

- *Locomotor play* This encompasses activities that involve all kinds of physical movement for their own sake and for the sheer physical pleasure of the experience.
- *Rough and tumble play* This is playful physical activity that often involves contact, usually between two children, such as touching and tickling and rolling. It is clearly enjoyable and is *not* fighting.
- *Games with rules* Both indoors and out children engage in games with rules that are predetermined by others (usually adults) or rules they determine for themselves. Games with rules can demonstrate great creativity – a bringing together of experiences and ideas from a range of previous experiences and activity. Children have very clear ideas about fairness and police their established rules often with great severity.
- *Freeflow play* In her influential book *Time to Play in Early Childhood Education* (1991), Tina Bruce puts forward a definition of 'freeflow' play as an 'integrating mechanism, which brings together everything we learn, know, feel and understand' (1991: 11) and in which children are 'wallowing in ideas, feelings and relationships'. A key feature of freeflow play is that children use the 'technical prowess, mastery and competence' that they have previously developed and that, in doing so, they are in control of the experience.

Different social contexts for play

Not only are there different types of play but, through observation, we see that children engage in play in different social situations. This does not mean that children's play evolves through simplistic or fixed stages of development. While there is a developmental influence here – with very young children displaying more engagement in play described at the top of the list – children throughout the foundation stage choose to be involved in all or any aspects of these social situations according to their mood and the purposes and nature of their play.

- *Solitary play:* children are engaged in their own play, without involvement of or reliance on others;
- *Spectator play:* children are often watching the play of others, onlookers who are absorbing what others are doing;
- *Parallel play:* children playing side by side often with similar resources or in the same space, but with little apparent interaction or engagement one with the other;
- *Cooperative play:* children sharing play space, resources and experiences, talking and playing together with often complementary roles.

Different cultural influences on play

The world in which we live and the culture into which we are born impact dramatically on our attitudes to all sorts of things, including the role and the status of play. The opportunities for play and the influences upon play come frequently from society's images, ideas and opinions. Some of these are very obvious but others are more insidious, though nonetheless profound for that. Marjatta Kalliala (2006: 10) identifies the following list of changes in society currently influencing children's play culture:

- how people earn a living;
- urbanization;
- more middle-aged and elderly people in the population;
- the increasing equality of women;
- the changing work patterns of women outside the home;
- changing class boundaries and social stratification;
- changing professions;
- changing sexual behaviour;
- changes in the nuclear family and childhood;
- no clear common ideology, religious movements or doctrines to give cohesion and shared understandings;
- changing institutions (e.g. church and state);
- changes in the welfare state and thinking what's best for society.

Changes in society

There are a number of changes in society that have become absorbed in children's play: the increasing number of women out at work and the increasing equality of women in all realms of society; advances in technology and the increasing reliance of all of us on its multiplicity of forms; attitudes to drugs, alcohol and smoking and how these are perceived by children via the media and advertising; the threat of increasing urbanization – pollution, child safety, spaces to play; the loss of influence of the church and the increase in secular behaviour, beliefs and attitudes towards right and wrong, good and evil. In the foundation stage, children are developing their own views about all of these things and these are often strongly influenced by the values and beliefs of their family and their community. In their role play, their socio-dramatic play and their pretend play, in particular, children represent their emerging ideas about relationships, about roles, about actions and consequences. They also inhabit roles and create situations which give them fresh powers and possibilities to be someone different or to change the course of events from those in their normal daily lives.

These types of play are about alternative worlds. They encourage children to use objects that represent other things and help them separate the difference between make-believe and reality. The key feature of play is that the child remains in control of events. Whether they want to take on a role which is the same as a significant adult in their life, or one that they have seen portrayed on the television or on film. Whether they want to imagine another's perspective and try out the powers that this new role might bring. Whether they want to create a character in order to give it the feelings of guilt, fear, anxiety or jealousy that they are currently working through. In all of these situations, the child has the power to make happen what, in the rest of their lives, they are only imagining and feeling and fearing. They have the power to experience the world from another's point of view and to control how much they engage with or discard this alternative persona and its imaginary consequences.

Gender

Attitudes towards gender and what is seen as gender-appropriate behaviour are formed in early childhood (Hutt et al. 1990; Holland 2003). Children learn most of their ideas from the stereotypes that surround them daily via advertisements, shop displays, television programmes and adult responses. Children begin to label themselves and others as male or female accurately from about the age of 2 and soon after this they begin to make links between these labels and different activities, toys and behaviours. Many girls will choose to play with dolls when boys will not. Many boys are drawn towards trucks, tractors and trains and girls are not. By the age of 5 most children have internalized gender-expected roles. Sometimes this is a result of the way in which boys and girls are treated in the family, with adults choosing to dress boys and girls in different colours, for example, and even the way in which adults touch and handle children – bouncing boys vigorously on the knee and cradling girls more gently and rocking them (Livingstone 2005). Vivian Gussin Paley in her evocative descriptions of play and learning in her classroom, reports that:

> Domestic play looks remarkably alike for both sexes at age three . . . [but] The four year old boy is far less comfortable in the doll corner than he was the year before; he may occasionally dress up in women's clothes or agree to be Daddy, but the superhero clique has formed and the doll corner is becoming a women's room . . . among five and six year olds . . . the girls officiate in the doll corner but the presence or absence of boys determines the character of the play . . .

As the superhero dominates boys' fantasy play the girls turn to dramatic plots that eliminate boys and bring in more sisters and princesses.

(Paley 1984: x–xi)

Paley goes on to suggest that 'No amount of adult subterfuge or propaganda deflects the five-year-old's passion for segregation by sex' (Paley 1984: ix). Every year, she recounts, 'the girls begin with stories of good little families, while the boys bring us a litany of superheroes and bad guys' (Paley 1984: 3).

Superheroes, war and weapon play

In the UK, it is the work of Penny Holland (2003) that has most challenged early years practitioners to face their own prejudices and ideologies when encountering superheroes in their settings and classrooms. Her research analysed the experiences of one inner London under-5s centre that decided to relax its 'zero-tolerance' approach to war, weapon and superhero play. In other words, challenging a policy that said 'we don't play with guns here'. Holland explains that, in common with most early years settings she had visited, this was not a policy that was written down. Rather it was a policy adopted consensually by early years staff – predominantly female – who saw their role when confronted with weapons and violent reenactments as peace-keepers, shunning violence or attempting to channel it into something more creative.

In seeking to question this policy, Holland first established the impact of a policy of zero-tolerance on the children and their play. She found that too many children, particularly boys, were receiving a disproportionate amount of negative attention; that these constantly negative interactions were damaging boys' well-being and self-esteem; and that following adult intervention, boys were more prone to disruptive behaviour. Finally, for many boys, this was their only outlet for sustained imaginative play and it was being removed. These concerns are echoed by others who write about war and weapon play (Paley 1984; Rich 2003). One key concern is for those children for whom there is a conflict of ideology between the early years setting with a policy of zero-tolerance and the home where such play is tolerated or encouraged or where it is modelled as necessary and appropriate by parents – for example, those serving in the armed forces.

Following the relaxation of the zero-tolerance policy in Holland's own setting, she reports that staff felt that children's self-esteem, especially that of the boys, increased; that children were learning about moral issues such as violence, aggression and justice through their play without this being controlled by adults; and that it was giving children conflict resolution strategies in genuine situations and that for boys, in particular, it was 'providing the seeds for rich imaginative play' (Holland 2003).

Media images

It is not only the world of superheroes that impacts on children's play culture. Media coverage of recent violent events has found its way repeatedly into children's homes and into children's play. Adams and Moyles (2005) describe very graphically how, since the events of 9/11, children seem to be struggling to find a response to the different images they have seen portrayed on television in particular, and that many were doing so through their play. Events such as 9/11, the BSE crisis in the UK – when many animals were seen being slaughtered – the Asian Tsunami in 2004 with its images of panic and destruction and the brutal killing of young people at a summer camp on the island of Utøya in Norway, provoke a range of emotions in adults and so we should not underestimate their emotional impact on children. While as adults we may have learned to manage and control our emotions, this may not be the case for young children and play becomes the only way in which they can act out what may have perturbed, frightened or bewildered them. Adams and Moyles' work sensitively questions practitioners about their responses to children's play, behaviour and language following the viewing of violent events. It challenges all of us to examine our personal prejudices and value-systems and asks where we individually draw the line between the tolerable and the unacceptable. Adams and Moyles (2005: 21) suggest twelve underpinning focus points for individuals and staff teams to consider when discussing this delicate subject. They are well worth reproducing here:

1 Violence portrayed in the media is powerful in terms of its visual imagery but can be viewed very impassively (or ignored) by adults. This could lead to adults or children becoming desensitized to violence and then not understanding right or wrong.
2 All children are exposed to violence portrayed through the media in ways that make it extremely pervasive.
3 Violence is promoted through fantasy (games such as Play Station, and traditional stories and rhymes), as well as news items reporting reality.
4 Practitioners have a responsibility for confronting their own feelings and making informed responses to children's representations of violence.

5 Practitioners are responsible for understanding their local communities and working in the best interest of that community.
6 Practitioners may feel insecure or disturbed by the strongly held beliefs of others, including children, and need opportunities to talk openly with other professionals.
7 Practitioners should set clear boundaries to protect the rights of all involved in their settings. Conflicts need to be addressed rather than appeased or ignored.
8 Children are more likely to express concerns or fears in an ethos of trust, reassurance and openness. They require time to explore their responses through play and talk.
9 Boys' and girls' experiences affect their attitudes to other people, faiths, cultures and ethnic groups; children's own experiences must be the starting point for discussion.
10 All children should be treated with equal respect and concern, although ways of expressing their feelings may differ. They should be allowed to represent violence through play or other means, in the curriculum.
11 Children are entitled to protected opportunities to express feelings of anger, frustration, fear, sadness or concern.
12 Cultural violence is all pervasive, influencing practitioners' construct of childhood and the role they have in supporting children's development and learning.

Ethnicity, culture and beliefs

Many of the issues raised in the section above relate to children who are from minority ethnic communities. Much of the confusion of 'right' and 'wrong' in recent media coverage stems from the demonization of certain ethnic groups and the polarization of views as to the outcome of, particularly, terrorist events. Liz Brooker (2002) reminds us that children can meet conflicting values and expectations between their own culture and that of the school/setting which can lead to confusion in identity and self-esteem. Families and children from minority cultural, religious and ethnic backgrounds may bring very different beliefs and attitudes into the settings they attend and these may not always sit comfortably with those of the practitioners. Furthermore, particularly after 7/7 in London in 2005 and the increasing hostility to minority ethnic groups generally, children may be made more aware of the way Muslims and others are often portrayed in the media and may be attending settings which such children also attend. Any resulting hostility may be reflected in their play. As Adams and Moyles (2005) argue, we must ensure that as adults working alongside young children we give children permission to play out their fears and their anxieties, their emotions and their feelings, even when these cut across our own personally held values and beliefs. But racial prejudice and discrimination are not the same as matters of differing (and sometimes conflicting) beliefs and values. Prejudice and discrimination are always unacceptable in any situation, so it is important to distinguish between them. While our concern is for the self-esteem and the well-being of each individual child, it is crucial that practitioners are sufficiently sensitive to intervene when there is evidence of racial prejudice or discrimination from whatever source (Lane 2005a, 2005b, 2008). Practitioners have to make very informed decisions about when one child's entitlement to express themselves interferes with another child's absolute right not to be oppressed or abused.

Playful environments

What we know about children is that they play naturally and instinctively. They only need to be observed in parks, in doctor's waiting rooms, in gardens and in shops. Children spontaneously find things to play with and create situations in which to be playful. Whatever is driving this – and the explanations outlined above are only some of many – children find in the most ordinary things the wherewithal to create alternative, imaginary scenarios which can absorb them for considerable periods of time. So what are the features of an environment that inspires children to be playful?

Time

There is no doubt that high quality play – using Tina Bruce's definition of freeflow play – needs time to evolve. It can start off as messing about or investigating or what Marjatta Kalliala calls 'dizziness' (2006: 94) but for children to become absorbed, it requires no time constraints and no deadlines. In most of our memories of childhood play there is an ephemeral feeling of timelessness that pervades our images of ourselves in playful situations.

Resources

It takes very little to inspire freeflow play. No toys are necessary. Sticks can be weapons or wands, a bundle of clothes can be a doll or a magic package, a tree can be a hideout, an empty box can be a treasure chest. In fact, the less structured the resources that children use, the more their imaginations can soar and their creativity can flourish. Certain more open-ended resources are often inspirational too – good quality bricks and blocks, construction equipment, sand and water – but their value as play resources comes from the fact that no adult has determined how they will be used and what their outcome should be. The outdoor environment is particularly ideal for playfulness. Trees, slopes, grass, logs, streams, sticks and bushes all inspire children to create alternative and fantasy worlds. The greater the expanse the better, the further from adults the better.

Being away from adults

Children do not need adults in order to play. Very often, children are at their least inhibited and at their most creative when adults are nowhere in sight. Being alone seems to lead children to be more adventurous, more inventive and to inhabit an imaginary world with less inhibition. Nevertheless, an attentive and interested adult will sometimes find themselves included in a play scenario either as 'audience' or as a co-player, providing rich opportunities to support and extend children's ideas and their thinking.

Other children

Other children are not essential to play but, more often than not, children from the age of about 2 years prefer to engage in play when other children are around. Pretend situations are so much easier when there is a friend to be the other witch, to be the baby, to carry your queen's train and to go into battle alongside you. Play that involves construction is easier when there is a friend to lift the other end of the wood, to hold the tower while you try and balance another brick, to dig beside you so you can get to Australia more quickly. Other children bring out playfulness in their peers. It seems a world they are instinctively at ease in co-inhabiting and co-constructing. It is a world that they own with confidence and surety.

Boredom

Sometimes children become most creative and playful when they are bored. Many children today are involved in a whole series of adult-directed play situations – football, karate, dancing, piano lessons and playgrounds. All of these are entirely valid but do not give children much opportunity to develop their own creative voice and their own imaginary alternatives. It can be when there are no planned activities, and when there is no television or computer at hand, that children turn to their own resources and develop play situations from the most unlikely beginnings. Very often the cry 'I'm bored' precedes some of the most creative play. It is not that boredom is a prerequisite for play but that being constantly in planned play situations can extinguish children's own imaginative energies.

Creating a playful environment in foundation stage settings

The great challenge for foundation stage practitioners is, once again, to emulate the most effective features of the best learning environments found in the home and the local community. In working alongside countless practitioners from nursery through to Year 1, I believe that the following are essential points for consideration when planning an effective environment for playful learning.

1 Play has to be the first *consideration in planning the environment*
When play is consigned to the corners of a classroom already set up for more formal learning, it doesn't work. Play needs more space than a squashed-up home corner in the only place not filled with tables. Start by identifying what play spaces children need and make these available. If some of them – for example, small world play – need table tops, then that is when to add some tables (see Chapter 5 for more ideas for planning the learning environment in general).

2 Play needs open-ended and adaptable resources
Play does not rely on resources. Children, especially in the outdoors, will often find their own. However, the world of the early years setting has, to some extent, to be 'manufactured' for learning and the practitioners within it must make informed choices about which play resources will stimulate deep level learning. I believe that any high quality play provision in the foundation stage needs the following:

- as large and natural an outdoor space as possible;
- a sandpit (not just a tray) outside;
- water play and resources such as gutters and pipes and pumps;
- wooden blocks of various sizes;
- a home corner that is lifelike and robust and large enough to accommodate a whole 'family' and their neighbours;
- endless supplies of dressing-up materials.

3 Play needs the opportunity to flow from one place to the next
Like most things in the life of a young child, play is not neat and tidy. One of the reasons that it is inhibited by small spaces is that play often moves about. It goes from the home corner to the 'shop' or 'travel agent' and back again. It goes from the sandpit into the outdoor house and back again. It goes from the woodwork table to the garden and back again. Play scenarios and play resources get transported from one place to the other and are often discarded en route. Play will flow as it develops, attracting children and losing others, moving from one idea to the next with the purposefulness that is only ever seen in child-initiated activity. Foundation stage learning environments need to ensure that play can move about in this way, uninhibited by tables,

other resources, adult rules and clutter. 'Only four can play' is a complete anathema to playful behaviour. Rules such as these are an indication of limited space or the adult's desire to control the play situation. If play is dominated by constraints of this nature, then this is what will dominate play and my experience is that children will spend longer talking about 'you can't play 'cos there's already four' than they will becoming immersed in playful activity.

4 Play must be the bedrock of children's learning experiences
Play will not be effective or of high quality if it is seen as having a different status to work (see Chapters 4 and 9). This means that play is what most children in the foundation stage should engage in most of the time. The environment should be set up so that the kind of play resources listed above and the kind of play opportunities listed on page 139 are available every day and so that children learn how to move purposefully and independently from one learning situation to another. Only when the play environment is truly absorbing and engaging for children can the adult then plan more adult-focused interventions. If practitioners attempt to plan this sequence the other way round, i.e. if they plan a more structured and adult-dominated environment first and then attempt to offer play opportunities in a limited way – maybe when adult-initiated work is finished or 'just before assembly' – then the play will be as impoverished as the time allowed for it.

5 Play is not 'as well as', 'instead of' or 'what comes after' work
There are some practitioners who say there isn't time for children to play as well as do everything else that the early years curriculum requires. This is to misunderstand entirely the purpose of play in an early years setting. Play is not 'something else'. It is not another Area of Learning but, rather, the *way* in which children will become scientists and designers and writers and mathematicians. It is concerned with the processes of learning and is not some additional subject that has to be covered 'as well as' the rest of the curriculum.

Neither does play take place 'instead of' work. It has different purposes. It has been said that play *is* the child's work (Isaacs 1929), but very often 'work' is seen by children as the activity which adults require them to do, while play is initiated and directed by themselves. We have seen that both adult-initiated and child-initiated experiences are necessary in the effective early years setting. While play is the bedrock of foundation stage practice, the 'work' comes when the adult plans activities that focus children's learning on a new skill or the repetition of a developing concept or the rehearsal of newly acquired knowledge.

Finally, play should never 'follow' work. It should not be dangled as the carrot to be won if and when the less appetizing tasks set by the adult are completed. Play will never have the status it needs and deserves if it fits into the spaces left when the work is finished. It needs children to be at their freshest and brightest, not weary from the completion of adult tasks. Not only do children need play to take place alongside adult-led and adult-initiated learning, but adults need it too. As we have seen in Chapter 4, if adults plan only for adult-led/initiated activities to take place all at the same time, they will be torn between which groups and individuals to support. Early years practitioners can give their attention to adult-led tasks most successfully when the other children are engaged in more independent learning – and the most effective independent learning takes place during high quality play.

6 Play resources and spaces should not be changed too frequently
One common mistake in the planning of play provision by those who are inexperienced is to change the resources for play too frequently. This is to confuse the fact that the early learning environment needs to be 'stimulating' with the belief that it needs to be ever-changing. Stimulation can be maintained for quite some considerable time if the opportunities are the right ones at the right time. A good rule of thumb is that while children are involved or engaged with certain resources or scenarios, then these are providing stimulation and do not need to be interfered with or changed. It is once they lose their cognitive shine that the skilled adult knows that fresh opportunities must be made available or that an existing play situation needs to be refreshed and extended by the addition of new materials or resources.

'Planned' and 'structured' play

One way in which many practitioners strive to justify play is by prefacing it with the words 'planned' or 'structured'. The two terms are often used interchangeably but, to me, they imply very different things. First, 'planned' play implies that play in an early years setting is not as likely to be as spontaneous or unstructured as it is in home or community environments. By very dint of the fact that all space and resourcing and timetabling are planned by practitioners, there will always be an element of adult intervention in foundation stage play. Nevertheless, practitioners can facilitate the kind of opportunities described above or constrain and inhibit play opportunities also as described above. Early years educators must make wise choices and have their principles about how young children learn firmly to hand if their planning is to be in the best interests of children's playful experiences.

'Structured' play suggests a very different emphasis. If play is 'structured' then it implies more than adult *intervention* and borders on adult *interference*. If practitioners structure play – if, for example, they say 'you can go to the home corner and act out the story of the "Enormous

Turnip"' – then the learning opportunity being provided for the children is not play. The children may be using play resources and they may be in a play space, but the experience they are having is not play. It has become, instead, an adult-initiated activity (see Chapter 4). In other words, the adult has a purpose for the activity; an outcome which he or she wishes the children to achieve and a set of learning intentions that prescribe and constrain what the children will do. Now, once again, there is nothing inherently wrong in an 'act out the "Enormous Turnip"' activity (although I do sometimes think that certain authors must be grieving for the purposes for which they originally wrote their classic tales), but practitioners must not plan for this kind of 'structure' and then try and pass it off as play.

Why is play challenging to early years practitioners?

One of the most important things to do if early years practitioners want to improve the quality of play in their settings is to confront the fears and anxieties that exist about introducing a more play-based curriculum. Nothing is ever gained by repeatedly extolling the virtues of play, only to leave the planned provision highly structured and controlled by adults rather than children.

Play does not have defined outcomes

Early years practitioners in the UK have identified skills, concepts and knowledge that young children should have acquired by the age of 5 (see the Early Years Foundation Stage, DfE 2012). Because of this there is a strong concern that if practitioners do not plan for and cover the curriculum in a structured way, that children will not achieve all their Early Learning Goals. There is a belief that when adults direct children's learning, that children will learn what the adult has planned that they should learn. Conversely, there is a fear that when children are playing that they will learn something completely unpredictable. That is, of course, the case. By definition, play has no defined outcomes and adults can have no idea what learning will take place when children are engaged in playful experiences. However, the first myth to dispel is that when they are playing, children will not learn anything that relates the curriculum. This is not true. The majority of the early years curriculum is in evidence whenever children are engaged in high quality play. For example, children:

- **negotiate** when sharing blocks in the block area;
- **calculate** when constructing models to their own specifications;

- **extend their vocabulary** when discussing who takes on which roles in the home corner;
- **investigate objects and materials** when creating a fantasy world in the sandpit;
- **use a range of large and small equipment** as they extend their physical skills in the outdoor area;
- **express and communicate their ideas, thoughts and feelings** as they play alongside each other in fantasy and small world play.

So, when children are playing, they are always learning something that is required by the 'educational programme' of the Early Years Foundation Stage. The task of the adult is to observe what that is and record it appropriately and use it to plan for the next stages of their children's learning.

Next, however, the notion that adults will know what children will learn if they direct their activity needs to be challenged. As I have said in Chapter 4, one adult alone cannot be sure what a whole group of children will learn, even if they are all being taught the same thing at the same time. The larger the group, the less likely it is that children will all gain the same from an activity or explanation or discussion, and there are likely to be a number of children who will gain little because the experience is too easy or too demanding. Even when adults direct learning with a small group of children, there is a chance that some children will misunderstand or simply not engage with the adult's agenda. We know that at different points of the day, or week, or their life, children are preoccupied with things that take their concentration away from the focus of the adult's preoccupations and reduce their capacity to learn.

Finally, when learning is directed by adults, then children's experiences are often inhibited by the learning intentions of the activity. In other words, children will learn what the adult has planned, no more and no less. In play, however, the boundaries of what children might learn are limited only by their own creativity and drive. Vygotsky asserts that 'a child's greatest achievements are possibly in play' (1966: 92).

Observation and first-hand evidence reveal how, when children are engaged in high quality play, they will be learning something meaningful and relevant – however unpredictable. So, it may not be that all children will learn what an adult intends all of the time, but at least if some children are engaged in play, then they will be learning something that is meaningful to them at that moment, and are more likely to retain and build on the skills or knowledge they have learnt because these have meaning and purpose for them.

Play can take a long time

Another grumble about play, from those who have yet to observe its potential, is that it takes a long time. Give a child a worksheet and they will complete it and then be ready to move on. Give a child an adult-directed task and they will finish as orchestrated by the adult and then move on. It is indeed true that high quality play takes time to evolve, but early years educators have to ask which is of more value – a large number of 'tasks' that are finished quickly but where learning is relatively superficial and not particularly engaging, or a play scenario that may stretch over days, seemingly concerned with one theme and yet incorporating many if not all of the Areas of Learning and meeting any number of adult learning objectives (see Box 7.1).

Box 7.1   Child-initiated activities involving learning in many curriculum areas

In this foundation stage setting, reception children are free to play indoors and out, with about an hour and a half in each session given to uninterrupted child-initiated activity, alongside the other 3- and 4-year-old children. The context for this play, is that building work had been taking place on site, including the building of an extension. The children had been able to watch the whole process through a mesh fence. A few weeks before, a huge cement machine had been used to pour cement into the foundations of the new extension through a large plastic pipe. On one afternoon, a group of reception children had gathered guttering, crates, spades and a wheelbarrow and were transporting sand from the sandpit. They spent an hour patiently bringing sand up to the top of the mound in the school garden which, on the one side, is the back of an 'amphitheatre'. They used the wheelbarrow and poured sand down the guttering angled on the crates with the aid of spades. The steps for the amphitheatre have vertical wooden panels at the front, filled in with 'hogging' – gravelly sand, this had got scattered and had left the panels sticking up and easy to trip over. The children had noticed this and said they were 'making the steps safe'.

   In the course of this extended activity the children were talking to one another, negotiating roles and working as harmonious team. They were exploring scientific ideas of how to transport and funnel the sand into the right place, and problem-solving the challenge of the hazardous step and how to make it safe. They were drawing on their recent observations of building work and role-playing being builders. They were exploring the physical skills necessary to manoeuvre the wheelbarrow up a steep grassy slope, and how to balance the guttering on the crates. Throughout they were focused, self-motivated, involved and persistent.

Play does not guarantee to 'cover' the curriculum

I hope I have already dispelled this concern. With very few exceptions – certain aspects of calculation or phonological awareness or correct spellings, for example – play cannot help but address all aspects of the early years curriculum, especially with the judicious selection of resources and opportunities that early years educators have to make every day in their planning. Play may not 'cover the curriculum' in any prescriptive or predictable manner, but no high quality playful scenario takes place without a wealth of language, social inter-action, emotional involvement, mathematical and scientific applica-tion, physical manipulation and creative imagination. This does not mean, however, that there is no place for adult intervention. What effective adults do is to observe the emerging patterns or schemas in children's play (Nutbrown 2006; Athey 2007) and use this to plan for extending or supplementing play provision on future occasions. Adults also draw together and emphasize key aspects of learning at appropriate moments. This may be during a review time with an individual child or group of children when play is in flow or when it has drawn to a conclusion. It may be at the end of a session, in order to give status to the play experiences children have had as they played independently. It may be that, during observation of children's play the adult observed that a child has struggled with a something they are trying to achieve and that this would benefit from direct teaching or support. It may become apparent that a number of children have reached a similar point in their conceptual development and would benefit from a more focused activity to reinforce their developing awareness. It may be that the adult wants to introduce their group to some new materials or some different opportunities that are available and can do this best with a group in a more focused way. The skilled early years educator emphasizes, reinforces and rehearses different aspects of the curriculum with children at key moments. But these moments are only identifiable when children's play is observed suffi-ciently well and understood as the basis for all key learning experiences and opportunities (see Chapter 2). In this way, adults can ensure that children are introduced to aspects of the curriculum in systematic ways alongside the more spontaneous and unpredictable opportunities offered by play.

Play can be messy

Play has already been identified as 'messy' in the context of planning described above. Play is difficult to manage if you are someone who likes order, control and predictable outcomes. In addition, play can be literally messy. We know that most young children do not place a high priority on tidying up as they go along. Clothes leave a trail from one play space to another. Resources find their way from the inside to the outside, from the sandpit to the water tray. Resources are used and discarded as other props and materials come to hand. This is part of the creativity of play, this taking up and putting down of tools that serve a purpose and enhance the moment. When play is in full flow, any requests to tidy up can completely cut across children's creative intentions and interfere with their action and activity. There will be time for tidying up at certain points in the day that do not interfere with children's playful preoccupations. Children need to understand that sharing play space means leaving it sufficiently tidy for others to access. However, it is a mistake to expect the tidying up to take place while the play is taking place. Early years practitioners need to be sensitive to the right moment to ask for the communal good to be considered.

There is often an expectation in early years settings for spaces to be tidied at the end of the session or the end of the day. While this can seem necessary or desirable when planning for a different group of children in the afternoon, it can destroy the flow of play for those children who want to pick up where they left off the next day. Where possible, play spaces and play scenarios should be respected and, if the end of the session interrupts a particularly valuable play situation, then adults need to find ways of protecting the space and the resources so that children can start again when they return the next day.

The early years is not the place for adults who are obsessed with tidiness and predictability. It is one of the chief challenges we face when evaluated or inspected by people who like order and precision and outcomes. The joy of the early years is in its spontaneity. It is what makes working alongside children such a delight and keeps us so fresh and engaged in our work. Adults should resist the urge to tidy up as they go along or to bring order to the play environment just because it makes *them* feel better or because they think it will persuade a visitor that something more worthwhile is going on.

Play can be boisterous

Finally, play can be boisterous. For some early years practitioners this can be as disconcerting as the fact that it can be messy. However, if adults try and stop boisterous play, then they are removing valuable opportunities for children, particularly boys, to let off steam, to use up supplies of testosterone and to develop their physical powers and prowess. Play spaces in the home and the community are under increased threat from urbanization. Traffic, stranger danger and synthetic play areas have reduced play opportunities for children away from adults and out of doors. There is a growing concern among play organizations that the simplistic pursuit of 'safety' across play provision – staffed and unstaffed – has the unintended consequence of making provision so boring that children are denied the opportunity to engage in 'beneficial risk-taking' (for more detail, visit www.playlink. org.uk) in formally provided provision and seek out more dangerous play situations to give themselves the challenge and excitement that play can and should provide. Children need to experience risk and personal challenge in their play and outdoor play can and should provide this.

The provision of an outdoor area that is constantly available to children instantly increases the size of the learning environment. If space indoors is cramped, then an outdoor area expands the learning opportunities in a trice. Children become used to moving between the outside and the inside areas and take both resources and experiences from one location to the other. But the outdoor area does not just provide more space, it also provides different opportunities to the inside. Outside there is room for children to experience large-scale movements that are often impractical indoors. They can paint with big brushes, draw and crayon on large rolls of paper, walls or the ground, run and skip and jump and balance, roll down slopes and clamber up ropes. Outdoors, children can experience fresh air and vigorous activity. They use more oxygen, strengthen large muscles and increase their blood supply to the brain. At a time when there are such concerns for children's sedentary lives, early years practitioners should be overjoyed that they are being encouraged to provide boisterous play opportunities for children in their settings. However, boisterous play needs to be channelled purposefully and there is no better place to do this than in a good quality outdoor area for learning. If children are inclined to be boisterous, then the best thing to do is to provide them with the opportunities to be so in the outdoor area and not to suppress this drive as it will only spill out into more aggressive behaviour at another time and in a more negative way.

The role of the adult in supporting children's play

The role of the adult in children's play is difficult to describe. It is as complex and varied as play itself. We have already considered in this chapter how, if adults dominate play or seek to control it, then it becomes another activity altogether. Activities that adults direct are adult-initiated or adult-led, they are not play. So how does the adult intervene to improve the quality of play? How does the adult ensure that these interventions do not end up being interference?

Adult as facilitator

The primary role of the adult is in providing an environment conducive to high quality play. This means facilitating the time, space, resources, experiences and opportunities outlined above. The adult has been responsible for developing the environment – both indoors and out – and selecting the resources, but it is the *environment* that stimulates and entices the child to be playful rather than any adult direction.

Adult as observer

The adult understands that at play, children reveal the true level of their competence and skill. Observation of children in a range of play situations is crucial if the adult is to understand what a child knows, understands and can do. Play also shows the extent of children's social and emotional development. If adults observe children at play, then they will be in the best position to identify which aspects of learning need reinforcement, repetition or extension and these can become the focus of adult-led planning at a later date.

Adult as responder

When an adult sits alongside children at play they can act as a catalyst for questions, conversation and ideas. Sometimes the adult does nothing and the children simply invite the adult into the play through their ideas and suggestions. Sometimes the adult talks aloud as they play, in parallel to begin with, commentating on what they are doing with the blocks, in the water tray, and so on. In either case, the adult is alert to the children's ideas, moods and activity and can respond, maybe just by nodding and smiling, but offering reassurance that the play has value.

Adult as protagonist

Following a period of careful observation, the adult may feel that the play has lost its momentum or needs a fresh idea in order to maximize its potential. This can be a very delicate decision. All too often adults can misunderstand the children's purposes or the direction of their play and the adult intervention then destroys the play situation altogether. Sometimes the adult offers an idea or poses a question and children ignore it, preferring to stay with their own focus and their own direction. However, a well-timed comment or question, or the addition of new resources, can fan the flames of the play and give play a fresh impetus and new energy.

Adult as co-constructor

Sometimes, the adult's parallel play or their close and sensitive attention to children's play results in an invitation to become more closely involved. Children may give the adult a role in pretend play; may invite the adult to join in the construction of a model; may suggest the adult tries different resources or a new challenge in the water tray. The adult and child together then become playful in their interactions and co-construction of shared playful experiences.

Raising the status of play

In order to raise the status of play, early childhood educators need to have first-hand experience of its value. It is no good reading about play but never seeing it in action; to provide for it in the corners of the environment or the timetable and not observe its potential when resourced and supported in the ways described above. If you have never seen high quality play, then go and visit a nursery school or a foundation stage setting where it is the bedrock of practice. The development of high quality play needs a commitment to it as being central to the curriculum for young learners. Box 7.2 suggests a charter for play that may support practitioners in raising the status of play in the foundation stage.

Box 7.2   A charter for play

1   *Acknowledge* its unique contribution as a process by which young children learn.
2   *Plan* for it as an integral part of the curriculum and not an 'added extra'.
3   *Facilitate* it with appropriate and high quality resources.
4   *Act* as a catalyst when intervention is appropriate and a scaffolder when expertise is required.
5   *Observe* it in order to have first-hand evidence of children's learning.

6 *Evaluate* it in order to better understand the needs of the learner.

7 *Value* it through comment and commitment in order for its status to be appreciated.

8 *Fight* for it with rigorous, professional argument in order to bring about deeper understanding and acceptance by colleagues, parents, managers and the community at large.

Conclusion

Play is the natural way in which children go about the business of learning. It enables them to integrate and consolidate a wealth of experiences that enhance their cognitive, physical, social and emotional development. It naturally encourages cooperation and collaboration, requires the use of fine and gross motor skills and demands cognitive application. It is pleasurable, but also helps children channel pain and sorrow. It is consuming and challenging and motivating. The relevance of play to early years education is unquestionable and its status in foundation stage provision in the classroom should be assured. This chapter has considered the complexities of play and suggested – and hopefully refuted – some of the reasons given for it not to be at the heart of children's learning experiences in all foundation stage settings.

Having addressed its complexities and many forms, it may be helpful to conclude this chapter with a definition of play that I have found to be in tune with the high quality experiences I see in the best early years provision. It comes from one of the last documents published by the National Strategies – *Learning, Playing and Interacting* (DCSF 2009: 10):

Play is freely chosen by the child, and is under the control of the child. The child decides how to play, how long to sustain the play, what the play is about, and who to play with. There are many forms of play, but it is usually highly creative, open-ended and imaginative. It requires active engagement of the players, and can be deeply satisfying.

In Chapter 8, we look at other situations in which children can have power and control in their settings and ask whether children can be motivated by the negotiation of elements of their learning and their learning environment.

Questions to Challenge your Thinking

1   Why do you encourage play in your setting? Is the learning potential of play clearly visible in displays and photographs around your room?
2   Are you comfortable and confident with your role in supporting and extending children's play?
3   Is play given the time, space and resources it needs – both indoors and out?
4   Do senior staff – and parents – understand the necessity for and benefits of play? How can you improve their understanding?

8

THE NEGOTIATED LEARNING ENVIRONMENT

Issues of ownership, power and control

Introduction

The idea of learning being negotiated is a challenge to any curriculum that prescribes the process and content of experiences without taking into account the current needs and interests of children. A developmentally appropriate curriculum, as described in Chapter 3, is built on what individual children know and need to know next. It is a curriculum that starts from the child rather than expecting the child to start from the curriculum. When early years practitioners see the desirability of motivating children in this way, then the learner is placed in a powerful position. Rather than being a passive recipient of someone else's decision-making and control, the learner is an active participant in the formation of their own experiences. When young children exercise control in the learning environment, it determines the relationship between educator and learner. The relationship becomes a partnership in which children can negotiate input and outcomes in ways that increase their autonomy and sense of purpose. This does not diminish the role of the adult but alters it. The idea that learning is controlled by the learner

> presupposes that knowledge is not transmitted directly from the teacher to the learner. It demands that both teacher and learner recognize that the subject matter of learning resides outside their 'circle of intimacy', rather than exclusively in the teacher.
>
> (Rowland 1984: 149)

The effectiveness of children's first educators

As we have seen in Chapter 1, one of the reasons parents and carers are so often successful as children's first educators is that learning that takes place in the home is embedded in real-life situations. The parent is frequently part of the context in which the child is exploring and thinking and the parent's support of the child is contingent upon their deep knowledge of the child's linguistic and cognitive competence. Most importantly perhaps, most of the learning stems from the child's own interests and preoccupations. It is the child who initiates conversations and asks questions and the parent who is there to supply answers, solutions and ideas.

This is possible because, with the exception of those parents who have a very clear educational agenda mapped out for their own child from an early age, most parents are content to take on the role of expert, support or facilitator for their child rather than 'teacher'. Many parents are very surprised when you suggest they have been an influential teacher because, to them, 'teaching' has a very overt purpose, involves a very prescribed curriculum, has clear goals and objectives, whereas what they think they do as parents is far more haphazard and spontaneous and 'un-expert'.

Yet, as we saw in Chapter 1, learning is in fact haphazard, spontaneous and unpredictable. Real-life learning involves coming upon something you find interesting, finding out more about it, or trying to learn how to do it, seeing whether what is new sits comfortably with what you already know, and making any necessary adjustments to assimilate the new in with the old. In real life, each person does this in very different ways. Some people are systematic and enjoy learning through books, manuals and training courses. Some like to just 'have a go' and adopt the trial and error approach. Some learners like to see the 'big picture' and then fill in the detail, while others like to start from the beginning and work systematically to the end before seeing 'the whole'. Some like to work alone, others thrive in company. This is true of adults and it is true of children. In the home, it is easier for parents and carers to be flexible and adaptable in response to their child's individual pursuit of knowledge and understanding. First, there are usually only a small number of children in a family to respond to, rather than a whole class. Second, parents are usually fascinated by everything their child says or tries to do, so are amused and delighted by their idiosyncrasies whereas, for the educator, the challenge of differentiation (as we saw in Chapter 3) is significant in classes of 30 or more. Finally, parents are not accountable, as educators are, for teaching something that is laid down by others. Despite increasing evidence of the importance of parents as educators and the importance of early experiences on the life chances of children, most parents still see their role as being loving and responsive to their children and, if any 'educating' takes place, that this is more often through following their children's interests and fascinations rather than leading them.

Negotiating learning in the nursery or classroom

So, from their earliest days, children in loving, responsive families are used to negotiating the learning space, to having control over the learning agenda, to having the power to choose what is talked about and what is tried out. Very often through play, but also through everyday experiences, children find new things to be interested in, to ask questions about, to try and accomplish. So, when these same young children arrive at nursery or school, it can take some considerable personal, social and emotional adjustment to de-centre and to make space for the learning interests and preoccupations of others – including the adults. That is why good early years practitioners offer children learning experiences that are similar to those they have experienced at home. They offer considerable amounts of child-led learning – the freedom, the control, the power to be in charge of their own activities and explorations, plus some adult-led ideas that come from knowing what a child of 3 years or 6 years might be interested in, but may not have experienced.

Children retain this drive to have control over their own learning until around the age of 7 years (Bredekamp 1987; Tassoni 2007; Robinson 2008). It is not until children reach the end of Key Stage 1 that they become more responsive to someone else initiating the learning rather than constantly pursuing their own interests. This does not mean that before this age they cannot or will not take heed of an adult. They are often intrigued by something an adult introduces and try hard to learn about or learn from an adult whom they see as significant to them. But until the age of around 7, the balance of learning power needs to lie with the child.

Early childhood educators spend considerable time following children's interests but, at times, also need to focus their interest on something external to that child's individual agenda. It is this balance between child-led and adult-led learning; it is the negotiation of time, objectives and purposes, that characterize the early years classroom. Indeed, effective early years practitioners do not just follow children's interests at times and then ignore them when introducing the adult-led agenda. Children's interests and fascinations can also be harnessed to make the adult-led agenda more relevant and meaningful and to help the child see connections between his or her learning intentions and those of the adult world.

The problem comes when adult learning is decontextualized from the reality of the child's world; when the child cannot see the purpose or the benefit of spending time on something that the adult wants to pursue. There are times when practitioners have to work particularly hard to help children see the connections between what is to be learned and the interests the child or the group is currently pursuing or might want to pursue. While there is much that is highly relevant and appropriate to young children in the EYFS, the fact remains that there are certain aspects of the 'Development Matters' (which it should be remembered is guidance only and *not* statutory), and of initiatives outside the EYFS such as 'Sounds and Letters' (DfES 2007c) (also *not* statutory) which children might not discover through self-initiated exploration or play or, indeed, which children might not choose to learn at this particular moment in their learning lives. Most of the elements of teaching and learning that early years educators find challenging in the UK at present are concerned with introducing children to learning for which many are not developmentally ready. Certain aspects of literacy and numeracy in particular would be far more easily and readily learned if this country just allowed children to become a little older, more developmentally mature and better able to understand the purpose of that learning. It is salutary to remember and always important to point out, that in most countries in Europe children do not begin compulsory school until age 6 or 7 (Sharp 2002; Sharp et al. 2009), whereas in England, while the compulsory school age is still the term after a child's fifth birthday, the reality is that for most children school begins on the September after reaching the age of 4. When goal posts are set unreasonably high, and the children expected to jump them are younger and younger, then there will be casualties. The great concern is, that while UK governments continue to remove children from high class, outstanding nursery provision in order for them to start school at a younger and younger age, there is no evidence that this is in any way beneficial to standards – or to children. Indeed, although the evidence surrounding age of starting school is complex (Sharp 1998, 2002; Elley 1992; Sharp et al. 2009), most researchers agree that in those countries where children start school later, children 'catch' up with other 'earlier' countries by age 9 with less damage to children's emotional well-being (UNICEF 2011).

Making the transition from home to a new early years setting

So it can be seen that learning in the home offers a child more opportunities for negotiation and for control over a learning situation than is sometimes offered once the child moves to nursery or to school. This readjustment to new relationships and new levels of power and influence is just one of many readjustments to be made by young children when they move away from the home and into an educational setting. The older the child when this transition occurs, then often the greater the gap between the informality and spontaneity of the home environment and the more orderly, planned surroundings of the new educational environment. Settings that exclusively care for and educate children below the age of 5 usually make strenuous efforts to create an environment that mirrors the home and community, with comfy areas for sharing books and talking together, areas for boisterous play, trips out to the shops and all manner of other real-life experiences that offer children rich learning opportunities.

But making the transition from home to a new learning environment is fraught with possible setbacks and needs to be carefully thought through (Selleck 2006; Dunlop and Fabian 2007; Brooker 2008; O'Connor 2012). There are many adjustments that both children and their parents and carers need to make in order to adapt to this new cultural situation. Vygotsky (1978) suggests that the historical, cultural and institutional context shapes children's individual development and their view of the world and yet many practitioners still underestimate the huge cultural shock that children sometimes experience in the transition from home to nursery or early years classroom. Bronfenbrenner (1979) explains that the transition from home to nursery is usually the first and major ecological transition in children's lives. Children are suddenly faced with making new relationships and finding themselves in a new position in the social hierarchy. As home and nursery have different purposes, children may be confronted with a totally different cultural model of expectations from the adults around them.

When thinking about the transition that children make from home to the early years setting or classroom, practitioners might reflect on the following in order to minimize the cultural shock of transition.

- identifying a Key Person (see Elfer et al. 2003; Lindon 2010), who will have a close and loving relationship with the child and their family for the duration of the child's time in the setting;
- undertaking home visits, which will introduce the Key Person to the family at home and enable them to see the child in familiar and secure surroundings so that the Key Person is already a familiar figure;
- having conversations with parents and carers to learn as much about the child as possible before they visit the setting;
- arranging as many visits to the new setting as necessary for the child and their primary caregiver to be confident and secure before the child begins at the setting;

- offering the opportunity for the parent or caregiver to remain as long as necessary (each day and over days) once the child starts at the new setting until everyone is sure that the transition is secure.

Transition between settings in the foundation stage

The transition from home to early years setting is not the only transition that children will have to face in their foundation stage years. Of great concern to many early childhood educators is that, due to a number of social and political pressures, too many children are currently making several transitions during their foundation stage career, at a time in their lives when they most need stability and security. It is not just the case that children make a number of significant transitions in a linear way, i.e. from a childminder at age 2 to a playgroup at age 3 to a nursery class at age 4 to a primary class at age 5. This would be bad enough with all the social and cultural confusions that this can entail. But our youngest children are also making vertical transitions. In other words in the course of one day, many of them make the transition from home to a childminder, then to a morning preschool, then to an afternoon nursery class, then back to the childminder and then home. In her powerful article 'Key Persons in the Early Years Foundation Stage' (2006) Dorothy Selleck describes these transitions as 'serial care', as children are moved from pillar to post very often for the needs of the adults in their lives rather than their own. Selleck challenges these practices by saying that 'I can think of no other adult scenario in which constant transitions would be thought of as desirable, ethical or healthy' (p. 12).

When practitioners realize just how many adjustments and readjustments young children are making as they try to settle into their particular setting, then staff need to work hard to reduce the discontinuities children might face. This can only be achieved if practitioners, across all sectors, work closely together to iron out the discontinuities that are unnecessary and undesirable. The best place to start is from the child's perspective. Many practitioners have revolutionized their practice having once tracked a single child across their foundation stage experiences in one day or one week. Only when we see the world through the child's eyes do we truly understand just what is involved in making adjustments from one setting to the next.

Becoming a 'pupil'

No matter how much work is undertaken to make children's first transitions as smooth as possible, within the first few hours of being in their new early years setting young children pick up messages that life here is going to be different. Most notably, the number of children around is different from home. In addition, the environment is probably more extensive and there are more adults around. Then there are the expectations of those adults. Not only are these different between home and the early years setting but very frequently they can be different between settings too. One of the hardest points of transfer for children, especially when this is happening in one day, is when expectations of them and their behaviour are different between one set of adults and the other – as confusing as it can be when two parents have different boundaries and sanctions. Where in one setting, for example, children have to ask to go to the toilet and in another, do not. Where in one setting children are expected to find and replace their own resources and in another they are found and replaced by the adults. Where in one setting guns and sword play are permitted and in another they are banned. But not only are adult expectations of behaviour frequently a cause of bewilderment, but young children learn that in their different settings there are expectations to become a different sort of person, to take on new roles. No longer are they culturally secure in their role as daughter, son, granddaughter, nephew, but they become a 'pupil'. While most early years settings outside of the state sector do not use that word, the expectations can be similar. Children find they have to wait their turn for something rather than receiving it instantly; they have to accommodate the preferences of other children rather than having their own way; they have to wait for certain times to eat or to have a snack. If children make a transition directly into an early years classroom, then the differences can be even more dramatic. This title 'pupil' carries with it attitudes and expectations, not their own, but learnt from the attitudes and expectations of those around them – 'when you're at school you won't be able to do that'; 'at big school they keep you in at dinnertime if you haven't finished your work'; 'now you're at school you'll learn proper things like sums and writing' – a mass of expectations that usually come in the form of well-meaning advice, but can also carry the undertones of threat.

In this way, children arrive at school with a notion, correct to a lesser or greater extent, about what it means to be a pupil. Many children – and certainly many parents – believe that children are in school to learn and the teacher to teach. The active role is that of the teacher and the appropriate role for a pupil is to be passive and receive the teaching. Children will find their own ways of managing this new world. They may follow, negotiate, transform or reject becoming a 'pupil' but the process of negotiating their position in this new learning environment is a continuous process. Pollard and Filer (1999) point out that adaptation is actively, not passively, fitting in. Therefore, how children cope with and adapt to, the new learning environment is crucial to their 'career' as a lifelong learner.

What all early years practitioners can do is to make the learning experiences in the early years setting as similar to those of the home as they can, to make learning lifelike and authentic, and to replicate the positive atmosphere and the genuine responses of parents and carers. All too often children who move directly into school can see few similarities between learning in the home and learning at school. The new learning environment can sometimes be full of secondhand experiences; of interruptions by adults; of writing down rather than acting out; of learning what the adult directs rather than what the children initiate. Good early years practitioners recognize that this is not an effective learning environment for young children. If children are to continue to be interested, excited and motivated to learn, then practitioners must do everything possible to replicate the effective learning environment that has made them competent learners from birth.

Changing a child into a 'pupil'

As we have seen, there are many aspects of a foundation stage setting that tell a young child that their role in this place is somehow different from their role at home. Particularly for those practitioners who work in the school sector, it can be illuminating to reflect on how many practices insidiously turn the young enthusiastic spontaneous learner into a more passive and reactive 'pupil'. Some of these changes are necessary if children are to learn the social skills necessary for playing and learning and living alongside others other than their family members. Some, however, are simply designed to maintain the traditional status quo of classrooms, which is that teachers have the power and control, and the role of the child, as pupil, is to learn from the adult's greater skill and knowledge. One of the first rules that children are introduced to – and one of the most entrenched – is that of 'putting your hand up'. Sinclair and Coulthard (1975) call this 'bidding', which is an excellent description. The child is bidding for the adult's time by raising a hand in response to the demand to do so. It is a request to hold the floor and have the adult's attention. Putting up your hand demands an understanding of two basic rules: one, that in order to speak to the adult, this is what you need to do; two, that there are times when you can talk to other children and times when you cannot, and this is one when you cannot unless you are told you can, in which case you must but only when you're told!

Because the rules and routines are bewildering, many children resort to imitation. Sometimes that imitation is of other children who have been in the setting longer or who have simply cottoned on faster. Children offer responses 'that clearly enough imitate those that have recently been offered and have seemed to please the teacher well enough to get positive feedback' (Willes 1983: 186). Sometimes the imitation is of the adults who, as Mary Willes describes, through their 'intonation, gestures and expression' give out clues that the child is left to guess about and test the meanings of.

The rules and routines are frequently non-negotiable. They are the prerogative of the practitioner, and often they do not choose to or think to divulge them. Thus becoming a pupil is seen by Willes as learning these adult initiatives as rapidly as possible:

> The minimal, inescapable requirement that a child must meet if he [sic] is to function as a participating pupil is not very extensive. It is necessary to accept adult direction, to know that you say nothing at all unless the teacher indicates that you may, to know that when your turn is indicated you must use whatever clues you can find, and make the best guess you can. There are prerequisites to learning this. It is necessary to want adult attention and approval, and to be able to attend to a person or to a topic for more than a moment or two.
>
> (1983: 83)

This is 'training' in the true sense of the word. It is learning to respond in a given way to a given signal – behaviour with Pavlovian overtones.

Pleasing adults

The notion of pleasing adults is also a very important one in the discussion about power and control in environments for early learning. Holt (1982: 70) suggests that 'it is only when pleasing adults becomes important that the sharp line between success and failure appears'. This implies that children's perceptions of their own success or failure, their own worth and value come from the values and perceptions of the early childhood educators whom they encounter. We know that there is evidence of a self-fulfilling prophecy that operates in any educational environment. Tell a child that they are good, will succeed, are doing well and the child obliges by responding with enthusiasm and proving you right. Tell a child that they are worthless, useless, hopeless or any other damning adjective directed at a certain group of children daily in their educational lives, and lo and behold they prove the adults right again. Holt suggests that being incompetent has two advantages: first, it reduces what others expect of you and second, it reduces what you expect or even hope of yourself. When you set out to fail, he says, one thing is certain – you cannot be disappointed.

Chapter 1 showed that, whatever their experiences, most young children arrive at their early childhood class or setting as enthusiastic and energetic learners. Their early experiences in that setting can bring about a transformation in their attitudes and behaviours so that they become a shadow of their former competent selves. Much of this is a result of the transference of learning power and control, from the child to the adult. Janet Meighan (1993: 43) suggests that once children begin school, 'Learning how to learn gives way to learning how to be taught.'

So we return to the main question of this book. Why, when children in their early, formative years have achieved what Gardner calls a 'breathtaking array of competences with little formal tutelage' do some of those same children suddenly become dependent, passive learners, reliant on the adult for success and self-esteem? Gardner (1993: 3) suggests that 'schools were instituted precisely to inculcate those skills and conceptions that, while desirable, are not so readily and naturally learned as [their] intuitive capacities'. There is more than an element of truth in this. Schools, and now the whole range of foundation stage providers, are devices of society and therefore must respond to the requirements of that society and of the cultures it serves. Unfortunately, in fulfilling this requirement, these settings can denude children of all their inherent powers as learners and make them feel as though their needs and their interests no longer have a place. For some children, the transition from home to school or setting marks a transition from success as a learner to failure. All too often it is the child who is a truly intuitive learner who is at greatest risk. Early years settings, particularly schools, do not always cater for individuals. Because of their very nature they demand a good deal of conformity, and early childhood settings that are not sufficiently flexible to allow for the idiosyncrasies of learners are likely to alienate some of the most creative and free-thinking children.

Disaffected learners

Feelings of alienation come about when there is a mismatch between the child's expectations of their new early learning setting and the setting's expectations of the child. According to Willes (1983), some children step out of line because they do not know where the line is drawn. Some children, however – those who are already having feelings of alienation because they do not fit with the setting's expectations – know where the lines are drawn, but deliberately cross them. In the introduction to her book on disaffection in the early years, Gill Barrett defines disaffection thus:

Fundamentally the word implies a negative state of something that was once positive. Thus affection for something has been reversed to become disaffection. Here we are concerned with disaffection in the early years of schooling. Thus, instead of affection for the activities of schooling, disaffection implies a dislike and hence a turning away from the activities and learning expectations of the classroom and school.

(1989: xiv)

If one considers that some children have only just started at school or their new setting, the implication of this definition is that the 'affection' was for learning that happened in contexts prior to and outside the setting. Disaffection therefore comes hard on the heels of affection for situations in which the child saw him or herself as competent. Running right through this book is the notion of the young child as both a competent and motivated learner, and it is a dreadful indictment of the early childhood setting which can turn that motivation and competence so quickly into disaffection.

So how is this disaffection likely to manifest itself? Young children are unlikely to withdraw themselves from the environment as older children might do, as most young children choose to remain within the security of their early years setting even when feeling very aggrieved. Their most likely response is to reject or withdraw from the activities or tasks they are being required to perform. If this withdrawal is 'active', the children can throw tantrums, disappear under tables or absent themselves into another room. Barrett (1989: 30) claims that the early years setting or classroom

with all its new expectations and people, is likely to provoke strong responses such as crying, hitting other children and removing oneself from the source of frustration. If the child knows that these strong responses have always been responded to by an adult in the past, and the cause of frustration removed and dealt with, then it may cause even stronger response behaviour in school when the initial crying or attempted withdrawal fails to remove the expectation.

This is a terrible picture of the distress that some children feel and the anger they consequently display. If the rebellion is more passive, then children simply stop doing what is asked of them, do it extremely slowly or make sure they disrupt as many other children as possible in the process.

There can be no doubt that disaffection arises because children are asked to do things that make little sense to them. It is no justification to say that children have to learn to do this in life and therefore they should start now. This rationale is used for an astonishing range of experiences, from sitting still for long periods of time to enduring competition in games. Children may have to face a myriad of unpleasant and unhappy experiences before they grow old and die but this is no justification for inflicting such experiences on children just so they can practise for future unhappiness.

One of the greatest frustrations for young children is that often they cannot articulate their own feelings. They find it hard to explain or describe what they feel and why. Gill Barrett's important study and the more recent work of Penny Lancaster and her team on *Listening to Children* (2010) show that if adults are patient enough to ask, and willing to find out the answers, as to why children are not responding positively, then they are half-way to resolving the problem for the child and, of course, for themselves and the rest of the children.

A further frustration for young children is the amount of interruption they get from adults when they are engaged in activities. We have seen that one important principle of early childhood education is that the young learner has time for periods of sustained activity. Whether this is initiated by the child or the teacher, an adherence to the principle is crucial if children's experiences of learning in their early years setting are to emulate their experiences at home and if the practitioner is to give positive messages about the worth of the activity or experience in which the child is engaged. Barrett gives examples of the intense frustration young children feel when their experiences are interrupted:

> Daniel and Carl have found a book on New Zealand (Carl's homeland). They start to read when the teacher calls, 'Time to put them away'. Daniel's face and comment show disappointment. 'But I've only just got it.'
>
> There are always too many people in school to take things properly. You have to stop too soon. Someone always spoils it.
>
> (1989: 10)

Many early years educators are addressing the issue of interruptions to the learning day. Research by Campbell and Neill (1990) confirmed what all practitioners know, that there always seems to be insufficient time in the day for all that has to be done. An audit of how time is spent in school, in particular, can reveal how much learning time is fragmented by the school timetable. Assemblies, playtime, lunches, television, and so on, all interrupt the flow of learning for children. Each break requires teachers and children to wind themselves down and then to wind themselves back up again to achieve the momentum that was stopped. This is not an efficient use of time and it is a useful exercise to examine the interruptions in a classroom or within the school, and see if there are ways in which such interruptions can be minimized (see Chapter 5).

The negotiated classroom

The early learning environment, as we have seen, is a place where rules and expectations can be governed exclusively by adults and where children are unable to stake a claim. It is usually adults who create the learning environment for children, who decide what activities and opportunities are available and who decide what should be done where and with whom. But what happens if adults consciously and deliberately give children a stake in the process? What is possible if, in order to maintain and sustain their motivation, application and *rights*, children are taken on as partners in the shared negotiation of practice and behaviour?

The notion of negotiation

Sylvia Warham (1993: 35–6) suggests that in some ways teaching and learning are in themselves a negotiation because 'the process requires the consent of both the teacher and the learner'. The negotiation of the learning context between the early childhood educator and the children is a negotiation of what the children will allow the adult to do and what the adult will allow the children to do. Successful negotiation requires messages to emanate from the adult. When children are listened to and respected (Lancaster 2010) and their ideas and interests absorbed into the fabric of their learning experiences, then this is a positive starting point for the negotiation of a more reciprocal partnership between educators and learners.

The identity of the adult as educator

There is a whole range of things in the context of the early years setting that can be negotiated with children. The extent to which these are adopted depends very much on the style of the early childhood educator responsible for establishing the learning environment, and her or his personal identity. Warham (1993) identifies educators who have 'dominant identities' and those who have 'less dominant identities'. She suggests that those who have dominant identities 'created inequality. The children found that only one person at a time could be dominant and they had to compete with one another and the teacher if they wanted to take part in the [class] discussion' (Warham 1993: 35–6). On the other hand, the less dominant educators appear to have 'no control over the situation', but in fact use a far greater range of strategies in interaction with children than the dominant educators. By encouraging children to be independent thinkers and learners, the control that less dominant educators exercise is far more subtle, but far more effective. Effective educators, says Warham, adopt both dominant and less dominant strategies in different situations, but she warns that it is important to be conscious of the positive effects of habitually less dominant strategies which, she claims

- foster trust, confidence and security;
- encourage in children a sense of self-worth and respect for others;
- encourage independence and self-reliance;
- encourage children to develop their own initiatives; and foster a sense of equality.

(Warham 1993: 37)

While habitually dominant power strategies may not prevent children from learning, it is possible they carry with them certain inherent risks. Warham suggests that it is possible they may

- foster competition to the point of confrontation;
- damage group and individual relationships;
- discourage the children from taking initiatives;
- make the children dependent upon their teacher; and risk damaging the child's future attitude towards teachers and education.

(Warham 1993: 37)

The notion of negotiation can only sit comfortably with the less dominant strategies described above. The remainder of this chapter is devoted to looking at ways in which early years practitioners can move towards the kind of learning environments that acknowledge children's competences, respect their rights as individuals and see education as a collaborative venture between learners.

Negotiating learning and the learning environment

The possibilities for negotiation within the early learning environment fall into three broad categories:

- *organization*: when and how things are to be learnt;
- *context*: where and with whom they are to be learnt;
- *curriculum*: what is to be learnt.

Organization

The start of the day

At the beginning of the day children are full of energy and, we hope, enthusiasm. If they arrive at their setting and are required to sit down, sit still and – probably – sit quietly, then immediately they are having to adopt behaviours that suit the purposes of the adults rather than themselves. The children's needs are subsumed beneath the needs of the practitioner to sort out the early morning issues, to juggle children and parents, and to be seen as having a calm, controlled group. The beginning of the day establishes the tone for much that will follow. If the day begins in ways that repress children, for whatever purposes, then this sends negative messages to children about those in power and control in the room, and in some children can set up feelings of frustration, alienation and resentment before the day has hardly begun.

In most early learning environments, children on arrival get straight down to activities that they choose themselves. Parents are encouraged to stay for as long as they can or want, and while children are engaged independently or with their parents or carers, the practitioner can get on with her administration or organization in the knowledge that the children are playing purposefully. If a child is new or younger and less settled, then this also gives the practitioner the opportunity to settle and calm them and have conversations on an individual level until the child is reassured and comforted. Some adults are concerned about starting the day in this way because of their responsibilities over completion of the register. However, completion of the register does not rely on children sitting on the carpet and responding to their names. There is a whole range of strategies for recording the arrival of children, from hanging names on a 'tree', to posting names in a letter box, to writing names on a white board. Any strategies such as these can help practitioners start the day in a less formal and frequently less stressful way.

The organization of the learning environment

When I was in my first year of teaching I used to spend days before the beginning of each term organizing my classroom. I drove the caretaker mad by arranging and rearranging my room. I made labels, signs and charts, spent a fortune on card and pens and tacky-backed *everything*. I believed that it was part of my professional responsibility to make the room as 'ready' for the children as I could, so that it would be a welcoming environment in which we could all get down to play and work. As I began to give more and more time and thought to the involvement of children in decision-making processes within the classroom, however, I realized just what wonderful learning opportunities I was taking out of the hands of the children. Real-life problem-solving situations frequently stare us in the face in classrooms, and instead of responding to them as heaven-sent opportunities, we subject children to the contortions of 'identifying a need' for a problem for which they will rarely realize a solution and which they would never have identified for themselves.

Early learning environments *need* organizing, however. As Chapter 5 describes, there are decisions about space and resources that are fundamental to the establishment of spaces and areas that are conducive to independent learning. Since these are environments in which children are to learn, then it seems entirely logical that they should be environments that they help to create. Once I realized this I left the furniture where the caretaker had left it – in a heap in the middle of the classroom (yes, that really *was* his practice!). Then when the children arrived, we worked together to decide what learning areas were needed and where resources should go. Then came the business of sorting, locating and labelling resources which, because the children were so involved, gave them a sense of ownership over the classroom that they never had when I made the decisions and took the action, when they were not around.

Discipline: rules and sanctions

One successful way of helping children to respect and adhere to rules and sanctions is not to impose them from on high, but to negotiate them. Children can become involved in establishing rules that they perceive to be necessary in order for their learning environments to run smoothly and for the benefit of all. Children's rules sometimes reveal interesting insights into their perceptions of what is or is not important and what is or is not likely to happen when in their settings. 'The children mustn't spit', said one 4-year-old recently arrived at school – now where did *that* idea come from?

The sanctions that children work out for themselves can be very enlightening. I had endeavoured, as a headteacher, to alter my role within the school in the disciplining of children. Rather than seeing children only when they had been naughty, I asked the staff to send me children with whom I could share something positive and celebratory. This seemed to be working well, so I was dismayed when the reception class, on negotiating their own sanctions, ended a long list of mounting retribution with 'No. 6: Send them to Miss Fisher for telling off.' Children's perceptions are not altered overnight.

If rules make sense to children and if sanctions seem appropriate, even if not necessarily 'fair' in adult terms, then children are more likely to feel a sense of responsibility in maintaining them. One last word about rules, and that is – it is best to keep them positive. It contributes so much more constructively to the ethos of the classroom if the list talks about what we *will* do and be like, rather than what we must *not* do or be like.

Order of experiences

As we have seen, there are many worthwhile reasons for encouraging children to be independent in their movement from one activity or experience to the next. The necessity to do this of course will vary according to the age of the children within the foundation stage. For the 3- or young 4-year-old in a preschool or private nursery or nursery school, children will be encouraged to move from experience to experience, that is either adult- or child-initiated, as they choose. If practitioners want to work alongside specific children for an adult-led activity, then this can be planned for the beginning of sessions so that children's independent learning is not interrupted. For older children in the foundation stage, those in their reception year or in Year 1, then adult-led learning can successfully take place alongside more independent learning and, as we have seen in earlier chapters, each will benefit from the quality of the other (see Fisher 2010).

Whether or not the learning day incorporates a number of adult-led or adult-initiated experiences, children should still be given as much autonomy over when they engage in other learning as is possible. If practitioners attempt to organize a 'carousel' of activities so that all children complete the same tasks in a day, then many of children's spontaneous interests and much of their self-initiated learning will fall by the wayside. Not only that, but the adoption of a 'carousel' approach usually results in children's activity being stopped all at the same time and children being moved on to the next activity, irrespective of whether their activity/task has ended.

Letting children negotiate the order in which they do things presupposes an element of trust between practitioners and children. If there are some adult-initiated tasks for reception or Key Stage 1 children to complete, then children have to understand that these need to be fitted into the day. If children know that they are being trusted and are being given the opportunity to make their own choices and decisions, then they also know, because it is a part of the 'negotiation' made explicit by the practitioner, that they have to fulfil their side of the bargain. Negotiation can never be one-sided, and a learning environment where children do their own thing, but not the adult's, is not a negotiated environment. Part of the developing relationship between the early years practitioner and the children must include discussions about what choice and decision-making mean, and it includes the responsibility to fulfil all sides of the bargain and to complete the tasks that the adult initiates as well as the tasks children want to initiate themselves. On the practitioner's side, the bargain is that she or he does not set up so many adult-initiated activities that time for child-initiated activity is squeezed out. Planning is critical. If time has been allowed for a balance of activities (see Chapters 4 and 9), then it is perfectly appropriate for an adult to remind a child that there is only x amount of time now in the day/week and there is still y to be done. Most children, given the self-respect that comes from making their own decisions, respect in turn their educators and will complete what is outstanding – even if reluctantly at times. In negotiated early learning environments, where children can choose the order in which they do their various activities, there is a purposeful and dynamic atmosphere. It is rare to see the persuasion and coercion that can go on in classrooms where children are required to complete successive tasks set by the adult with no room for negotiation or using their initiative.

Length of time on different activities

When children can negotiate the order in which they go to different activities and resources, then it is implicit that they will be able to determine how long they will spend there. Time management is something that many adults could usefully learn, but even young children can develop this skill when given experiences that leave decisions in their hands. Most children learn to pace themselves given sufficient experience of having control over time and their own learning activities.

As we have seen earlier in this chapter, children need sustained periods of time in order to produce work or to engage in learning of quality and depth (EYCG 1992; Early Education 2012). It is up to the early childhood educator to plan for the delicate balance between sufficient time being given to the needs of the child and sufficient time being given to the demands of the external agenda. Some practitioners worry about the child who, despite reminders or help with time management, still stays all day on a child-initiated activity. If there are a lot of interesting and absorbing experiences and opportunities both indoors and out, then most children want to experience more than one thing in any one day. However, if a child is genuinely reluctant to move and clearly is gaining something valuable from their self-selected activity, then what is this telling us about the child? Children who need to repeat experiences may be in need of reassurance of something familiar. They may be feeling unsettled or unwell and simply find the repetition of something they know offers them the security they temporarily need. If the behaviour is out of character and continues, then this should alert the practitioner to investigate reasons for the child's behaviour. Forcing children simply leads to alienation. It may bring about a temporary result, but will not enhance the children's attitudes or approaches to learning. As Holt says, 'If the situations, the materials, the problems before a child do not interest him [*sic*], his attention will slip off to what does interest him, and no amount of exhortation or threats will bring it back' (1982: 265). Children can be trusted to set their own pace. They will need opportunities from the adult to manage and organize their time, but as with all elements of independent learning, this is time well spent.

Context

Places to learn

Where we choose to engage in activities can have a significant bearing on our application to a task. I am sure I am not alone in feeling that I cannot do my own writing unless I am in the relative tranquillity of my study, and cannot settle to read the Sunday papers unless I have my legs up on the sofa and the cat on my lap. Locations can promote or inhibit learning and, as with everything else, what is desirable for one person can be thoroughly undesirable for someone else. If an early learning environment is designed along the lines of the 'workshop' approach outlined in Chapter 5, then children will already have the freedom to move around the indoor and outdoor space in order to find resources and use equipment. However, this freedom is fettered if children are then required to go back to a predetermined place to complete the task in hand. If a child truly concentrates best sitting alone, lying on the floor, working with a friend, then the environment should be designed so that this can happen. Part of negotiation is being able to justify a decision made (on the part of the adult as well as the child) therefore a child who chooses an unusual location to learn may be required to justify it to his or her peers and the adult. If the quality of everyone's learning is not compromised, then the decision is justified. If learning is adversely affected, then the practitioner and other children are at liberty to challenge the decision and suggest a different one.

Sometimes, in settings where children are getting used to their independence, there can be children who seem to be 'flitting' – to be going from place to place without settling for long, or who go and watch other children without actually joining in themselves. This situation is another learning opportunity for the practitioner. Children who flit fall generally into two categories. There are those who are unsure of themselves and need to see the range of what is possible but do not yet have the confidence to try something for themselves. In this case flitting is very valuable because it means that the child comes to gain confidence through observations and imitation and almost always joins in once this is achieved. Then there are children who need supporting towards independence. Perhaps they are given little independence at home, are used to having things done for them and need support to make decisions for themselves. In this case the practitioner needs to make it part of her or his 'teaching' that the child is helped in small stages to begin to make decisions and to act on their own initiative. One of the most important parts of this is to gain the understanding of parents so that they extend independence to the child's life at home.

With whom to learn

Most of us work, play and learn better when we are alongside people we like and trust. You only have to try and separate practitioners who work together at the same setting when they attend in-service training courses to realize just how much we like to be alongside people we know! If children are not in adult-directed groups for a specific purpose (see Chapter 6), then for most of the day they should be able to learn alongside those with whom they want to learn. If they are working on a task or playing as an individual, then it makes no odds whether they are sitting next to somebody doing something different. However, for most of the time children benefit from playing and learning alongside others. They will collaborate readily when they see the need to do so and will organize themselves very effectively for the purpose. So, being able to be with someone you choose usually gives children an added sense of motivation. Of course there are some exceptions to this. Once again it is part of the negotiation process. If children do not work in cooperative and constructive ways with the person or people whom they have chosen, then the other children and/or the practitioner can suggest alternative ways of learning.

The curriculum

The topic

In Chapter 3, I expressed certain reservations about topic work, in that it can be hijacked by adults and have little relevance to children.

I believe that topics for young children can inhibit and constrain their learning as adults seek to link together areas of the curriculum in ways that become unnatural and illogical. For 3- and young 4-year-olds the cross-curricular nature of their interests can be captured best by short themes that run for a matter of days or for the duration of the children's interests. For older children, a topic can usefully emphasize the links between areas of learning and the application of skills and understandings across the curriculum. Children of this age really enjoy choosing a topic or saying what they already know about a topic, suggesting ideas for what might be learned and involving people at home in finding resources and materials to bring into school. In one of the schools where I was headteacher, staff would suggest a few topics to the children and, when they found the topic that had most interest amongst the class, the children would pose questions that they wanted answered, e.g. why do leaves fall off trees in winter? How do spacecraft know where to land? Do all police officers need to know how to ride a horse? These questions were written on huge bits of card and hung from the classroom ceilings so that they became the focus of the class's investigations over the coming weeks. No matter how bizarre – or challenging – some of the questions were, the teachers found that by starting from the children's questions, they still 'covered' all the skills, concepts and knowledge that they would have planned themselves (and often in more interesting and thought-provoking ways).

Criteria for success

One of the ways in which early years practitioners display control in their settings is by being in charge of what is deemed to be good, appropriate or sufficient with regard to children's play, work and learning. Children come to rely too much on the adult's judgements for affirmation and approval and do not believe that their own opinion matters (Dweck 1978; 2006). Practitioners sometimes use words like 'good', 'well done', 'brilliant', and so on, and children can be left bemused as to *why* this effort was 'good' and this 'not your best'. Some practitioners draw smiley faces and award stickers which also send out the message that it is what the adult thinks that matters; that judgements about value and worth are by the adult's criteria. When children are reliant on the adult's evaluations in this way, they are usually left in no uncertain terms about whether the adult is pleased or not.

In an interesting article called 'In praise of praising less' (1991), the author Mark Tompkins warns against empty praise. The article suggests that practitioners should give their *opinions* rather than their *judgements* and make specific reference to the details of the child's activity or the process the child has used. If children have negotiated the purpose of the work and understand why they are doing what they are doing, then they are far more likely to be able to give a rationale for when something has been undertaken or achieved to their own satisfaction. In some effective settings working with older foundation stage children, practitioners negotiate with children the 'success criteria' *before* an adult-led or adult-initiated activity begins. In other words, they ask 'What do you think will make this an effective chair for the bear to sit on?'; 'What do you think will need to happen for you all to collaborate on designing this map?'; 'What will make this an interesting story for the readers in Class 4?'

When children select their own 'success criteria', if it is appropriate to an activity, then it helps give them a clear framework in which to evaluate and review their own efforts. This notion of making explicit what has been achieved and what might be achieved next has, however, been taken to extremes recently in ways that are neither helpful not beneficial to younger learners. The introduction of the Assessment for Learning initiative (Black et al. 2002) and, more recently, target setting with children (DfES 2006), have led to the introduction of practices in foundation stage classrooms that were originally designed for older learners and have not always been sensitively or fruitfully adapted for those who are younger. When introduced appropriately, both initiatives encourage children to articulate what they are good at, where they need to improve and what help they need to do so. Such strategies, in the hands of sensitive early years practitioners, can boost children's self-esteem and lead them to new ways of thinking and learning. However, there are real dangers in the use of both initiatives in the hands of those who succumb to practices such as displaying individual targets on the wall of foundation stage classrooms, or using a 'traffic light' system that says – I 'must', 'should' or 'could'. Targets (or even 'next steps') for foundation stage children should not be displayed, for all the world to see, if they are in any sense pejorative. A public display of what a child cannot do is hardly likely to raise a child's self-esteem. If we want confident and motivated learners, then what goes on the wall should be what that child *can* do and what he or she *has* achieved. Indeed, the imposition of external criteria for success (for this is what targets are) goes against the grain of promoting intrinsic motivation, which is a fundamental principle of high quality early education.

What happens to the outcomes of children's efforts?

Sometimes children are pleased with their efforts and want to share what they have done. Sometimes they are dissatisfied and want to start again. Sometimes they are dissatisfied and want to do something else. If children make a decision that their efforts are not acceptable to them, then in almost every case they should be at liberty to dispense with them as they choose. Some children screw up or dismantle what they have been working on because they are so lacking in self-esteem that they cannot believe they have achieved anything of worth. Whatever the reason for satisfaction or dissatisfaction, choosing what happens to their various efforts should be the child's decision. Yet so often that drawing, or mark-making or number story automatically becomes the property of the adult. 'I just want to borrow it for the colour display'; 'you can take it home at the end of term'; 'mummy will be so pleased to see it on the wall'. The 'I just want to borrow this for the wall/portfolio/ book' puts the adult very firmly back in control of what happens to children and their learning efforts. There are legitimate reasons for adults wanting children's work for display. These should be explained to the children. But if children then decide they would rather keep their efforts to themselves, or take them home, or throw them away, then they should be allowed to do so.

Conclusion

If children are to emulate their early success as learners once they start in their new early years class or setting, then practitioners need to ensure that there is not a great gulf between being a child and becoming a pupil. Children who are expected to behave in ways that are alien and irrelevant to them may become disaffected learners and this disaffection frequently occurs when children have no control over their own experiences. When early childhood educators are committed to a learning partnership with their children, then there are many ways in which children can negotiate learning. The power and control this negotiation gives children can be a powerful and motivating force for learning and is likely to lead to positive, lifelong attitudes towards learning and accomplishment (Schweinhart et al. 1993; Dweck 2006). Some practitioners believe that giving children control means that they themselves will lose it. My experience is that this could not be further from the truth. One practitioner in a reception class who evolved a negotiated classroom with her children remarked, 'The more control I give away, the more in control I am.' The next chapter draws together the many practical aspects of previous chapters in suggesting how children can be helped to organize their own learning experiences.

Questions to Challenge your Thinking

1 How do you support children's (and parents') transitions in to and out of your setting? Are you confident about supporting the particular needs of vulnerable children?
2 How do you ensure children's learning experiences are relevant and meaningful to them as individuals? How do you engage them in learning?
3 Which elements of learning and the learning environment are negotiated with children? Could children's voices be heard more in your setting?

9

THE ASSESSMENT OF CHILDREN'S LEARNING

What practitioners need to know about children and their achievements

Introduction

We have already established that assessment should come at the beginning of the cycle of teaching and learning (Chapter 2), as well as at the end of it. It is rather like a sandwich in which observation is the first slice of bread, planning and implementation constitute the filling, and evaluation and assessment are the final slice of bread (Fisher 1998a; 1998b; 1998c). In order to plan effectively, early childhood educators need to know what children already know and can do and this is established through rigorous observation-based assessment of children in action. However, there is also an important place for assessment that comes at the end of the cycle of teaching and learning, when it is used to review what a child has learned and what progress they have made.

Assessment *for* Learning and Assessment *of* Learning

Recently, the distinction between assessment that takes place *before* learning is planned and implemented and that which takes place afterwards, has been clarified by the use of the terms – Assessment *for* Learning (before) and Assessment *of* Learning (after) (Black et al. 2002). These different types of assessment each serve a distinct purpose.

Assessment for Learning

Assessment *for* Learning happens all the time in good early learning environments. It is rooted in the observation of children and the sticky notes, quick jottings and ongoing records that practitioners gather as evidence of development and progress. Importantly, it involves children in their own self-evaluation. Early years practitioners are responsible for ensuring that – in developmentally appropriate ways – children are helped to reflect on what they have done, what skills and materials they used, what they might like to do differently next time, and so on. This continuous assessment by both the practitioner and the child ensures that children's development is kept under constant review and the evidence gathered is at hand to inform the ongoing plans that are made for the learning environment and the learning needs of individual children. This ongoing Assessment *for* Learning is often called '*formative* assessment'.

Assessment of Learning

Assessment *of* Learning, on the other hand, is usually carried out once children have been introduced to or experienced something new. It is used to establish what a child *now* knows and can do – after a new topic perhaps, or after the introduction of some adult-led work on, say, some aspect of 'materials' or the 'use of technology'. Assessment *of* Learning is also used at the end of a particular phase in children's educational experience – i.e. the end of term, the end of a year, when making a transition to a new setting. As such, it often means that the practitioner is summing up all the evidence that has been gathered over a period of time in order to make a judgement about where the child is now. Because of this, Assessment *of* Learning is often termed '*summative* assessment'.

Different uses of assessment

Early years practitioners, then, are responsible for using assessments for two key purposes – formative and summative:

- *formative assessment* – used on a daily and weekly basis, by the practitioner, to inform what is planned for the learning environment and for children's individual needs;
- *summative assessment* – used to inform others such as parents, other professionals or the practitioner in the setting to which a child will transfer, and by the practitioner to 'sum up' children's progress at key points such as the end of a term.

The quality of summative assessment relies on the quality of formative assessment. If a practitioner needs to summarize a child's achievements at a certain point in time, they can do so far more easily if they have good ongoing, formative assessments to refer back to. In addition, the regular and systematic use of observation ensures that practitioners know their children well rather than being uncertain about their skills and knowledge when asked to make a judgement for summative purposes. I want to look at the two purposes of assessment in more detail as, when practitioners are clear about these two types of assessment, then they find it easier to gather appropriate evidence and that evidence is more useful for the purpose to which it is put.

Formative assessment

Formative records give ongoing information about a child's progress and attainment. Most formative assessments are used *by the practitioner* in everyday practice to 'observe children's learning, strive to understand it, and then put our understanding to good use' (Drummond 1993: 13). The Early Years Foundation Stage (DfE 2012) says that:

> Ongoing assessment (also known as formative assessment) is an integral part of the learning and development process. It involves practitioners observing children to understand their level of achievement, interest and learning styles, and to then shape learning experiences for each child reflecting those observations.
>
> (p. 10, para 2.1)

Formative records are necessary because they give practitioners daily information about what children know and can do and, therefore, provide the necessary information on which to build and adjust short-term plans. As we saw in Chapter 3, short-term plans are concerned with differentiation and in order to plan activities and experiences that are appropriate for different children, the adult has to have detailed knowledge of their current learning needs. Ongoing records provide such information and are the foundation of all good planning. By dint of their concern with the detail of children's development, formative records are often quite lengthy, but these records are not for onward transmission to somebody else. The practitioner uses these records either to make plans for the learning environment, to make decisions about the current learning needs of individual children or to make judgements about children's attainment for summative purposes. The records for formative assessment then, can be summarized as follows:

- ongoing, cumulative notes, taken throughout the teaching day;
- narrative records of what children do and what children say;

- including contributions from parents, children and other adults who work with the child;
- providing evidence on which to base future planning;
- incorporating analysis and planned action.

Summative assessments

By definition, summative assessments are summaries of achievement. Very often they are required in order to pass on information about a child and, therefore, need to be relatively brief. In the course of a child's educational life, summative information needs to be passed regularly to a number of different people. Parents have a legal right to receive an annual report on their child's progress including the child's attainment, if appropriate, on the Early Years Foundation Stage Profile (DfE 2012). The next foundation stage setting or the new school or the next practitioner needs a summary of a child's attainment on transfer in order to help them plan the next stages of the child's education. There are often concerns expressed about how much these transfer records are read. The practitioners who have completed a profile of a child's achievements during their time in the foundation stage or during their time in one particular setting often feel that they want to share all their information with the next practitioner. The practitioner who receives the records sometimes feels that they have too much information passed on and cannot possibly absorb all that is being reported. So, there is a necessity for practitioners who are forwarding information to the next setting or practitioner to be sensitive to what is reasonable and practical. The best way to judge this is to have conversations together and decide from one setting to the next, from one practitioner to the next, what is desirable yet manageable.

Even when records are read by the next practitioner, there is another debate about *when* they should be read. Some practitioners say they will not read records before they meet and get to know new children so that they can make up their own minds about the child and form their own relationships. On the other hand, if a practitioner does not know the new children and does not read the information to hand about their abilities on leaving their previous setting, how can they plan appropriately for the first days of the child's new learning environment? In addition to this, it is important to have a summary of each child's attainment for those times when progress is not smooth and decisions have to be made about appropriate intervention and support. Summative records of progress, written at regular intervals, can give a good indication of strengths and weaknesses, developmental patterns and gaps in knowledge and understanding, all of which provide a foundation for the diagnostic assessment of children's current needs. The records for summative assessment then, can be summarized as follows:

- brief statements made to summarize information gained through formative records;
- a summary of the most vital and relevant information about what the child knows, understands and can do at regular points throughout the year;
- often made at a point of transfer, for example, on entry, change of setting, change of school;
- designed to inform others, for example, parents, next practitioner/setting, outside agencies.

Recording formative and summative assessments

Formative assessments

As we have seen, formative assessments are based on the ongoing observations that early years practitioners make of children in action. Recording these is a demanding task, but one that practitioners need to make part of their everyday practice if they are to plan a curriculum that is relevant and appropriate to the children in their class.

The initial recording of an assessment is often very informal. It is as a result of an observation – whether planned or spontaneous – that is frequently captured on sticky notes, sticky labels or in notebooks. Equally, the observation may focus on one child for a considerable length of time – say, 20–30 minutes – in order to capture in depth a child's approach to and achievement in learning. Many nurseries plan systematically for children to be the focus of a long observation in rotation, with one or more members of staff focusing on that child for a pre-planned length of time. In some classrooms, the long observation is used to find out more about a particular child causing concern, where greater depth of knowledge and understanding are needed on the part of staff. It is, of course, preferable that every child is regularly the focus of such observations because often it is only over time that new insights are gleaned and new understandings are reached.

What happens to observations once they are made is dependent on their type. Long observations should be acted upon, used to inform the planning process and then filed for future reference if necessary. Brief observations should also be used for analysis and to inform the next steps of children's learning experiences. Once analysed, these temporary jottings are either filed or (more sensibly) thrown away, because action has been taken, or the most significant assessments of steps in children's learning are transferred onto a more permanent record.

These permanent records need to demonstrate progress. They need to show:

- date;
- observation (although this may be on the sticky note that is then thrown away);
- analysis (learning achieved not activity undertaken);
- future action.

The *date* ensures that a child's rate of progress is recorded and that each individual spurt or plateau can be seen as part of the child's overall development. The *observation* captures what the child says and does and sets the action in context. This can be written straight on to the record sheet or it can be written on a sticky note which is then transferred to the record sheet. The *learning analysis* uses the practitioner's professional judgement to identify the skills, concepts, knowledge and attitudes which the observation represents (see below). This analysis will be done at a later stage than the observation and will be used by the practitioner to inform the action column. The *action* column is completed as a result of the analysis by the practitioner, hopefully with other adults who share responsibility for the assessment of the foundation stage children, of the learning needs of an individual child. Completion of this section prompts the adult to fine-tune the short-term planning. The practitioner should ask:

- What does this observation mean for this *child*?: Does an activity or an experience need to be planned that will support this child's learning in different ways?
- What does this observation mean for the *environment*?: are any additional resources required to extend, or rejuvenate play and exploration?
- What does this observation mean for me as the *practitioner*?: was I in the right place at the right time for this child? Does the child need me to support their learning more at this stage or does the child need me to back off so they can learn or consolidate their learning more independently?

Taking action as a result of observations ensures that assessment influences the curriculum. Sometimes no action is required above and beyond the introduction of the next planned part of the curriculum. At other times, children unexpectedly reveal that they know or do not know something and the practitioner needs to adjust their plans accordingly. There is no point at all in doing observations of children if they have no impact on the planning process. Ofsted inspection reports repeatedly criticize practitioners for gathering file-loads of observations that sit and gather dust and have no impact on children's experiences in the days that follow. The purpose of observations is to improve the quality of learning and the quality of teaching. Equally, when summative records are written, they draw on these detailed, ongoing notes and this is why the quality of summative records is heavily dependent on the quality of formative assessments.

Summative assessments

The recording of summative assessments is much more dependent on the purpose of the assessment. It is best if, once a purpose is established, practitioners design a format that will best capture the evidence that is necessary. At its most straightforward, a summative assessment would record:

- date;
- period of time to which the assessment refers;
- summary of evidence – across all areas or learning and/or characteristics of learning.

(DfE 2012: 7, para 1.10)

As electronic data systems come increasingly online, there is a temptation to leave the recording of children's progress to prescribed tick boxes, formats and formulae. However appealing these systems may be initially in seeming to save time, they have their limitations. Children are far too individual and idiosyncratic to be summed up by a pre-determined list of characteristics, skills and knowledge. If a practitioner wants to use such a list, they would soon find that a child had an attribute that was not written down and that there were attributes on the list that did not adequately describe the child. In addition to the failure of pre-designed checklists (electronic or otherwise) to give a full and rounded picture of an individual child's personal achievements, the information gathered is limited in its uses, for it does not offer the richness of ongoing formative assessments that capture all the uniqueness of the individual learner. Without this rounded and individual picture of each child, it is not possible to plan for their specific learning needs. Electronic assessment of children's learning may have its uses in providing data for external and internal scrutiny, but it lacks the rich, personal illumination of an individual child's learning journey.

The Early Years Foundation Stage Profile

The Early Years Foundation Stage Profile (EYFSP) is the statutory assessment of children completed at the end of their time in the foundation stage. It was introduced in 2003 and replaced national baseline assessment on entry to primary school and has been revised since the introduction of the most recent Early Years Foundation Stage in 2012. The EYFSP is a combination of both formative and summative assessment. It requires all practitioners working with foundation stage children to undertake observations of children in order to record their attainment and progress. It then places a statutory duty on all foundation stage providers to make a summative judgement at the end of the foundation stage of every child's achievements against prescribed assessment scales.

When the Foundation Stage Profile was introduced in 2003, the National Assessment Agency (NAA), gave practitioners some valuable guidance when describing the practice best suited to gathering the evidence necessary to complete the Profile. It bears repeating in this current era:

- The FSP (as it then was) is *not* a test. It is not completed on one day at the same time for all children as, for example, the national tests at the end of Key Stage 2.
- The starting point for assessment is *the child* – not a predetermined list of skills.
- Products such as *test materials* that require foundation stage children to respond to a series of pre-set questions using a computer screen or booklet are contradictory to NAA guidance. No supplementary assessments are required in addition to completing the FSP, nor is there any expectation that they should take place.
- The FSP is not a *one-off* assessment. It cannot be completed in an instant as it relies on the accumulation of evidence over time. Judgements are made through assessing behaviour that is demonstrated consistently and independently in a range of situations. A judgement will need to demonstrate the child's confidence and ownership of the specific knowledge, skills or concept being assessed. The only part that is completed 'in a moment' is the summative score, which will be completed most easily when the quality of formative assessments is good.
- When *making a judgement* for FSP, practitioners should draw on at least 80 per cent of evidence from knowledge of the child, observations and anecdotal evidence and no more than 20 per cent from adult-directed or focused assessments.
- *Observations and records* show what a child can do – their significant achievements – not what they cannot do.
- Practitioners observe children as part of their *daily routine*.
- *Parents' contributions* to the assessment process are central.
- *Children are involved* and encouraged to express their own views on their achievements.

Moderation

Assessment of children's attainment and progress is a complex and demanding task. While the use of practitioner-based judgements is to be welcomed in the foundation stage (rather than the use of more objective tests) there are potential weaknesses in this mode of assessment. The weakness lies in the vast number of practitioners making the judgements, many of whom have different levels of training and expertise in observational techniques. While the Early Years Foundation Stage Profile documentation has emphasized the great skill involved in this kind of assessment, the EYFSP process has highlighted significant variation in the skills demonstrated by the range of practitioners who make the assessments. For this reason, the EYFSP process has included the necessity to moderate the assessments made.

Moderation is a way of agreeing the assessment judgements made by different practitioners in order to try and ensure that any practitioner observing the same child engaged in the same learning would make the same judgement. Currently this is not the case. As schools and settings have started to take moderation more and more seriously, there has been a realization that sometimes *within* the same setting – let alone *between* settings – practitioners are not agreeing about the judgements they would make. Good moderation comes when practitioners have regular conversations together about children, their learning and the developmental stage they have reached. It means, in most cases, that practitioners within the same setting need to agree their judgements first. Then, when there is a consensus between practitioners in the same setting, that setting needs to link up with other foundation stage providers working in the same community to moderate between settings.

It is important that everyone in the Early Years Foundation Stage becomes confident in the assessments that others are making. Because of the number of transitions that children face during their time in this phase of education (see Chapter 8), practitioners in different settings need to believe they can rely on the summative assessments passed onto them and to use these with confidence when planning for the child's next learning steps.

One very effective way to strengthen the moderation process is the use of videos. By watching someone else's children at play, it can give practitioners the opportunity to comment on and test out their own theories about what a child knows and can do without this being a judgement about them and their own children. When practitioners in a setting are more confident, then best practice would include videoing themselves and their own children so that the knowledge they bring to the assessment and moderation process is more rounded and extensive. Such confidence takes time, but it is important that all practitioners appreciate that their own judgements can be highly subjective, affected by all manner of prejudices, bias and preference and, therefore, that they need to subject these judgements to scrutiny by others to ensure that their assessments are valid.

Who contributes to observations and assessment?

The assessment of children's achievements does not rest with the practitioner alone. While theirs might be the most pivotal contribution, all of the following people can and should help to build a profile of the individual learner.

The child

Getting the child to evaluate their own learning is an important developmental skill. We know from research (Dweck 1978; 2006, for example) that success in learning is often based on self-esteem and self-motivation. Those children who believe that they are competent and successful as learners do better than those who are uncertain and rely too much on adults and other children. This is the case even when the more confident child is not necessarily the more able. Self-belief overrides the lack of expertise and frequently leads to the child achieving more than the child who is more able but less confident in their own ability. When children believe that intelligence is a malleable quality – something over which they have control – then, says Dweck, they adopt a disposition of 'mastery' over whatever it is that they want to learn. They believe they can achieve and they do. On the other hand, when children believe that intelligence is a fixed trait, then they often feel 'helpless' in the face of learning that challenges them. They are motivated, not by the drive to succeed that comes from within, but by more external factors, such as the adult's praise or rewards such as stickers or stars. When children become overly reliant on the adult for a sense of their own worth, these 'helpless' learners will often choose tasks that conceal their ability or protect it from negative evaluation by adults or their peers.

If children are to believe in themselves as learners and if they are to rely on their own judgements about their achievements, then their learning environments need to support their 'mastery' and not create 'helplessness'. Practitioners might consider the following:

- Do I praise children too much? Do I say 'that's lovely' to almost everything in a mistaken attempt to boost children's self-esteem? Will children know *what* I think is good about their work and why? Why should my opinion as the educator give status to a child's achievement?
- Do I rely on external rewards such as stickers or star charts to motivate children? Have children become more anxious to achieve a sticker than they are to achieve something for their own satisfaction or for its own worth?
- Do I talk to children about what they are trying to achieve, what skills and knowledge they have used that has made them successful and what they might need to know more about?
- Do I support children to reflect on their achievements and activity during a session or a day? Does each child get a regular opportunity to review what they have achieved; where they might want support; what they might want to return to tomorrow; what they felt went really well?

All children need the opportunity to self-assess their own efforts in developmentally appropriate ways. Sitting and listening while large number of children talk about their own activities is unlikely to lead to greater self-awareness. However, being given the opportunity to talk to an attentive adult during or after an activity – with maybe the other children involved at the time – will make a review time far more relevant and meaningful. When adults regularly review children's efforts and achievements with them, then children begin to internalize this for themselves and come to ask the questions internally that adults have asked out loud.

In order to self-assess, children need to be clear about what they are trying to achieve, to have a sense of their own 'success criteria' – what makes the activity or experience worthwhile for them, what they might have learned from what they have done and how they might like to build on that in the future.

Parents and carers

Both the Early Years Foundation Stage (DfE 2012) and the EYFSP documentation (DfE 2012) emphasize the importance of parental contributions to the assessment of their children's learning.

Parental contributions to the assessment process do not consist of the parent sitting and listening to a practitioner telling them about their child. The parent or carer has a view of the child that is quite unique. It is usually gained from a lifetime's experience with that child and this knowledge has to be respected and included. Even if the knowledge of the child is gained over a shorter period of time, maybe because the child is adopted or is being looked after by grandparents or a foster family, the knowledge of that child's particular needs will be far greater than any knowledge that can be accumulated by the practitioner alone. It may be that the child has emotional needs that he or she masks well in the context of the setting and are only known to the parent or carer (O'Connor 2012). It may be that the child responds differently to the learning environment of the home and that this will give the practitioner insights into how to stimulate and motivate the child in the setting. It may be that the child or the family has cultural expectations that do not match the expectations of the setting. It might be that the child has just experienced something – a trip, a visit, a family occasion – which could provide the stimulus for play or activity in the setting and on which the practitioner might build. There are characteristics and attributes of each child that are only ever seen at home and practitioners must never ignore the parent's perspective even if – and probably especially when – it differs from their own.

Indeed, it is not unusual to hear a parent say that their view of the child is quite different from the view of the practitioner – and vice versa. Given the different roles that parents and practitioners play and their different intentions for the child, this is not surprising. However, it is all too easy to hide behind a professional smokescreen for fear that parental involvement means parental interference. Sometimes practitioners do not want to know there is another point of view as it will mean adjusting their own preconceptions, plans and ideas. Early childhood educators must be open to the challenge of parental opinion and be able to value and respect the contribution they make. In this way, children will come to see that their parents, carers and practitioners all have their interests in common and will be working together to bring about the best educational experiences possible.

Other adults

Concern is sometimes expressed by practitioners that assessment should not be in the hands of those who are not adequately trained. However, it is important to separate out making assessments from making observations. All adults who work alongside a child should be capable of making an observation of what they are doing and saying. The skilled part for the practitioner comes in the analysis of these observations in order to decide what implications there are for future planning of the environment and the curriculum. The more views of the child, the better, as this will only enrich the rounded picture that practitioners are trying to achieve.

Box 9.1   Example 3: Focused teaching and assessment 1

A student had planned that a group of children should bake cakes. Her lesson plan identified the following intended learning outcomes:

1   The children will understand more fully the concept of change.
2   The children will use the scientific skills of observing, hypothesizing, predicting and investigating.
3   The children will record their findings in ways which are relevant to them in order to report back to their peers.

The lesson was well planned and the children became engrossed in their task. The student asked open-ended questions and answered the questions that the children raised. In her profiles, however, the student did not record the achievement of the children in relation to the intended learning outcomes of the lesson. Instead, she recorded the children's success in relation to the quality of the cakes that they had made. While this was important for those tasting the cakes, it was not the purpose of the lesson and the information recorded was of little value when the student came to plan the children's next scientific experience.

Box 9.2   Example 4: Focused teaching and assessment 2

A group of 4-year-olds were to design their own Christmas wrapping paper. The purpose of the activity was for the children to use pattern in their design. The adult had brought into the class a whole range of wrapping paper as a stimulus for the children so that they could see different patterns. Following a look at this wrapping paper, it was put to one side and the children began to print their own paper. From that moment on, the support of the adult lost its focus. Rather than reminding the children about pattern and showing the purchased wrapping paper as a reminder, the adult prompted the children to use more of this colour or that shape, to fill in the spaces and to press harder to get a clearer print. In other words the adult had become more concerned with artistic rather than mathematical achievements and the potential for reinforcing a key mathematical concept (the purpose of the activity) was lost. When making assessments of that session the adult focused on the quality of the printing rather than the children's understanding and application of pattern.

Box 9.3 Example 5: The cross-curricular nature of learning

When engaged in a cooking activity the children may gain experience of English (when discussing the processes involved or consulting the recipe), maths (when counting out spoonfuls, comparing sizes, weights, etc.), science (when observing changes or dissolving substances), design and technology (when observing the effects certain tools such as a whisk have on the ingredients), history (when discussing how cake mixture was beaten before we had whisks), geography (when discussing which part of the world certain recipes come from and finding these on a map), personal and social development (when learning about the hygiene aspects of food preparation, and about which foods are most and least healthy), music (when comparing or imitating vocally sounds made by different utensils), physical education (when learning to control whisks, knives, cutters, etc.) and art (when discussing patterns made by different implements, or decorating cakes or biscuits).

(Hurst and Lally 1992: 55)

Making time for assessment

Chapter 2 explained why observation and conversation are the key strategies on which early years assessments should be based. Both of these require practitioners' close attention and this is not possible in a busy learning environment unless the children are encouraged to be independent learners. Chapter 4 suggests that in order for practitioners to give observation the time it needs and deserves, then time must be planned for that purpose. While some observation clearly takes place when an adult is working or playing alongside a group, this is not sufficient. Some observations require the adult to be independent of children in order to focus on what they know and do independently.

Assessment on entry

On entry to any setting it is important to establish a baseline of what children currently know and can do. Without this, it will not be possible to plan a curriculum to meet the individual child's learning needs nor will it be possible to make judgements later about how much progress they have made while in the setting.

If children are coming from home to a new setting, the gathering of evidence about what they currently know and can do, what they are interested in and what they enjoy is particularly important.

Home visits

Home visits are one key way in which practitioners gather such information for, at this stage, it is the parent or carer who clearly knows the child best and has all the information that the practitioner needs. Home visits should be offered to all parents of children on entry to a new setting in the foundation stage, although they should never be mandatory as there are occasionally parents who, for a variety of reasons, choose not to have visitors in their home. However, most parents and most children are more than delighted to welcome a practitioner into their home to find out more about the child, but this visit is a privilege that must not be abused. Such a visit is an occasion for listening to what others have to say and not going in with a predetermined agenda. Practitioners who are sensitive to the invitation into the homes of their new children will learn much if they look and listen to what is being told to them, what they are shown, the toys and books that are around, the way in which children's behaviour is managed, the way in which the family communicates and relates. This rich source of evidence will help a practitioner to understand how much of a transition a child is making from one place to the next: whether expectations of children in the home and the setting are similar or not, whether the language used is similar or not, whether the attitude towards books and play are similar or not. However, this must not lead to pejorative feelings or comments about the home. It does not make the home 'wrong' and the setting 'right', but it can indicate where the culture of the home and the culture of the school are at variance making it harder for the child to access the world of the early childhood setting and make progress there without appropriate support. Home visits give practitioners a privileged insight into the different worlds of family life. They should lead to greater understanding of the adjustments that children sometimes have to make, for example, the child who comes from a minority ethnic group and whose first language is not English, who may be relied upon at a very young age to communicate on behalf of his parents and to translate between the different adults in his or her life. Or the only child who isn't played with by the adults in his life and who may find sharing his possessions with a number of other children a real challenge. Or the child who doesn't have access to books, doesn't see her parents read and doesn't visit the library and who may find the language of books and stories used in the setting or school difficult to understand and unfamiliar to use. All of these insights into children's lives should lead the practitioner to make professional judgements about the needs of the child in the setting rather than prejudicial judgements about the attitudes and approaches and behaviour of the family. If families sense a respect for them, their homes and their communities, then word will soon spread that the home visits help the family as well as the child to feel welcomed and included in the setting and will provide a rich reference point for all involved in the child's ongoing learning.

Other strategies on entry

In addition to home visiting, there are a range of other ways to gather evidence about a child on entry to a setting or class. These are just some of the many suggestions that practitioners have made in discussion about this aspect of assessment:

- photographs taken of children before they start at the setting, so that these can be displayed alongside their peg on arrival, or made into a display to greet the new children on arrival;
- visits made to the setting from which the children are transferring (if not the home);
- visits from the child's current practitioner to their new setting (in both these cases practitioners are seeking to ease the discontinuities in some transitions, see Chapter 8);
- observations made of some children in their current setting in order to have some evidence on which to base initial planning;
- joint observations between practitioners from different settings to moderate their judgements of the children they are 'sharing' in the foundation stage;
- records from the previous setting – where the summative information to be passed on has been agreed between practitioners from the two settings as being useful and relevant;
- questionnaires for parents to complete with their child and before the child's arrival at the setting;
- conversations with parents before the child's arrival at the setting;
- information and records from any other professionals who may have already been working with the child, e.g. educational psychologist, preschool teacher counsellor, social worker, health visitor;
- local cluster meetings between all foundation stage providers in an area who 'share' children – to agree, for example, ways of planning and assessing and to discuss behavioural expectations, routines and procedures.

Planning the use of time for observation

The following is a useful checklist for planning the use of time for formative assessment:

- What evidence is required?
- Is the assessment to find out what children *already* know/can do or what they know/can do *after* a period of teaching?

- Is the evidence best gathered during or after the activity?
- Who will gather the evidence?
- What technique best serves the assessment purpose?
- How and by whom will the evidence be recorded?

Gathering evidence of children's learning

What evidence is required?

There is a difference between obtaining *information* about children's learning and gathering *evidence* of their learning. We collect *information* about children's learning:

- from previous summative records;
- from parent consultations;
- from conversations with the child.

Previous assessments are important but are not sufficient. Information can be dated or open to misinterpretation. Effective planning is based on current *evidence* and is gathered in a variety of ways:

- through the collection of tangible end-products;
- through photocopying pictures/writing/mark-making, etc.;
- through taking photographs;
- through making audio/video recordings;
- through observation of what children do:
  - the process of learning;
  - their learning styles and strategies;
  - their knowledge and understanding;
  - their skills and attitudes;
- through recording what children say:
  - their developing understandings;
  - their misunderstandings;
  - their explanations;
  - their enthusiasms.

Who will gather the evidence, where and when?

- Who? (adults)
  - the practitioner;
  - other adults/practitioners who work with the child;
  - parents/carers;
- With whom? (the children)
  - child alone;
  - children in a group;

- children with an adult;
- children without an adult;
• Where?
  - inside and out;
  - in the hall (if appropriate);
  - in the home (parental and child contributions);
• When?
  - on entry to the setting (establishing a baseline);
  - regularly during the child's time in the setting (tracking progress);
  - at the end of the child's time in the setting (judging attainment and progress);
  - before or after teaching (Assessment *for* learning or Assessment *of* learning);
  - while working with child/children;
  - while child/children working independently.

What technique best serves the assessment purpose?

There are a variety of assessment techniques which all have their value. The decision that teachers have to make is which technique will give them the evidence they need. For excellent descriptions of different techniques and their uses, for example, time sampling, frequency sampling, audio-taping, videoing and targeted observation, see Drummond et al. (1992), Bartholomew and Bruce (1993) and Hutchin (1996 and 1999).

Building a profile of the child as a learner

Keeping a record of children's learning throughout their time in the foundation stage is more than just completing a series of checklists. As we have seen already in this chapter, the individual child is too rich and complex a learner to be represented by a list of somebody else's predetermined skills.

Certain kinds of evidence 'speak for themselves'. Pieces of writing, photographs, tape recordings and photocopies only need annotation to make them valuable evidence of the stage in a child's development. The annotation is important, however, for without it the precise context for learning will be forgotten and there will be little evidence of the trajectory of progress made from one piece of evidence to another. A profile should be more than a random selection of paper and photos but show the child's learning journey through words and pictures. Evidence within a child's profile should be annotated with:

• the name of the child;
• the date;

- the learning context;
- child's comments (if any);
- level of support from adult(s)/other children (if any);
- stage of development – using the Early Years Foundation Stage 'Development Matters' (Early Education 2012).

In different countries, a focus on gathering evidence has resulted in processes which can enrich our understanding and thinking about the assessment process here in England. In particular, the work of Margaret Carr and her colleagues in New Zealand, on 'Learning Stories' and the work of the educators in Reggio Emilia, Italy, on 'Documentation'.

Learning Stories

Learning Stories are narrative-style observations of children in everyday settings, designed to provide 'a cumulative series of qualitative "snapshots" or written vignettes of individual children' (Carr 2001: 96). As such, they sound similar to the child profiles often created by English early years practitioners. But to complete a Learning Story, the evidence base has to focus on some very particular characteristics of learning. Rather than accumulating evidence across areas of the curriculum, Carr and her colleagues suggest that assessment should concentrate on five particular dispositions which they believe underpin successful learning in all other domains. For the purpose of Learning Stories, these five dispositions are translated into actions:

- taking an interest;
- being involved;
- persisting with difficulty or uncertainty;
- expressing an idea or a feeling;
- taking responsibility or taking another point of view.

Carr proposes that these five dispositions demonstrate to what extent a child is ready (their inclination to learn), willing (their sensitivity to what is around them and what can be investigated) and able (the repertoire of skills they have) to optimize their learning opportunities. As we have seen earlier in this chapter it is often those children who are motivated by an inner self-belief who succeed over and above those who are more able but may be inhibited by self-doubt (Dweck 1978; 2006).

The completion of Learning Stories lies in the hands of many people:

- the child
- the practitioners
- the family.

Each 'story teller' is seen to have a unique contribution and the emphasis is on participation and a shared enterprise. The Learning

Stories provide a discussion point at staff meetings, and at meetings with the child and with the parents. The purpose of Learning Stories, as with all other formative assessment, is to support practitioners in deciding what to do next in planning for the child's learning.

Learning Stories include photographs, photocopies of mark-making and other recorded work and comments from children and from parents. They also include the context of learning, they highlight the activity or task at hand and they include an interpretation from a story teller (the person completing that element of the Learning Story), focusing on evidence of new or sustained interest, involvement, challenge, communication and responsibility. Learning Stories, says Carr, need to 'capture the complexity of situated learning strategies plus motivation' (Carr 2001: 95). By doing so, they 'acknowledge the unpredictability of development (thus reflecting) the learning better than performance indicators' (p. 101).

Documentation

This richness of accumulated evidence from a range of significant people is also a characteristic of the Documentation in the preschools in Reggio Emilia. The material for the Documentation is gathered during the experience of learning and, as with Learning Stories, read and interpreted at the end of the experience in order to make judgements about children's next steps for learning. Rather than focusing on the developing child as an autonomous learner, the educators in Reggio Emilia see education as a communal activity, a sharing of culture through collaboration among children and also between children and their teachers. Documentation is used for collaborative reflection upon what the evidence might show and enables staff to support the learning process by checking the connections between 'the theories, the hypothesis and their outcomes' (Rinaldi 2001).

> Whenever we can we have these daily reconnaissance meetings while everything is still fresh. In discussing events together our individual interpretations and hypotheses can be compared and consequently take on new substance and meanings.
>
> (Malaguzzi 1997: 31)

The evidence base is not referred to just once, but brought back for rereading, revisiting and reconstruction of the experience in order to fully understand what the evidence suggests (Rinaldi 2001). The evidence may be in the form of videos, audio recordings, written notes or drawings. There are contributions from staff, from parents, from children and from members of the community. One of the key purposes of Documentation is to support the preschools in their search for meaning in addition to supporting the child in their individual and personal search for meaning. The process of Documentation originated through a desire to make visible the way in which the preschools approached learning and teaching and, to this end, Documentation is displayed openly on the walls of all the preschools, and staff, children, parents and the community are encouraged to read about what is taking place and to contribute their thoughts and feelings about it. Though Documentation may have originated as a way to offer children an opportunity to evaluate their own work and to keep parents better informed about preschool experiences, it was soon discovered to be 'an extraordinary opportunity for teachers to revisit and re-examine their own work with children, offering unquestionable benefits in terms of professional development' (Malaguzzi 1997: 11).

The educators in Reggio Emilia believe that Documentation leaves examples of the school's history and gives their institutions a sense of their heritage. But, of course, it is more than simply a record or an archive, for it demonstrates to children the value of their contributions and encourages them to contribute to the process. The evidence that is accumulated evaluates not just what the child knows and can do now, but what they could do 'if . . .'. As such, it builds on the work of Vygotsky (1978) and Bruner (1986) in giving the adult a pivotal role in facilitating and scaffolding learning.

The educators in Reggio Emilia stress, as others do (Drummond 1993; Carr 2001), the complexity of assessing young children's learning journeys. They emphasize in particular the difficulty of knowing and understanding what a child is thinking, and are 'suspicious' of the value of Documentation that offers a linear description of a child's development. They admit that what counts in education is often that which escapes being photographed or tape recorded because it belongs to the world of possible interpretations:

> If we are interested in exploring the genesis and development of means that children construct in their encounters with reality, if we want to know more about the procedures of thought and action used by individual children in their learning processes, then we must document not only that which took place *around* the child, but above all that which we think has taken place *within* the child.
>
> (Malaguzzi 1997:11, original emphasis)

Using assessment to inform planning

The whole purpose of observing, assessing and analysing children's learning is to plan a learning environment that stimulates children in relevant and appropriate ways, and to plan for the needs of individual children within that learning environment. The paragraphs on Learning Stories and Documentation (above) have emphasized the importance of collaborative reflection on practice. In many early child-hood settings there is a team of practitioners who work together to discuss and analyse the impact of their planning on both the learning environment and on individual children.

Planning the learning environment

In daily or weekly staff meetings, staff share their views of the learning that has taken place as a result of the planned and the unplanned inter-actions of children with both the indoor and the outdoor environ-ment. These discussions lead practitioners to extend children's learning through:

- the addition of resources to play that is already in full flow;
- the removal of some resources in order to give more space and possi-bilities to others;
- the planning of new experiences that meet current interests and preoccupations;
- the linking of activities indoors with those outside (or vice versa).

Planning for individual children

Planning alone

All early years educators are responsible for planning for a group of children. Sometimes this is a group of eight or ten children, sometimes – and often in a reception class – for a whole class of 30 children. Practitioners need to look daily at their notes and sticky notes, gath-ered during planned and spontaneous observation of children. Planning then needs to be amended if it does not meet the current needs of individual children. Plans are there to be written on. It is not possible to predict with total accuracy what the needs of all children will be even a few days or a week in advance. So practitioners must be sufficiently flexible to change their plans and put something else in their place if this is what is needed.

Planning with the staff team

Many early years educators are fortunate enough to work as part of a team. In this instance, the practitioner responsible for a group of children will not be the only one making observations and gathering evidence. Where there is a foundation stage team, then all practitioners in the setting can share their views of individual children whom they may have worked alongside or observed at play. Different staff can bring their sticky notes and observational notes and support the lead practitioner in planning appropriately for his or her group or for one individual.

However, even if the discussion of individual children and some subsequent planning are done as a staff team, it is important to remember that this does not mean that all staff within one year group in a school will end up with the same plans. While children within the same year group are entitled to the same curriculum (see Chapter 8), this does not mean that the curriculum must (or should) be taught through the same activities, themes or experiences. These should be relevant to the children in each individual class and may on many occasions be different from the class next door. The activity, experience, theme or topic are merely vehicles for learning the curriculum, and observations and assessment enable practitioners to fine-tune planning on a daily basis to meet the needs of their particular class.

Whatever strategies are used to share information and evidence, the single most important thing is that observations and assessments are not wasted. There is no point in gathering information about a child's learning journey if that evidence is not going to be put to good use. The two key processes of assessment and planning should be linked inextricably together for the one cannot be robust without the other.

Planning for adult support

Observation and assessment also reveal the level of support needed by an individual child or a group of children. As the practitioner observes how a child tackles an activity; whether a child can manage the planned learning alone; how well a group cooperate together, so decisions can be made about the level of support necessary from adults in the next steps of learning. The practitioner may decide any of the following:

- the child is managing well alone and does not need me at present.
- the child understood the concept taught today so I will see how they manage alone tomorrow.
- the child was struggling today . . . I will give them close attention tomorrow.
- the group is struggling to be independent and needs support from me to learn further skills of cooperation and collaboration tomorrow.

Evaluating the level and type of adult support is a notable feature of a setting where observations and assessment truly inform planning.

Conclusion

The assessment of children's learning is a challenging task for early childhood educators. Time must be created to observe each child with care, for without time, assessments will be superficial and of little value when planning for the next steps in children's learning. Practitioners must be clear about the different purposes of assessment in order to gather evidence that is fit for that purpose. Whether assessments are *for* learning or *of* learning, the quality of those assessments will be determined by the quality of the observations on which they are based. Observation and assessment are both time-consuming and this time is wasted if what is learned about children is not used to make planning for their individual needs relevant and purposeful. But the best early years practitioners not only observe children, but they turn the spotlight on themselves. They reflect on their own practice and the impact it makes on children's learning and children's lives. In the final chapter of this book, we consider what practitioners need to know about themselves and their own practice in order to meet the developmental needs of children and extend their learning.

Questions to Challenge your Thinking

1 Are your assessments valuable to *you* (formative) in planning for children's learning, and relevant and valuable for *others* (summative) such as parents/carers, practitioners in the next setting?

2 Do your recorded assessments clearly show children's progress?

3 How do you ensure that your judgements are valid and consistent with other practitioners – both within your setting and between settings?

4 Do children and parents make a valuable contribution to children's profiles? Are their contributions used to shape children's future learning experiences?

10

REFLECTION AND EVALUATION

What practitioners need to know about their practice, their provision and themselves

Introduction

Effective early childhood educators are continuously reflecting on their practice. Because the environment of early learning is multilayered and multifaceted, practitioners need to have a constantly questioning heart and mind in order to evaluate the quality of children's experiences and the quality of their own contribution to children's learning.

Reflective teaching

Some of this reflection takes place in the bath, on the train, walking along the beach or in the middle of a supermarket aisle. The ongoing quest for more appropriate resources, a more interesting way to introduce a mathematical concept, a more challenging way to extend children's physical prowess means that good early childhood educators never miss the opportunity to spot learning potential in the most unlikely places. Sometimes the reflection is about the emotional needs of a child. How can David be encouraged to play less aggressively with other children? How can I support Georgia as she grieves for the loss of her grandma? How can I encourage children to include Sundeep in their play when he doesn't yet communicate in English? All of these questions, and thousands more, teem through the working mind of the early years practitioner, very often at a subconscious level and most often when we are trying to get to sleep. This constant reflection is necessary because our working environment is neither repetitive nor predictable. We can plan well and with thought and care, but children can hijack that planning and take their learning on a course that we have not anticipated. We can visit other settings – even other countries – to look at different practice, but it is not until those ideas are applied to our children and our learning environments that we can evaluate whether the additions, adjustments and alterations are working. It is one of the main reasons, of course, why working in early childhood education keeps practitioners interested in and stimulated by their work. But it means that we will never get it entirely 'right'. There is never a moment when we can say – 'I've cracked this now. I can do it like this for ever.' Even if our learning environment is effective and challenging and appropriate this year, it may need complete re-evaluation next year with a different group of children with different needs and expectations.

We have seen in Chapters 2, 3 and 9 that observation of individual children is central to the planning process in the early years. However, there are times when early childhood educators carry out other observations in their settings that are not specifically to do with the development of individual children. These are concerned with how smoothly the setting runs, whether good use is being made of space and resources and whether – as the practitioner responsible – children's learning has been supported in the most appropriate and effective ways.

Observation of resources

This observation provides evidence of different children's responses to a key resource – such as a water tray or the blocks. It shows whether the resource is still used effectively or has become rather 'tired' and the play repetitive:

- How effectively is the resource used by different children?
- Is there any dominant use by, e.g. boys as opposed to girls, younger children as opposed to older, children with special needs, children with English as an additional language?
- Is the resource sufficiently challenging for more able children to think creatively, to investigate and to play?
- Are there pieces missing? Do construction toys still fit well together? Are resources a little tatty or bent or 'tired'? Do they need replacing?
- Is the quality of play enhanced by this resource?
- Do resources consolidate children's skills and understanding as well as challenging and stimulating them?
- Are resources of a suitable variety and do they encourage choice?
- Are there sufficient resources?

Observation of the environment – indoors and out

This observation is planned to highlight issues of space, resourcing and independence:

- Is there sufficient space in the learning environment – both indoors and out – for children to engage in active learning?
- Is there easy access to an outdoor area for learning and is it constantly in use?
- Is the outdoor area safe and secure?
- Is outdoor equipment suitable for the age of the children?
- Are areas for play indoors constantly available?
- Are tables and heavy furniture (such as cupboards) used, or are some wasting space?
- Are resources – both in and out – easily accessible for children?
- Do children find and return resources to their appropriate location?
- Are children able to manage themselves independently?

Observation of children's experiences

This provides evidence of the general quality of planning and provision for children's learning needs:

- Is the planned curriculum based appropriately on the Early Years Foundation Stage?
- Is the curriculum planned with full regard to children's gender, race, ability and needs?
- Does planning give children opportunities to work alongside adults who have initiated activities as well as to initiate learning themselves?
- Is the full curriculum represented both indoors and out?
- Do the experiences on offer stimulate, interest, intrigue and engage children?
- Do children have sufficient opportunity to consolidate learning as well as to extend it?
- Do children have sustained opportunities for learning, without unnecessary interruptions?
- Is there flexibility within the planned curriculum to respond spontaneously to children's interest and preoccupations?
- Is the curriculum inclusive with full regard to the needs of each individual child?
- Do curriculum experiences promote process over product?

Observation of relationships and attitudes to learning

- Do children make constructive relationships with one another and with adults?

- Are children able to concentrate and persevere on both adult-initiated and child-initiated learning?
- Do children show initiative and are they given responsibility?
- Do children have the confidence and motivation to pursue their own play intentions, ideas and interests?
- Does each child feel valued and supported by the care, routines and rhythms of the day?
- Are the rights of children embedded in everyday practice in a way that supports the growth of positive self-esteem, confidence and mutual respect?
- Are children given the freedom to take risks, make mistakes and learn from these?
- Are the diverse needs, abilities, differences and contributions of all children taken into account, valued and respected?

Observation of the practitioner – by the practitioner!

This is perhaps the most challenging but potentially the most enlightening observation of all. Many early childhood educators are now using video cameras to make a record of their interactions with children in order to evaluate some of the following:

- What do I spend my time doing?
- Do I spend more time talking than the children?
- Do I listen to children as well as initiate conversations?
- Do I tune in to children and their thinking before deciding whether to intervene?
- Do I respond positively – both in my body language as well as my words?
- Do I ask children questions that show my interest in their thinking and learning?
- Do I answer children's questions properly?
- Do I challenge and extend children's thinking?
- What strategies am I using to make children more independent?
- Am I having fun? Are the children having fun?

Action research

One way in which some practitioners choose to reflect on their practice, in a more systematic way, is to engage in some action research in their own classrooms. The work 'research' can sound daunting. But what action research requires of practitioners is very straightforward. In settings and schools, action research gives practitioners a framework to follow a self-reflective cycle (Carr and Kemmis 1986; Whitehead and McNiff 2006) of:

- planning
- acting
- observing and
- reflecting.

In order to undertake action research, the practitioner *plans* what they would like to alter or amend about their current practice or their learning environment. They evaluate what they are doing now and what the children are achieving now, as a baseline against which to judge the impact of any changes.

The practitioner then *acts* to intervene in the current way of working. They may decide to open the doors to the outdoor area for the whole of the teaching time of a session, rather than just for an hour in the middle. They may decide to give children greater autonomy in their choices – of where to play or with whom to play. They may decide to ask more open-ended questions and see if this improves children's thinking skills. The subject matter for action research can be whatever a practitioner has identified as being in need of development in their setting.

Next the practitioner *observes* the impact that the intervention has had. It is down to the practitioner to decide how long the intervention needs to last before any change is discernible. But when sufficient time has elapsed, the practitioner observes the child, or the group or the environment and sees how children are behaving now as opposed to at the start of the research.

Finally, the practitioner *reflects* on the changes that have taken place – if any, and asks what impact the evaluation has had. This analysis asks not only whether any changes have occurred but what that might be and whether there have been any surprise outcomes as a result of the intervention. This reflection might lead to another cycle of action research or a period of consolidation while the changes bed down.

In Oxfordshire, some 76 foundation stage practitioners took part in a year-long action research project led by Professor Guy Claxton (Fisher et al. 2005). The first term (in the summer) was spent on an initial investigation and this became refined in the autumn and spring terms of the following year. The aim of the project was to increase the 'learning power' of children (Claxton 2002) and enable them to be more resourceful and independent in their learning. We have seen throughout this book that evidence points to young children being naturally both resourceful and independent in their learning. What the project identified is that it is often the practitioners who put barriers in the way of children's competencies and the practitioner who has to change the way they plan for and organize learning to permit what Claxton calls 'learnacy' to flourish.

As their contribution to the project, which was called 'Playing for Life', each practitioner undertook a piece of action research in their own setting or classroom which they wrote up as a case study. The headings from those case studies reports may prove helpful to others wishing to take a first step into action research:

- *Focus of the enquiry* What is the question you are asking about your practice? What is the planned impact on the development of children as learners?
- *Context of the enquiry* What kind of setting are you working in? Are there any special circumstances?
- *Initial investigation* How did you start off? What were you originally interested in? Why was that?
- *Initial findings* What kind of things did you begin to find out as you studied your children more carefully during the summer term? How did these findings change your question or focus?
- *Main investigation* What became the final focus for investigation in the autumn and spring terms? What changes in the children as learners did you hope to bring about? What methods did you use? What intervention did you use? How did you evaluate whether there had been any changes?
- *Main findings* What changes did you actually observe in the children's attitudes to learning? What conclusions can your draw from your study?
- *Implications for our teaching* How will the outcomes of your study change your teaching in the future?
- *Reflections on our own learning* What has this project contributed to your own thinking and development?

The project revealed a great deal about action research. First, that the hardest thing is to decide what you want to research – and sticking to it. The second is not to make the focus of the enquiry too broad. Time is short and the focus needs to be focused. Third, good ideas for developing practice often come from others – from the books we read, from the journal articles we see, from the training we attend. No one practitioner can have all the ideas and all the know-how, and early childhood educators need to constantly update and refresh their professional knowledge about what research others have undertaken and about what ideas others have tried. We would all be very concerned if a doctor said he didn't know about the latest medical research because he was too busy in his surgery seeing patients! Finally, we learned that research in the real world is not easy. As Alison Price writes in the project publication (Fisher et al. 2005: 7), children involved in the project moved out of the class or setting, or out of the area, teachers became pregnant, teaching assistants fell ill. All of this meant that practitioners had to revise their plans and adjust their thinking. Any examination of practice in systematic ways can, of course, challenge practitioners' existing theories and beliefs. In action research, say Pollard and Tann (1993), practitioners must be prepared to explore the discrepancies between their current practice and the new insights that might be acquired. Whatever methodology is used, the notion of self-evaluation is every bit as critical for practitioners as it is for children. Reflection should lead to new ways of working (Adelman 1985) and in order for this to happen, early childhood educators need to be explorers and enquirers alongside their children.

The use of video for self-analysis

In my most recent research project (Fisher 2012a, b, c, d), practitioners working with children from 6 months to 6 years evaluated the quality of the interactions they have with the children in their setting. The methodology for this project was based once again on the cycle of action research but, at its heart, was the use of video technology to record the interactions in order to analyse and reflect on them at leisure. While other research methods were used – such as the keeping of practitioner journals detailing thinking over time – it was the DVD footage that practitioners said had the greatest impact on their practice. Not many educators have the opportunity to see themselves 'in action' in a work situation. It is daunting at first but, in time, practitioners find it reveals invaluable examples of habitual actions, mannerisms, tone of voice, approach and style that they would probably never have known about any other way.

In this particular project each practitioner was filmed over two years and the considerable amount of DVD footage gathered provided a basis not only for individual but for group analysis of behaviours and practices. Such was the impact of the filming on some of the project participants that they took this way of working back to their settings and have used it for whole staff development. One headteacher said: 'Nothing has changed our practice so quickly and with such positive impact than the use of videoing to analyse our practice.'

It goes without saying that for a practitioner to permit a film of themselves to be viewed and analysed by others takes courage. To begin with in our project, practitioners were more worried about what they sounded like or looked like than the quality of their interactions and their support of the children's learning. But attention shifted swiftly to the children and individuals became increasingly analytical about how their own contributions to a conversation enhanced or inhibited children's learning. When the project participants agreed to let their personal footage be shown to the larger group there was once again a crisis of confidence. So to begin with, other practitioners were very generous and kind and only made positive comments. But in time, when participants felt more secure and a feeling of trust was established, others felt able to make suggestions for improvement or pick out points for discussion, which helped the whole project team refine their thinking and understanding about practice. It takes brave and committed practitioners to allow themselves to go in front of the camera, but in terms of self-evaluation, it is one of the most effective strategies there is (Fisher and Wood 2012).

Self-evaluation

Another highly effective strategy for reflecting on practice in the early years is to devise a structured programme of self-evaluation. Using a quality assurance scheme or devising a self-evaluation policy for an individual setting can bring rich rewards in terms of the development of the setting, particularly in relation to staff working together to decide on their judgements about the quality of provision, procedures and practice.

Self-evaluation seeks to identify all aspects of the life of the school or setting. The early years practitioner may be responsible for one part of the process or for many aspects, according to the size of the setting and its age range. But the efficacy of the self-evaluation process lies in *analysing the impact* of what is being done in the setting, rather than *describing* what is being done. If the analysis is effective, then it gives a clear steer about what steps need to be taken to enable the setting to develop further.

A good self-evaluation or quality assurance programme supports a setting to focus on improvement and to work towards its vision for the future. In Oxfordshire (OCC 2005), the quality assurance programme 'Partners in Quality' focused on ten 'aspects of quality':

1 Interactions and relationships
2 Attitudes and dispositions
3 Opportunities and experiences
4 Support from adults
5 Children's well-being
6 Inclusion
7 Working with parents, carers and the community

8 The environment
9 Staffing and professional development
10 Leadership and management.

Like the Early Years Foundation Stage, 'Partners in Quality' built on the National Standards and included the principles from *Birth to Three Matters* (DfES 2003a) and the *Curriculum Guidance for the Foundation Stage* (DfES 2000). It led practitioners through a process of:

- *Audit* Where are we now? What is our evidence?
- *Action* What do we currently do well? What do we want to develop? Who is going to do this? When do we aim to finish?
- *Evaluation* What developments did we make? What impact has it made on the quality of our setting? What will we do in the future to further enhance this aspect of our setting?

Like all good quality assurance schemes, 'Partners in Quality' emphasized throughout the importance of staff working together to make their judgements and to gather their evidence. Self-evaluation is not a one-off process but one that continues in a planned cycle so that once one element is evaluated and reflected upon, the next is put under the spotlight. Self-evaluation is a very liberating and empowering process because it gives practitioners the evidence base for making judgements about their own setting and enables staff to challenge any external evaluation that may contradict their own view. It may be that outsiders, such as inspectors and advisers, have a different perspective and arrive at different judgements. But self-evaluation empowers staff to draw on their own findings and their own evidence base and to debate any judgements that they feel are not accurate.

The following prompts offer a framework for discussion between staff about what might constitute 'quality' in their own setting. It is reproduced with grateful thanks to Oxfordshire County Council Early Learning and Childcare Service:

1 *Interactions and relationships*
- The aims and values of the setting are open and inclusive. All children and adults should be able to participate and contribute to the work of the setting.
- Observations of children and adults are made regularly and are used to improve the quality of social interactions and relationships within the setting, and between home and setting.
- Transitions are handled sensitively.
- Practitioners provide good role models for behaviour and offer support, encouragement and guidance to parents and carers on positive behaviour strategies.

- Practitioners implement a behaviour policy and procedures that are shared with parents.
- Practitioners understand the social and emotional development of children and take into account the age and stage of children in their care.

2 *Attitudes and dispositions*
- Practitioners share observations of the children with each other and use these observations to support children to develop positive attitudes and self-esteem.
- Practitioners ask open-ended questions and encourage children to experiment and ask questions themselves.
- Practitioners provide a secure environment in which children are confident to try new things and learn from their experiences.
- The setting has flexible routines which give children time to develop their interests.

3 *Opportunities and experiences*
- Practitioners have a good understanding of the developmental needs of the children.
- The environment and activities are planned in response to observations of the children.
- Practitioners respond flexibly to the needs and interests of individual children.
- Children are given time to become involved in their play and learning.
- Opportunities reflect the social and cultural experiences of children and their families.

4 *Support from adults*
- All practitioners are involved in planning broad and balanced activities and experiences and making observations and assessments.
- Practitioners share daily plans and observations with parents and carers and respond to parents' and carers' knowledge of individual children.
- Practitioners plan experiences based on their knowledge of each child.
- Practitioners ensure that all children have access to a carefully planned Early Years Foundation Stage curriculum or planned activities/experiences appropriate to their age and developmental needs.
- Practitioners support and extend children's learning through play.
- Practitioners take part in ongoing professional development.

5 *Children's well-being*
- All practitioners contribute to the writing and implementation of statutory policies and requirements, e.g. child protection policy.
- Provision is made for healthy eating, sleep and exercise.

- Children have daily opportunities for play and learning indoors and out.
- Practitioners are knowledgeable about and respond to children's individual circumstances sensitively.
- Practitioners respond to the physical and comfort needs of children.

6 *Inclusion*
- The Equal Opportunities and Special Educational Needs coordinators have discussed their training with the full staff team.
- Practitioners are informed about the cultural, social and personal circumstances of individual families.
- The Inclusion/Equal Opportunities and SEN policies are implemented and evaluated.

7 *Working with parents, carers and the community*
- The setting works in partnership with parents, carers and the local community to identify and respond to the needs of all children.
- Parents and carers are given up-to-date and accessible information about the setting.
- Practitioners are informed about the cultural, social and personal circumstances of individual families.
- All parents and carers feel welcome and are invited to participate in the day-to-day work of the setting.
- The setting is responsive to the views and concerns of children, parents and carers.

8 *The environment*
- Facilities are provided that support children to develop their exploration, play and learning in all areas indoors and outside and are inclusive for children with special needs.
- Practitioners audit and evaluate the quality, safety and appropriate use of resources in all areas.
- All staff implement health and safety and security procedures.

9 *Staffing and professional development*
- All staff are involved in the self-evaluation process.
- Staff share a common vision and values.
- Staff have a commitment to ongoing training.
- All staff have the opportunity to contribute to planning for children's experiences and to suggest improvements.
- Staff are given support to fulfil their roles and responsibilities.

10 *Leadership and management*
- Procedures for appointing staff, committee members or members of the governing body are in place.

- Policies are regularly reviewed.
- Parents/carers are given regular information about the setting.
- The quality of education and care is monitored and action plans are created to sustain and improve quality.
- Staff are supported to fulfil their roles and responsibilities.

Evaluation by others

Self-evaluation empowers practitioners by giving them an evidence base which can be used to explain and justify best practice. It is increasingly important that practitioners have agency in this way as the yardsticks used to evaluate early years practice do not always reflect the priorities or principles of early childhood education (see Chapter 3), and those who are empowered to evaluate, monitor or judge quality are frequently neither trained nor experienced in working with young children. While this is a deplorable state of affairs, it means that early years practitioners need to be knowledgeable as well as confident and bold in standing up for what they believe to be in the best interests of their children.

Tools for evaluation

Until recently, both schools and settings had to complete a self-evaluation form before their inspection by Office for Standards in Education (Ofsted). These forms have now been removed but the requirement to self-evaluate still remains. Early years practitioners could draw on the quality assurance prompts above to offer a framework for that self-evaluation but it is always wise to include those criteria set by Ofsted to evaluate the quality of teaching and learning. Currently these are to be found in the Framework for School Inspection (Ofsted 2012a, 2012b).

The problem for those working in the early years is that these Ofsted criteria are generic and are intended to cover the inspection of schools educating children and young people from '0–19 years of age'. The descriptors for practice use language that does not always sit comfortably with those working with young children or, indeed, cover all the aspects of good early years practice that specialists would want to see. Nonetheless, the Framework for School Inspection identifies one principle of school inspection as 'taking account of schools' self-evaluation' (Ofsted 2012a: 11). As such, it is incumbent upon those who are the early years specialists in schools to ensure that they have evaluated their own practice with rigour and in ways that will be acceptable and palatable to Ofsted inspectors. I encourage schools to become very familiar with Ofsted criteria, to decide what the generic language means for young children, to find evidence of learning that meets these requirements and then to identify what is missing – what they believe as early years specialists Ofsted and other external evaluators should look for, listen for and note.

Box 10.1 gives the current criteria for a school to achieve 'outstanding', the top grade awarded by Ofsted, for the quality of teaching and learning (Ofsted 2012b: 12).

Box 10.1   Ofsted Grade descriptor for 'outstanding': quality of teaching in school

Evaluation Schedule January 2012

Much of the teaching . . . is outstanding and never less than consistently good. As a result, almost all pupils are making rapid and sustained progress . . . teachers have consistently high expectations of all pupils. Drawing on excellent subject knowledge, teachers plan astutely and set challenging tasks based on systematic, accurate assessment of pupils' prior skills, knowledge and understanding. They use well judged and often imaginative strategies that, together with sharply focused and timely support and intervention, match individual need accurately. Consequently, pupils learn exceptionally well across the curriculum. The teaching of reading, writing, communication and mathematics is highly effective. Teachers and other adults generate high levels of enthusiasm for, participation in and commitment to learning. Teaching promotes pupils' high levels of resilience, confidence and independence when they tackle challenging activities. Teachers systematically and effectively check pupils' understanding throughout lessons, anticipating where they may need to intervene and do so with notable impact on the quality of learning. Time is used very well and every opportunity is taken to successfully develop crucial skills, including being able to use their literacy and numeracy skills in other subjects. Appropriate and regular homework contributes very well to pupils' learning. Marking and constructive feedback from teachers and pupils are frequent and of a consistently high quality, leading to high levels of engagement and interest.

Together with a number of teachers, I have teased out those elements of this descriptor that need further consideration if they are to be applied to young children (see Table 10.1). It would be worthwhile considering these criteria yourself to see whether there is language used, or missing, which you think needs further explanation for an

Table 10.1

Ofsted grade descriptor	EYFS additions/explanations
'rapid and sustained progress'	'Progress' in the early years is *over time*.
	(a) We may not see the impact of an early years experience for *years* so often 'progress' will not be seen in the time an inspector spends in the classroom.
	(b) In the early years, consolidation is every bit as important as extension. So a definition of progress in the early years is learning that goes *deeper*, not always *higher*.
'teachers have consistently high expectations'	Practitioners should have high expectations of children as competent and confident learners in both adult-led *and* child-led situations. Every activity in an early years classroom should be engaging and absorbing (for both children and adults).
'drawing on excellent subject knowledge'	Early years practitioners need to be expert in the development of all Areas of Learning but also, and especially, in Child Development.
'teachers plan astutely'	In the early years this means flexibly and responsively (Chapter 3).
'and set challenging tasks'	*Not* always. Young children need to *consolidate* as much as *extend* their learning. The 'challenge' might be to repeat and rehearse what you already know. But tasks should always be involving and engaging.
'based on systematic, accurate assessment of pupils' prior skills, knowledge and understanding'	All planning should be based on daily observation and assessment that are *used* to inform planning. Planning should show this cycle in action (Chapter 3). 'Prior skills etc.' will have been acquired at home and away from the setting *not just* in school.
'sharply focused and timely support'	Support for children's learning should be both planned and spontaneous. Support for child-led learning cannot be 'sharply focused' (if this means pre-planned) as learning is unpredictable. Support for child-led learning should be flexible and responsive. It should indeed be 'timely' but this might mean that the practitioner waits to intervene until 'the time is right' or might decide not to intervene at all.

'match individual needs accurately'	High quality early years teaching is based on the quality of daily observations which should ensure plans are matched to individual needs.
'The teaching of reading, writing, communication and mathematics is highly effective'	Communication and Language is the *Prime* Area of these for young children. Literacy and Mathematics are now Specific Areas which rely on Communication and Language (as well as Physical Development and Personal, Social and Emotional Development) to 'build capacity to learn' (EYFS: 4) and to be 'highly effective'.
'Teachers and other adults generate high levels of enthusiasm for, participation in and commitment to learning'	The best early childhood educators are committed to and passionate about teaching young children and are fascinated by their thinking and their learning journeys.
'Teaching promotes pupils' high levels of resilience, confidence and independence when they tackle challenging activities'	Early childhood education has always been committed to promoting positive attitudes and dispositions to learning. Young children will develop resilience, confidence and independence when consolidating their learning in familiar situations as well as tackling activities that challenge them.
'Teachers systematically and effectively check pupils' understanding throughout lessons'	Early childhood educators need to observe and listen to young children in order to tune in to their thinking. This enables them to decide whether to and how to 'check' understanding (see Chapter 6).
'anticipating where they may need to intervene'	Intervening in early learning can so easily lead to interference. Early years practitioners need to make careful judgements about *whether* intervention will enhance learning and *when* that intervention would be most valuable (Chapter 6).
'and doing so with notable impact on the quality of learning'	Very difficult to judge in the early years. Sometimes an adult's intervention can be seen to have immediate impact but young children frequently 'take away' what is said, mull it over and put it on a 'back-burner' for some considerable time, returning to their thoughts days or weeks later. Their threads of thinking do not crystallize immediately. Impact may only be 'notable' to the adult who knows the child well and is alongside them when they make the links in their learning at some later date.

(Continued overleaf)

Table 10.1 Continued

Ofsted grade descriptor	EYFS additions/explanations
'Time is used very well'	Young children need sustained periods of time for uninterrupted learning particularly in order to develop high quality play. Time should not be interrupted unnecessarily (Chapter 2). Revising timetables can extend learning and teaching time for both practitioners and children.
'every opportunity is taken to successfully develop crucial skills'	Observation of children as well as working alongside them shows practitioners the skills needed to complete tasks, both those set by adults and those the child sets him/herself.
'marking'	Young children respond to verbal 'marking' rather than written. For a written message to have meaning, it is often too difficult for a child to read. If practitioners 'simplify' the message – with a star or sticker – then children can become reliant on adult approval and external reward which is undesirable (Chapter 9). Verbal feedback – at opportune moments – is best.
'constructive feedback from teachers [is] frequent and of a consistently high quality'	Not empty praise (see Chapter 9). Young children need to understand why they have 'succeeded' and how they can improve, not that they have been a 'good girl/boy'. Practitioners should offer opinions not judgements.
'constructive feedback from pupils [is] frequent and of a consistently high quality'	Young children should be included in the setting of success criteria of adult-initiated learning so they understand what they are trying to achieve. In play, children set their own success criteria and it is up to the practitioner to tune in to and support these efforts.
'leading to high levels of engagement and interest'	Early childhood education should be characterized by the high levels of engagement and interest of both adults and children – in both adult-led and child-led situations.

inspector, adviser or headteacher who is not an early years expert. These notes are intended to provoke discussion between early years practitioners but particularly between early years practitioners and those who come into their settings and classrooms to make judgements about the quality of teaching and learning. If judgements are made by those who have little experience of or expertise in the early years, then they will resort to what they know and understand, the easily measurable and the readily observable. But high quality early education is complex and challenging. It is neither easily measured nor readily observed. Every early years educator should take responsibility for explaining and justifying their practice and backing up the strategies they use with hard evidence of children's learning, development and progress. It is always best to be proactive. Talk to headteachers, curriculum coordinators, advisers and inspectors before they make judgements about you; tell them your philosophy of early childhood education; show them what to look for and explain what they otherwise might not 'see' or understand. Nothing is lost by being bold, but plenty might be lost if judgements of quality are left in the hands of those who do not know enough.

Young children deserve early childhood educators who are knowledgeable, articulate, brave and committed. As early years professionals, every one of us should see it as our personal responsibility to guide and steer those who are less knowledgeable to make more informed judgements about the quality of the education received by the youngest children in our education system.

Conclusion

However early childhood educators choose to evaluate their practice, one thing is for certain – it is a process that must never stop. Practitioners who continually question themselves and reflect upon their practice keep children's experiences stimulating and intriguing and absorbing. Throughout this book we have celebrated the competence of young learners. We have considered the central role of the adult in responding to children's learning needs with sensitivity and skill. We have understood that if every child is to be given strong foundations for lifelong learning, then adults must base their planning and their preparation on the daily observation of children. If children's learning experiences are to be relevant and meaningful, then what is taught and learnt in foundation stage settings across the country needs to start from the individual learner – it needs to start from the child.

Questions to Challenge your Thinking

1 Are you a reflective practitioner? Do you constantly evaluate and refine what you do?

2 Are you in a community of critical thinkers? If this is not possible in your setting, can you affiliate yourself to a group or an organization that supports you and your thinking (such as Early Education, see www.early-education.org.uk)?

3 Are you confident that you can articulate your philosophy of early childhood education and explain the rationale for your chosen practice to others who may not share the same values?

REFERENCES

Adams, S. and Moyles, J. (2005) *Images of Violence*. Lutterworth: Featherstone Education.

Adelman, C. (1985) Action research, in S. Hegarty and P. Evans (eds) *Research Methods in Special Education*. Windsor: NFER.

Anning, A. (1991) *The First Years at School*. Buckingham: Open University Press.

Athey, C. (2007) *Extending Thought in Young Children*, 2nd edn. London: Paul Chapman Publishing.

Ball, C. (1994) *Start Right: The Importance of Early Learning*. London: RSA.

Bandura, A. (1977) *Social Learning Theory*. London: Prentice-Hall.

Barnes, D. and Todd, F. (1977) *Communication and Learning in Small Groups*. London: Routledge and Kegan Paul.

Barrett, G. (ed.) (1989) *Disaffection from School? The Early Years*. Lewes: Falmer Press.

Bartholomew, L. and Bruce, T. (1993) *Getting to Know You*. London: Hodder and Stoughton.

Biddulph, S. (1997) *Raising Boys*. London: HarperCollins.

Bilton, H. (2002) *Outdoor Play in the Early Years*, 2nd edn. London: David Fulton.

Black, P., Harrison, C., Lee, C., Marshall, B. and Wiliam, D. (2002) *Working Inside the Black Box: Assessment for Learning in the Classroom*. London: King's College.

Blenkin, G.M. and Kelly, A.V. (eds) (1987) *Early Childhood Education: A Developmental Curriculum*. London: Paul Chapman.

Blenkin, G.M. and Kelly, A.V. (eds) (1994) *The National Curriculum and Early Learning*. London: Paul Chapman.

Bowlby, J. (1969) *Attachment*. London: Pelican.

Bowlby, J. (1975) The nature of the child's attachment to the mother, *American Journal of Psychiatry*, 132: 133–7.

Bowlby, J. (1981) *Attachment and Loss (Vol. 3): Loss, Sadness and Depression*. Harmondsworth: Penguin.

Bredekamp, S. (ed.) (1987) *Developmentally Appropriate Practice in Early Childhood Programs Serving Children from Birth through Age 8*. Washington, DC: NAEYC.

Brierley, J. (1994) *Give Me a Child Until He Is Seven*, 2nd edn. London: Falmer Press.

Bronfenbrenner, U. (1979) *The Ecology of Human Development.* Cambridge, MA: Harvard University Press.

Brooker, L. (2002) *Starting School: Young Children Learning Culture.* Buckingham: Open University Press.

Brooker, L. (2008) *Supporting Transitions in the Early Years.* Buckingham: Open University Press.

Bruce, T. (1987) *Early Childhood Education.* Sevenoaks: Hodder and Stoughton.

Bruce, T. (1991) *Time to Play in Early Childhood Education.* Sevenoaks: Hodder and Stoughton.

Bruce, T. (2004) *Developing Learning in Early Childhood.* London: Paul Chapman Publishing.

Bruer, J.T. (1999) *The Myth of the First Three Years.* New York: The Free Press.

Bruner, J.S. (1960) *The Process of Education.* Cambridge, MA: Harvard University Press.

Bruner, J.S. (1968) *Processes of Cognitive Growth: Infancy.* Worcester, MA: Clark University Press.

Bruner, J.S. (1977) Introduction, in B. Tizard and D. Harvey (eds) *The Biology of Play.* London: Spastics International Medical Publications.

Bruner, J.S. (1980) *Under Five in Britain: The Oxford Preschool Research Project.* Oxford: Grant McIntyre.

Bruner, J.S. (1985) Vygotsky: a historical and conceptual perspective, in J.V. Wertsch (ed.) *Culture, Communication and Cognition: Vygotskian Perspective.* Cambridge: Cambridge University Press.

Bruner, J.S. (1986) *Actual Minds, Possible Worlds.* Cambridge, MA: Harvard University Press.

Bruner. J. (1990) *Acts of Meaning.* Cambridge, MA: Harvard University Press.

Bruner, J. and Haste, H. (eds) (1987) *Making Sense: The Child's Construction of the World.* London: Methuen.

Cairns, K. (2002) *Attachment, Resilience and Trauma.* London: BAAF.

Calvin, W.H. (1996) *How Brains Think: Evolving Intelligence Then and Now.* London: Weidenfeld & Nicolson.

Campbell, R.J. and Neill, S.R.St.J. (1990) *Thirteen Hundred and Thirty Days: Final Report of a Pilot Study of Teacher Time in Key Stage 1, Commissioned by the Assistant Masters and Mistresses Association.* Warwick: University of Warwick, Department of Education.

Carnegie Corporation of New York (1994) *Starting Points: Meeting the Needs of our Youngest Children.* New York: Carnegie Corporation.

Carr, M. (2001) *Assessment in Early Childhood Settings.* London: Paul Chapman Publishing.

Carr, W. and Kemmis, S. (1986) *Becoming Critical: Education, Knowledge and Action Research.* Lewes: Falmer Press.

Central Advisory Council for Education (CACE) (1967) *Children and their Primary Schools* (The Plowden Report). London: HMSO.

Chang, G.L. and Wells, G. (1988) The literate potential of collaborative talk, in M. Maclure, T. Phillips and A. Wilkinson (eds) *Oracy Matters*. Milton Keynes: Open University Press.

Chilvers, D. (2006) *Young Children Talking: The Art of Conversation and Why Children Need to Chatter*. London: BAECE.

Claxton, G. (2002) *Building Learning Power*. Bristol: TLO.

Cohen, D. (1997) *The Secret Language of the Mind*. London: Duncan Baird.

Cousins, J. (1990) Are your little humpty dumpties floating or sinking? *Early Years*, 10(2): 28–38.

Cousins, J. (1999) *Listening to Four Year Olds*. London: National Early Years Network.

Cox, C.B. and Boyson, R. (eds) (1975) *The Fight for Education: Black Paper 1975*. London: Dent.

Cox, C.B. and Boyson, R. (eds) (1977) *Black Paper 1977*. London: Maurice Temple Smith Ltd.

Cox, C.B. and Dyson, A.E. (eds) (1969a) *Fight for Education: A Black Paper*. London: Critical Quarterly Society.

Cox, C.B. and Dyson, A.E. (eds) (1969b) *Black Paper Two*. London: Critical Quarterly Society.

Cox, C.B. and Dyson, A.E. (eds) (1970) *Black Paper Three: Goodbye Mr Short*. London: Critical Quarterly Society.

Darling, J. (1994) *Child-Centred Education and its Critics*. London: Paul Chapman.

Department for Children, Schools and Familes (DCSF) (2009) *Learning, Playing and Interacting*. Nottingham: DCSF.

Department for Education (DfE) (2012) *Statutory Framework for the Early Years Foundation Stage*. London: DfE.

Department for Education and Employment (DfEE) (1998) *The National Literacy Strategy Framework*. London: DfEE.

Department for Education and Employment (DfEE) (1999) *The National Numeracy Strategy Framework*. London: DfEE.

Department for Education and Employment/Qualifications and Curriculum Authority (DfEE/QCA) (1998) *Desirable Outcomes for Children's Learning on Entering Compulsory Schooling*. London: DfEE Publications.

Department for Education and Skills (DfES) (2000) *Curriculum Guidance for the Foundation Stage*. London: DfES Publications.

Department for Education and Skills (DfES) (2002) *Researching Effective Pedagogy in the Early Years*. London: DfES.

Department for Education and Skills (DfES) (2003) *Birth to Three Matters*. London: DfES Publications.

Department for Education and Skills (DfES) (2005) *Communicating Matters*. London: DfES.

Department for Education and Skills (DfES) (2006) *Independent Review of the Teaching of Early Reading*. London: DfES Publications.

Department for Education and Skills (DfES) (2007a) *Letters and Sounds: Principles and Practice of High Quality Phonics*. London: DfES Publications.

Department for Education and Skills (DfES) (2007b) *The Early Years Foundation Stage*. London: DfES Publications.

Department of Education and Science (DES) (1990) *Starting with Quality* (The Rumbold Report). London: HMSO.

Diamond, M. and Hopson, J. (1998) *Magic Trees of the Mind*. New York: Dutton.

Donaldson, M. (1978) *Children's Minds*. London: Fontana Press.

Donaldson, M. (1992) *Human Minds: An Exploration*. London: Penguin Books.

Dowling, M. (2010) *Young Children's Personal, Social and Emotional Development*. 3rd edn. London: Paul Chapman.

Drummond, M.J. (1993) *Assessing Children's Learning*. London: David Fulton.

Drummond, M.J., Rouse, D. and Pugh, G. (1992) *Making Assessment Work*. Nottingham: NES Arnold/National Children's Bureau.

Dunlop, A. and Fabian, H. (eds) (2007) *Informing Transitions in the Early Years*. Maidenhead: Open University Press.

Dunn, J. (1988) *The Beginning of Social Understanding*. Oxford: Blackwell.

Dweck, C. (1978) Children's interpretation of evaluative feedback: the effect of social cues on learned helplessness, *Merrill-Palmer Quarterly*, 22 (2).

Dweck, C. (2006) *Mindset: The New Psychology of Success*. New York: Ballantine Books.

Early Education (2012) *Development Matters in the Early Years Foundation Stage*. London: Early Education.

Early Years Curriculum Group (EYCG) (1992) *First Things First: Educating Young Children*. Oldham: Madeleine Lindley.

Edgington, M. (2012) Why is a reliance on numerical data unnecessary and potentially harmful in nursery education? *NCrNE Newsletter*, May: 5.

Edwards, C., Gandini, L. and Nimmo, J. (1994) Promoting collaborative learning in the early childhood classroom: teachers' contrasting conceptualizations in two communities, in L.G. Katz and B. Cesarone (eds) *Reflections on the Reggio Emilia Approach*. Urbana IL: ERIC/EECE.

Edwards, D. and Mercer, N. (1987) *Common Knowledge: The Development of Understanding in the Classroom*. London: Methuen.

Edwards, V. and Redfern, A. (1988) *At Home in School: Parent Participation in Primary Education*. London: Routledge.

Elfer, P., Goldschmied, E. and Selleck, D. (2003) *Key Persons in the Nursery*. London: David Fulton.

Eliot, L. (2009) *Pink Brain, Blue Brain*. Oxford: Oneworld Publications.

Elley, W.B. (1992) *How in the World Do Students Read? IEA Study of Reading Literacy*. The Hague: The International Association for the Evaluation of Educational Achievement.

Ellis, S. (2009) Policy and research: lessons from the Clackmannanshire synthetic phonics initiative, in F. Fletcher-Campbell, J. Soler and G. Reid (eds) *Approaching Difficulties in Literacy Development: Assessment, Pedagogy and Programmes*. London: Sage/Open University.

Entwistle, D. and Alexander, K. (1998) Facilitating the transition to first grade: the nature of transition and research on factors affecting it, *Elementary School Journal*, 98(4): 351–64.

Fabian, H. and Dunlop, A. (eds) (2002) *Transitions in the Early Years*. London: Routledge Falmer.

Featherstone, S. and Bayley, R. (2009) *Boys and Girls Come Out to Play*. London: A&C Black.

Featherstone, S. and Bayley, R. (2010) *The Cleverness of Boys*. London: A&C Black.

Fisher, J. (1996) Reflecting on the principles of early years practice, *Journal of Teacher Development*, 5(1): 17–26.

Fisher, J. (1998a) Seen and heard, *Nursery World*, 5 February: 26–7.

Fisher, J. (1998b) All part of the plan, *Nursery World*, 12 February: 12–13.

Fisher, J. (1998c) For good measure, *Nursery World*, 19 February: 14–15.

Fisher, J. (2000) The foundations of learning, *Early Education*, Summer.

Fisher, J. (ed.) (2002) *The Foundations of Learning*. Buckingham: Open University Press.

Fisher, J. (2006) Handle with care! Transitions in the early years, *Early Education*, Autumn.

Fisher, J. (2010) *Moving On to Key Stage 1: Improving Transition From the Early Years Foundation Stage*. Buckingham: Open University Press.

Fisher, J. (2012a) Time to talk, *Nursery World*, 23 January, 17–20.

Fisher, J. (2012b) In tune, *Nursery World*, 20 February, 19–22.

Fisher, J. (2012c) Under control, *Nursery World*, 19 March, 19–22.

Fisher, J. (2012d) Now you're talking, *Nursery World*, 16 April, 14–17.

Fisher, J., Claxton, G. and Price, A. (2005) *Playing for Life*. Birmingham: National Primary Trust.

Fisher, J. and Wood, E. (2012) Changing educational practice in the early years through practitioner-led action research: an adult-child Interaction project, *International Journal of Early Years Education*, 20(2).

Forman, E.A. and Cazden, C.B. (1985) Exploring Vygotskian perspectives in education: the cognitive value of peer interaction, in J.V. Wertsch (ed.) *Culture, Communication and Cognition: Vygotskian Perspective*. Cambridge: Cambridge University Press.

Galton, M. and Williamson, J. (1992) *Group Work and the Primary Classroom*. London: Routledge.

Gammage, P. (1999) After five, your brain is cooked, *Education Now*, summer (24).

Gardner, H. (1993) *The Unschooled Mind: How Children Think and How Schools Should Teach*. London: Fontana.

Geake, J.G. (2009) *The Brain at School: Educational Neuroscience in the Classroom*. Maidenhead: Open University Press.

Gerhardt, S. (2004) *Why Love Matters: How Affection Shapes a Baby's Brain*. Hove: Brunner-Routledge.

Gerhardt, S. (2010) *The Selfish Society*. London: Simon & Schuster.

Goddard Blythe, S. (2005) *The Well Balanced Child*. Stroud: Hawthorn Press.

Goddard Blythe, S. (2011) *The Genius of Natural Childhood*. Stroud: Hawthorn Press.

Gopnik, A., Meltzoff, A. and Kuhl, P. (1999) *How Babies Think: The Science of Childhood*. London: Weidenfeld and Nicolson.

Greenfield, S. (1997) *The Human Brain: A Guided Tour*. London: Weidenfield & Nicolson.

Gura, P. (ed.) (1992) *Exploring Learning: Young Children and Blockplay*. London: Paul Chapman.

Hall, N. (1987) *The Emergence of Literacy*. Sevenoaks: Hodder and Stoughton.

Harlen, W. (ed.) (1985) *Primary Science . . . Taking the Plunge*. Oxford: Heinemann Educational.

Hart, B. and Risley, T.R. (1995) *Meaningful Differences in the Everyday Experiences of Young American Children*. London: Paul H. Brookes.

Hastings, N. and Schweiso, J. (1995) Tasks and tables: the effects of seating arrangements on task engagement in primary schools, *Educational Research* (NFER), 37(3): 279–91.

Holland, P. (2003) *We Don't Play with Guns Here: War, Weapon and Superhero Play in the Early Years*. Maidenhead: Open University Press.

Holt, J. (1982) *How Children Fail*, 2nd edn. Harmondsworth: Penguin.

House, R. (ed.) (2011) *Too Much, Too Soon? Early Learning and the Erosion of Childhood*. Stroud: Hawthorn Press.

Howard-Jones, P. (2010) *Introducing Neuroeducational Research: Neuroscience, Education and the Brain from Contexts to Practice*. London: Routledge.

Hughes, B. (1996) *A Playworker's Taxonomy of Play Types*. London: Playlink.

Hughes, F.P. (2010) *Children, Play, and Development*, 4th edn. London: Sage.

Hughes, M. (1986) *Children and Number*. Oxford: Blackwell.

Hurst, V. and Lally, M. (1992) Assessment and the nursery curriculum, in G.M. Blenkin and A.V. Kelly (eds) *Assessment in Early Childhood Education*. London: Paul Chapman.

Hutchin, V. (1996) *Tracking Significant Achievement in the Early Years*. London: Hodder & Stoughton.

Hutchin, V. (1999) *Right from the Start: Effective Planning and Assessment in the Early Years*. London: Hodder & Stoughton.

Hutchin, V. (2007) *Supporting Every Child's Learning Across the Early Years Foundation Stage*. London: Hodder Education.

Hutt, J., Tyler, S., Hutt, C. and Christopherson, H. (1990) *Play, Exploration and Learning: A Natural History of the Preschool*. London: Routledge.

Inner London Education Authority (ILEA) (1990) *A Curriculum for Young Children: Outdoor Play*. London: Harcourt Brace Jovanovich.

Isaacs, S. (1929) *The Nursery Years*. London: Routledge and Kegan Paul.

Jones, P. (1988) *Lipservice: The Story of Talk in Schools*. Milton Keynes: Open University Press.

Kalliala, M. (2006) *Play Culture in a Changing World*. Maidenhead: Open University Press.

Karen, R. (1994) *Becoming Attached: First Relationships and How They Shape Our Capacity to Love*. Oxford: Oxford University Press.

Kotulak, R. (1997) *Inside the Brain: Revolutionary Discoveries of How the Mind Works*. Kansas City, MI: Andrews and McMeel.

Lancaster, Y.P. and Kirby, P. (2010) *Listening to Young Children*, 2nd edn. Maidenhead: Open University Press.

Lane, J. (2005a) 'I've just seen a wave as big as our house, Daddy': the importance of providing scope for children to talk about things that worry them, including disasters such as the tsunami, *Early Years Educator*, March.

Lane, J. (2005b) Facing terror: terrorist attacks are frightening and can have a big effect on children and adults, *Nursery Education*, November.

Lane, J. (2008) *Young Children and Racial Justice*. London: National Children's Bureau.

Lindon, J. (1993) *Child Development from Birth to Eight*. London: National Children's Bureau.

Lindon, J. (2010) *Positive Relationships: The Key Person Approach*. London: Practical Preschool Books.

Livingston, T. (2005) *Child of Our Time*. London: Bantam Press.

Mac Naughton, G. and Williams, G. (2009) *Teaching Young Children: Choices in Theory and Practice*, 2nd edn. Buckingham: Open University Press.

Malaguzzi, L. (1992) *A Message from Loris Malaguzzi*, video transcript, Reggio Emilia: Reggio Children.

Malaguzzi, L. (1993) History, ideas and basic philosophy, in C. Edwards, L. Gandini and G. Foreman (eds) *The Hundred Languages of Children: the Reggio Emilia Approach to Early Childhood Education*. Norwood, NJ: Ablex.

Malaguzzi, L. (1997) *Shoe and Meter*. Reggio Emilia: Reggio Children.

McMillan, M. (1919) *The Nursery School*. London: J.M Dent & Sons.

Meadows, S. (1993) *The Child As Thinker: The Development and Acquisition of Cognition in Childhood*. London: Routledge.

Meighan, J. (1993) The hijack of young children's learning, in R. Meighan (ed.) *Theory and Practice of Regressive Education*. Nottingham: Educational Heretics Press.

Mercer, N. (1995) *The Guided Construction of Knowledge: Talk Amongst Teachers and Learners*. Clevedon: Multilingual Matters.

Mercer, N. and Littleton, K. (2007) *Dialogue and the Development of Children's Thinking*. Abingdon: Routledge.

Moss, P. and Penn, H. (1996) *Transforming Nursery Education*. London: Paul Chapman.

Moyles, J. (ed.) (2010) *Thinking About Play*. Buckingham: Open University Press.

Newberger, E.H. (1999) *The Men They Will Become: The Nature and Nurture of Male Character*. Reading, MA: Perseus Books.

NIH/NIHM (2007) Sexual dimorphism of brain development trajectories during childhood and adolescence, *NeuroImage*, 36(4): 165–73.

Nutbrown, C. (2006) *Threads of Thinking*, 3rd edn. London: Sage.

O'Connor, A. (2012) *Understanding Transitions in the Early Years: Supporting Change Thorough Attachment and Resilience*. London: David Fulton.

Office for Standards in Education (Ofsted) (1994) *Assessing School Effectiveness*. London: Institute of Education.

Office for Standards in Education (Ofsted) (2004) *Transition from the Reception Year to Year 1: An Evaluation by HMI*. London: Ofsted.

Office for Standards in Education (Ofsted) (2012a) *The Framework for School Inspection*. www.ofsted.gov.uk/resources/110128 (accessed 1 October 2012).

Office for Standards in Education (Ofsted) (2012b) *The Evaluation Schedule for the Inspection of Maintained Schools and Academies*. www.ofsted.gov.uk/resources/110127 (accessed 1 October 2012).

Oxfordshire County Council (OCC) (2005) *What We Think about Starting School*. Oxford: Early Learning & Childcare.

Oxfordshire County Council (OCC) (2006) *Transition: Foundation Stage to Year 1*. Oxford: Early Learning and Childcare.

Oxfordshire Early Years Team (1996) *Curriculum Matters 13: Early Years*. Oxford: Oxfordshire Education Department.

Paley, V.G. (1984) *Boys and Girls: Superheroes in the Doll Corner*. Chicago: University of Chicago Press.

Palmer, S. (2006) *Toxic Childhood: How Modern Life is Damaging our Children . . . and What We Can Do About it*. London: Orion Books.

Pascal, C., Bertram, A., Ramsden, F. and Saunders, M. (1997) *Evaluating and Improving Quality in Early Childhood Settings (The EEL Programme)*. Worcester: Centre for Research in Early Childhood.

Phillips, T. (1988) On a related matter: why successful small-group talk depends upon not keeping to the point, in M. Maclure, T. Phillips and A. Wilkinson (eds) *Oracy Matters*. Milton Keynes: Open University Press.

Piaget, J. (1929) *The Language and Thought of the Child*. New York: Basic Books.

Piaget, J. (1951) *Play, Dreams and Imitation in Childhood*. London: Routledge.

Piaget, J. (1953) *The Origin of Intelligence in the Child*. London: Routledge and Kegan Paul.

Piaget, J. and Inhelder, B. (1956) *The Child's Conception of Space*. London: Routledge and Kegan Paul.

Pinker, S. (1997) *How the Mind Works*. London: Allen Lane, The Penguin Press.

Pollard, A. and Filer, A. (1999) *The Social World of Pupil Career*. London: Cassell.

Pollard, A. and Tann, S. (1993) *Reflective Teaching in the Primary School*, 2nd edn. London: Cassell.

Postlethwaite, K. (1993) *Differentiated Science Teaching*. Buckingham: Open University Press.

Pound, L. (2005) *How Children Learn: From Montessori to Vygotsky – Educational Theories and Approaches Made Easy*. London: Practical Preschool Books.

Pringle, M.K. (1992) *The Needs of Children*, 3rd edn. London: Routledge.

Pugh, G. (2002) The consequences of inadequate investment in the early years, in J. Fisher (ed.) *The Foundations of Learning*. Buckingham: Open University Press.

Read, V. (2010) *Developing Attachment in Early Years Settings*. London: Routledge.

Reggio Emilia Project Zero (2001) *Making Learning Visible: Children as Individual and Group Learners*. Reggio Emilia: Reggio Children.

Reid, J., Forrestal, P. and Cook, J. (1989) *Small Group Learning in the Classroom*. Scarborough, WA: Chalkface Press.

Rich, D. (2003) Bang! Bang! Gun play and why children need it, *Early Education*, Summer.

Richards, M. and Light, P. (1986) *Children of Social Worlds*. Cambridge: Polity Press.

Rinaldi, C. (2001) Infant-toddler centers and preschools as places of culture, in Project Zero and Reggio Children, *Making Learning Visible: Children as Individual and Group Learners*. Reggio Emilia: Reggio Children.

Roberts, R. (1995a) *Self Esteem and Successful Early Learning*. London: Hodder and Stoughton.

Roberts, R. (ed.) (1995b) *A Nursery Education Curriculum for the Early Years*. Oxford: National Primary Centre.

Robinson, E.J. and Beck, S. (2000) What is difficult about counterfactual reasoning? in P. Mitchell and K.J. Riggs (eds) *Children's Reasoning and the Mind*. Hove: Psychology Press.

Robinson, M. (2003) *From Birth to One: The Year of Opportunity*. Buckingham: Open University Press.

Robinson, M. (2008) *Child Development from Birth to Eight*. Maidenhead: Open University Press.

Rogoff, B. (1990) *Apprenticeship in Thinking*. Oxford: Oxford University Press.

Rogoff, B. (1997) Cognition as a collaborative process, in L. Duhn and B. Siegler (eds) *Handbook of Child Psychology*. New York: John Wiley & Sons.

Rogoff, B., Paradise, R., Arauz, R.M., Correa-Chévez and Anelillo, C. (2003) Firsthand learning through intent participation, *Annual Review of Psychology*, 203(54): 175–203.

Rogoff, B. and Toma, C. (1997) Shared thinking: community and institutional variations, *Discourse Processes*, 23: 471–97.

Rose, J. (2006) *Independent Review of the Teaching of Early Reading*. London: DfES.

Rousseau, J.J. ([1762] 1976) *Emile* (translated by Barbara Foxley). London: Dent.

Rowland, S. (1984) *The Enquiring Classroom: An Introduction to Children's Learning*. Lewes: Falmer Press.

Sanders, D., White, W., Burge, B. et al. (2005) *A Study of the Transition from the Foundation Stage to Key Stage 1*. Slough: NFER.

Santer, J., Griffiths, C. and Goodall, D. (2007) *Free Play in Early Childhood*. London: Play England/NCB.

Schweinhart, L.J., Barnes, H. and Weikart, D.P. (1993) *Significant Benefits: The High/Scope Perry Preschool Study Through Age 27*. Ypsilanti, MI: High/Scope Press.

Selleck, D. (2006) Key Persons in the Early Years Foundation Stage, *Early Education*, Autumn.

Shaffer, D.R. (1999) *Developmental Psychology: Childhood and Adolescence*, 5th edn. Pacific Grove, CA: Brooks/Cole Publishing.

Sharp, C. (1998) Age of starting school and the early years curriculum. Paper presented at the NFER's annual conference, London, 6 October.

Sharp, C. (2000) When should children start school and what should we teach them?, *Topic*, 23, Spring.

Sharp, C. (2002) School starting age: European policy and recent research. Paper presented at the LGA Seminar 'When Should Our Children Start School?', LGA Conference Centre, London, 1 November.

Sharp, C., George, N., Sargent, C., O'Donnell, S. and Heron, M. (2009) *International Thematic Probe: The Influence of Relative Age on Learner Attainment and Development*. Slough: NFER.

Sinclair, J.McH. and Coulthard, R.M. (1975) *Towards an Analysis of Discourse: The English Used by Teachers and Pupils*. London: Oxford University Press.

Siraj-Blatchford, I. (1994) *The Early Years: Laying the Foundations for Racial Equality*. Stoke-on-Trent: Trentham Books.

Siraj-Blatchford, I., Sylva, K,. Muttock, S., Gilden, R. and Bell, D. (2002) *Researching Effective Pedagogy in the Early Years*. London: DfES.

Smith, A.B. (1993) Early childhood educare: seeking a theoretical framework in Vygotsky's work, *International Journal of Early Years Education*, 1(1): 47–61.

Smith, H. (1995) *Unhappy Children: Reasons and Remedies*. London: Free Association Books.

Smith, P.K., Cowie, H. and Blades, M. (2010) *Understanding Children's Development*, 4th edn. Oxford: Blackwell Publishing.

Spaggiari, S. (1997) The invisibility of the essential, in Reggio Children *Shoe and Meter: First Approaches to the Discovery, Function and Use of Measurement*. Reggio Emilia: Reggio Children.

Stern, D. (1985) *The Interpersonal World of the Infant: A View from Psychoanalysis and Developmental Psychology*. New York: Basic Books.

Stewart, N. (2011) *How Children Learn: The Characteristics of Effective Early Learning*. London: Early Education.

Sylwester, R. (1995) *A Celebration of Neurons: An Educator's Guide to the Brain*. Alexandria, VA: ASCD.

Tassoni, P. (2007) *Child Development 6 to 16 Years*. Oxford: Heinemann.

Tizard, B. and Hughes, M. (1984) *Young Children Learning: Talking and Thinking at Home and at School*. London: Fontana.

Tompkins, M. (1991) In praise of praising less, *Extensions* (newsletter of the High/Scope Curriculum), 6(1): 1–3.

Trevarthen, C. (1980) The foundations of intersubjectivity: development of interpersonal and cooperative understanding in infants, in D. Olsen (ed.) *The Social Foundations of Language and Thought*. New York: W.W. Norton.

Trevarthen, C. (1992) An infant's motives for speaking and thinking in the culture, in A.H. Wold (ed.) *The Dialogical Alternative*. Oslo/ Oxford: Scandinavian University Press/Oxford University Press.

UNICEF (2011) *Children's Wellbeing in UK, Sweden and Spain: The Role of Inequality and Materialism*. Ipsos MORI.

Vermes, S. (2008) What are the features of the adult's contribution which create good interactions during child-initiated activity? MA dissertation, Oxford Brookes University.

Vygotsky, L.S. (1962) *Thought and Language*. Cambridge, MA: MIT Press.

Vygotsky, L.S. (1966) Play and its role in the mental development of the child (translated by Catherine Mulholland), *Voprosy psikhologi*, 12(6): 62–76.

Vygotsky, L.S. (1978) *Mind in Society: The Development of Higher Psychological Processes*. Cambridge, MA: Harvard University Press.

Warham, S.M. (1993) *Primary Teaching and the Negotiation of Power*. London: Paul Chapman.

Watson, R. (1998) Rethinking readiness for learning, in D. Olson and N. Torrance (eds) *Handbook of Education and Human Development: New Models of Learning, Teaching and Schooling*. London: Blackwell.

Wellhousen, K. (2002) *Outdoor Play Every Day*. London: Thomson Learning.

Wells, G. (ed.) (1981) *Learning Through Interaction*. Cambridge: Cambridge University Press.

Wells, G. (1985) *Language, Learning and Education*. Windsor: NFER/ Nelson.

Wells, G. (1986) *The Meaning Makers: Children Learning Language and Using Language to Learn*. Sevenoaks: Hodder and Stoughton.

White, J. (2008) *Playing and Learning Outdoors*. London:Routledge.

Whitehead, J. and McNiff, J. (2006) *Action Research, Living Theory*. London: Sage.

Whitehead, M. (1993) Why not happiness? Reflections on change and conflict in early childhood education, in P. Gammage and J. Meighan (eds) *Early Childhood Education: Taking Stock*. Ticknall: Education Now Publishing.

Willes, M.J. (1983) *Children Into Pupils: A Study of Language in Early Schooling*. London: Routledge and Kegan Paul.

Wood, D. (1998) *How Children Think and Learn*, 2nd edn. Oxford: Blackwell.

Wood, D., Bruner, J.S. and Ross, G. (1976) The role of tutoring in problem solving, *Journal of Child Psychology and Psychiatry*, 17(2): 89–100.

Wyse, D. and Styles, M. (2007) Synthetic phonics and the teaching of reading: the debate surrounding England's 'Rose Report', *Literacy*, 47(1).

INDEX

Locators shown in *italics* refer to boxes, figures and tables.

abilities, child
  educators as students of
    child abilities, 25–46, *29–30,
    32*
  impact of school timetabling
    upon, 34–6
  see also assessments
action research
  use as method of critical
    reflection, 212–15
activity
  importance as part of learning
    process, 17–18
activity, learning
  adult-led and initiated, 33–4,
    78–80
  balance and organization of,
    81–5, *82, 84, 85*
  child- initiated, 33–4
  observation of as element in
    assessment, 26–7
  salience for education
    planning, 64–6
  see also specific activities e.g.
    play; reading and writing;
    topic work
Adams, S., 144–5, 145–6
adaptability
  salience for play environment,
    148
'adaptive plasticity'
  salience in relation to brain
    development, 5–6
adult-initiated learning
  implications of, 78–80

role and use of educator time,
  87
role of differentiation in, 85–6
adult-led learning
implications of, 78–80
  role and use of educator time,
    86–7
  role of differentiation in, 85–6
  salience for planning, 65
adults
  as co-constructors and
    protagonists supporting play,
    157–8
  as facilitators and responders
    supporting play, 157
  as observers supporting play,
    157
  importance of communication
    of, 121–9
  planning for learner support
    by, 207
  role in group learning, 74–6
  role in independent learning,
    74–6, 89–90
affective theories of play, 138
agendas, external
  managing children learning
    alongside, 57–9
analysis, self-
  use as method of critical
    reflection, 216–20
  use of videos for, 215–16
assessments
  characteristics and tools for
    external, 220–25, *221, 222–4*

need for to inform planning, 70

role of educators, 26

strategy and organization in learning situation, 198–205

use in planning teaching and learning experiences, 205–7

see also elements and players e.g. conversations; educators and education; observers and observations; parents; questions and questioning

see also type e.g. formative assessments; summative assessments

assessments, self-

use as method of critical reflection, 216–20

use of videos for, 215–16

Athey, C., 22–3

attitudes, learning

acquisition among young children, 11

role and importance of reflection concerning, 211–12

see also behaviours, learning

attributes, personal

implications for successful conversation, 128–9

attunement

importance for successful conversation, 124–5

Barrett, G., 170–1, 172

Bayley, R., 7

behaviours, learning

salience of outdoors in improving, 103

see also attitudes, learning

beliefs, personal

implications for successful conversation, 128–9

influence on child play, 145–6

Birth to Three Matters (2003), 137, 217

Blenkin, G., 56–7

Blythe, G., 67, 119–20

boisterousness, child

as consideration in class play, 155–6

boredom

as pre-requisite for 'successful' play, 147

boys

brain differences with goals, 6–9

brain

growth and development in children, 4–10

Bristol Language Study, 18

Bronfenbrenner, U., 165

Brooker, L., 30, 42, 145

Bruce, T., 18, 43, 54, 137, 140

Bruner, J., 12, 19, 20, 39, 53

Campbell, R., 172

carers

as evaluators of offspring learning, 195–6

role of parent–teacher conversations, 42–5

significance as child educators, 15–16

case studies and examples

documentation in learning assessment, 204–5

focused teaching and assessment, *197*

impact on nature of learning, *198*

ineffective conversations, 39–41

Carnegie Corporation of New York, 3–4

centrality

salience for play environment, 149–50

change
  salience of limited for play
    environment, 150
charters
  successful play, *158–9*
child-centeredness
  significance in education, 51–4
child-initiated learning
  implications of, 80–5, *82, 84,*
    85
  role and use of educator time,
    87
  role of differentiation in, 85–6
child-led learning
  salience for planning, 65
children
  as evaluators of own learning,
    194–5
  importance of conversations
    with, 121–9
  see also development, child;
    learners and learning
Children and Their Primary Schools
  (1967), 51–2
Children's Minds (Donaldson),
  52–3
Chilvers, D., 131
classrooms and nurseries
  creation and design of, 98–115
  negotiating learning in, 163–4
  see also rules, classroom;
    sanctions, classroom
Claxton, G., 213, 214
climate, the
  consideration in learning
    environments, 100–1
co-constructors
  adults as in supporting play,
    158
communication
  educational importance of
    adult–child, 121–9
  educational importance of
    child–child, 129–31

see also interactions
see also particular e.g.
  conversations
communities, social
  significance as child educators,
    15–16
concepts
  learning of among young
    children, 11
  salience of intended for
    education planning, 64
confidence
  importance for learning
    success, 29–30, *29–30*
contexts
  priority of education, 131
control
  application to learner
    socialisation, 168–70
  see also negotiations
Convention on the Rights of the
  Child (UN), 30
conversations
  characteristics of effective,
    122–9
  educational importance of
    adult–child, 121–9
  educational importance of
    child–child, 129–31
  role within ability assessment,
    37–46
  use as information about child,
    200
cooperative play, 140
Coram Family Research Unit, 23
Coulthard, R., 168
culture
  impact on nature of learning,
    198
  influence on child play,
    141–6
curiosity
  outdoor learning as venue for,
    103–4

curricula
  characteristics and planning
    stages, 60–66
  influence of play in, 154
  need for spiral, 6
  organization and balance,
    81–5, *82, 84, 85*
  scope for content negotiation,
    180–81
  socio-educational impact on
    child, 45
  see also differentiation; topic
    work
*Curriculum for Young Children:
  Outdoor Play* (ILEA), 99
*Curriculum Guidance for
  Foundation Stage* (2003),
  217

Darling, J., 51, 52
decision-making
  child involvement, 112–13
Desirable Learning Outcomes
  (1998), 47
development, child
  influence of experiences and
    heredity, 2–4, *3*
  see also components e.g. brain
*Development Matters in Early Years
  Foundation Stage* (2012), 49
Dewey, J., 51, 54
differentiation
  planning of curricula
    embracing, 66–9, *68–9*
  role in child- and adult-
    initiated learning, 85–6
  salience for education
    planning, 64
diffidence, learner
  challenge for class teaching,
    120
directness, interaction
  importance for successful
    conversation, 122–3

disaffection
  among learners, 170–3
discipline
  scope for negotiation, 176–7
discovery
  need for outdoor resources to
    encourage, 102
documentation
  role in learning assessment,
    201–3, 204–5
  use as information about new
    child, 200
  see also stories, learning
Donaldson, M., 12, 13, 21, 52–3
dramatic play, 139
Dweck, C., 194

Early Childhood Education (Bruce),
  54
Early Learning Goals (2000), 47,
  53, 151
Early Years Foundation Stage (EYFS)
  (DfES)
  on curricula planning, 60–6
  on learning assessments, 187,
    191, 195–8, *197, 198*
  on young children's feelings
    and attitudes, 29
  principles and practitioner role
    in relation to, 35, 47–50
  see also elements and action e.g.
    assessments; curricula; play
Early Years Foundation Stage
  Profile (EYFSP)
  definition and characteristics,
    191–2
  role in assessment moderation,
    193–4
educators and education
  as evaluators of fellow
    practitioner teaching, 196–8,
    197, 198
  as learners of child abilities,
    26–46

characteristics and significance,
51–4
effectiveness of child's first,
162–3
implications of learning
processes, 20–23
importance of expertise, 15–16
models of, 72
priority of contexts, 131
problems of whole class,
118–21
role in child learning success,
31–2, *32*
role in outdoor education, 100
theories and principles, 54–7,
54–6
types and role of educator
time, 86–9
see also learners and learning
see also influences e.g. culture
*see also strategies and
considerations e.g.*
assessments; groups and
grouping; observers and
observation; time,
organization and
management; planning;
reflection, critical; time,
organization and
management
Edwards, D. 22
egocentricity, learner
challenge for class teaching,
119
Eliot, L., 7–8
Emile (Rousseau), 51
environments
importance for successful
conversation, 123
influence on child
development, 2–4, *3*
environments, learning
challenges of child transitions
to and in, 164–6

creation and organization of
appropriate and effective,
76–8, 98–115
power, organization and scope
of negotiation, 168–70,
173–83
pre-schooldays, 96–7
role and importance of
reflection on, 211
salience for education
planning, 65
salience for independent
learning, 95–6
significance for learning
success, 27–9
see also experiences, learning
see also elements and location
e.g. classrooms and nurseries;
indoors; outdoors; resources;
spatiality
equipment
nature of for 'play', 146–7
requirement for and
organizational implications,
101–2, 107–10, *108, 110*
role and importance of
reflection on, 210
use review, 113–14
see also spatiality
ethnicity
influence on child play, 145–6
evaluations *see* assessments
'excess energy' theory of play,
138
evidence, documentary
role in learning assessment,
201–3, 204–5
examples *see* case studies and
examples
excess energy theory of play, 138
exploratory play, 139–40
experiences
importance of reflection on
childhood, 211

influence of personal on child
development, 2–4, *3*
experiences, learning
balance and organization of,
81–5, *82, 84, 85*
independent learning as
replicating, 96–8
negotiation over sequence of,
177–8
pre-schooldays, 96–8
salience of prior for education
planning, 63
use of assessment in planning
of, 205–7
see also environments, learning;
organization, learning
experiences and
environments
exploration
importance as part of learning
process, 17
need for outdoor resources to
encourage, 102
expression
need for outdoor resources to
encourage, 102
EYFS (*Early Years Foundation Stage*)
*see Early Years Foundation
Stage*
EYFSP (Early Years Foundation
Stage Profile)
definition and characteristics,
191–2
role in assessment moderation,
193–4

families
challenges of child transition
outwith, 164–6
significance as child educators,
15–16
facilitators
adults as in supporting play,
157

Featherstone, S., 7
Fisher, J., 122
'fixed grouping'
as educational strategy,
133–4
'flexible grouping'
as educational strategy,
134–5
flow
salience for play environment,
148–9
formative assessments
definition and characteristics,
185–9, 194–8, *197, 198*
moderation of, 193–4
recording of, 189–91
Foundation Stage of learning *see
Early Years Foundation Stage*
Foundation Stage Profile (FSP)
characteristics and purpose,
191–2
role in assessment moderation,
193–4
free flow play, 140
Free Play in Early Childhood
(Santer), 137–8
Froebel, F., 51, 54
From Birth to One (Robinson), 9
frustration
among learners, 170–3
FSP (Foundation Stage Profile)
characteristics and purpose,
191–2
role in assessment moderation,
193–4

Gardner, H., 170
Geake, J., 5, 7
gender
influence on child play,
142–3
Gerhardt, S., 10
girls
brain differences with boys, 6–9

goals, learning
'desirable learning', 47
'early learning', 47
strategies for ensuring, 92
Gopnik, A., 9
grades, quality
of Ofsted classification, *221,
222–4*
groups and grouping
as organizational and
educational strategy,
131–5
importance of conversations
with, 118–21
role of adult in learning of,
74–6
salience of child's choice of,
135
see also requirements e.g.
'security'

Harlen, W., 11–12
Hart, B., 18
Hebb, D., 5–6
heredity
influence on child
development, 2–4, *3*
hierarchies
human need, 3, *3*
Holland, P., 143
Holt, J., 169
home life
challenges of child transition
outwith, 164–6
significance in child education,
15–16
How Babies Think (Gopnik), 9
Hughes, B., 139
Hughes, M., 12, 117, 118
Hurst, V., *198*

ideas, child
salience for education
planning, 64

image, self-
importance for learning
success, 29–30, *29–30*
images, media
impact on child play, 144–5
imagination
need for outdoor resources to
encourage, 102
independent learning
creation and organization of
environments, 76–8, 98–115
definition and characteristics,
94–5
effect on child of encouraging,
89–92
role as replicating early
experiences, 96–8
role of adult in, 74–6, 89–90
role of educator in
encouraging, 114–15
salience of environment for,
95–6
salience of out doors for, 103
see also barriers to achieving e.g.
interruptions
*Independent Review of Teaching of
Early Reading* (2006), 49
indoors
considerations of spatiality,
104–6, *105, 106*
importance as site for learning,
36–7
salience for education
planning, 65
Inner London Education
Authority (ILEA), 99
In Praise of Praising Less
(Tompkins), 181–2
intention
as outcome of child-initiated
learning, 83
interactions
challenge for class teaching,
120

characteristics of effective,
122–9
impact on classroom practice
of child need for, 22–3
importance as part of learning
process, 19–20
role in child- and adult-
initiated learning, 88–9
see also particular e.g.
conversations
'interpretive' model of teaching,
72
interruptions
avoidance for encouraging
independent learning,
111–12
effect upon young learners,
172–3
investigation
importance as part of learning
process, 17
involvement
outdoor learning as venue for,
103–4

Kalliala, M., 141, 146
Kelly, A., 56–7
'Key Person'
importance for successful
conversation, 123–4
role in child transition from
home to early years setting,
165–6
Kirby, P., 23

Lally, M., 198
Lancaster, Y., 23, 172
language
importance as part of learning
process, 18–19
Language at Home and At School
(Wells), 117
Learning, Playing and Interacting
(2009), 159

learners and learning
characteristics of successful,
13–15, 29–30, 29–30
child readiness for, 12–13
child transformation into,
168–9
implications of for classroom
practice, 20–23
managing alongside external
agendas, 57–9
process of among young
children, 10–12, 16–20
scope for negotiation over
fellow, 180
social expectations of learner
roles, 166–8
see also activity, learning;
assessments; curricula;
groups and grouping;
observers and observation;
relationships, learning
see also drivers and barriers to
success e.g. communication;
culture; disaffection;
discipline; environments,
learning; frustration;
interruptions; praise
see also players and
organizational procedures e.g.
educators and education;
families; peers; planning;
questions and questioning
see also type e.g. adult-initiated
learning; adult-led learning;
child-initiated learning;
child-led learning;
independent learning
Letters and Sounds (2007), 49
Lindon, J., 2–3
Listening to Children (Lancaster),
172
listening
socio-educational importance,
131

Listening to Children (Lancaster),
23, 172
literacy, teaching of
impact of timetabling on
learning ability, 34–6
Littleton, K., 122–3
locomotor play, 140

McMillan, M., 98
Malaguzzi, L., 13–14, 121, 204,
205
Maslow, A., 3
media
impact of images on child play,
144–5
see also type e.g. videos
meetings, cluster
use as information about child,
200
Meighan, J., 170
Mercer, N., 22, 122–3, 125
messiness
as consideration in class play,
155
models and typologies
child development needs,
2–4, *3*
independent learning
environments, 76–8
successful play, *158–9*
teaching, 72
moderation (verb)
of learning assessments,
193–4
Montessori, 54
Moyles, J., 144–5, 145–6

National Assessment Agency
(NAA), 74, 192
*National Curriculum and Early
Learning, The* (Blenkin),
57
Neill, S., 172
National Oracy Project, 117

needs
hierarchy of human, 3, *3*
typology of child development,
2–4, *3*
negotiations
organization and scope in
learning, 173–83
role in deciding of learning
context, 173–83
see also control
notes, taking of
salience for education
planning, 66
numeracy, teaching of
impact of timetabling on
learning ability, 34–6
nurseries and classrooms
creation and design of,
98–115
negotiating learning in, 163–4
see also rules, classroom;
sanctions, classroom

observers and observations
adults as in supporting play,
157
educators as, 73–4
need for to inform planning,
70
purpose and role in ability
assessment, 26–37, *29–30,
325*
salience in support of
planning, 63, 65–6
strategy and organization in
learning assessment,
198–205
Ofsted, *221*
open-endedness
salience for play environment,
148
opportunities, learning
salience of intended for
planning, 64

'oracy' (Wilkinson), 129
organization (concept)
    process of for educator as
        observer, 73–4
organization, learning
    experiences and
    environment
    involving adult–child
        conversations, 121–9
    scope for negotiation, 175–9
    see also activity, learning;
        decision-making;
        environments, learning;
        groups and grouping; time,
        organization and
        management
Osborne, R., 11–12
outcomes, learning
    'desirable learning', 47
    'early learning', 47
    strategies for ensuring, 92
outdoors
    characteristics of resources for,
        101–4
    importance as site for learning,
        36–7
    salience in education planning,
        65
Oxfordshire Adult–Child
    Interaction Project, 124,
    125–7, 128–9
Oxfordshire County Council
    'Partners in Quality'
    programme, 216–17

Paley, V., 142–3
parallel play, 140
parents
    as evaluators of offspring
        learning, 195–6
    role of parent–teacher
        conversations, 42–5
    significance as child educators,
        15–16

partnerships, parent–teacher
    strategies for success, 44–5
'Partners in Quality' programme
    (Oxfordshire County
    Council), 216–17
peers
    role and significance in
        learning success, 31
Pestalozzi, J., 51, 54
philosophies and theories
    early child education, 51–7,
        54–6
    of play, 137–9
photographs
    use as information about new
        child, 200
Piaget, J., 17, 19, 52–3, 58
Pinker, S., 8
'planned' play, 150–51
planning
    characteristics and stages of
        curricula, 60–66
    for adult support for learners,
        207
    of teaching and learning,
        205–7
    see also factors affecting e.g.
        differentiation; negotiations;
        timetables and timetabling;
        topic work; worksheets
plasticity ('adaptive')
    salience in relation to brain
        development, 5–6
play
    contexts and types, 139–41,
        150–1
    environmental elements and
        challenges, 146–50
    importance as part of learning
        process, 17–18, 21
    need to raise status of,
        158
    pedagogical and organizational
        challenges, 151–6, 153–4

role of educators in supporting, 156–8
theories of, 137–9
see also influences e.g. beliefs; culture; ethnicity; gender; media; society and socialisation; superheroes
'play as catharsis' theory, 138
'play as pleasure' theory, 138
'Playing for Life' Project, 214–15
Plowden Report (1967), 51–2
Pollard, A., 215
potential
as outcome of child-initiated learning, 83
power
application in learning environments, 168–70
see also negotiations
practice, classroom *see* educators and education
practice, reflective
role and importance in education, 209–25, *221, 223–4*
practice theory of play, 138
practitioners, education *see* educators and education
praise
use in learning contexts, 181–2
preparation theory of play, 138
pretend play, 139
Pringle, M., 2, 54
prioritization
salience for play environment, 148
processes, learning *see* learners and learning
programmes, learning *see* curricula
protagonists
adults as in supporting play, 157–8
pupils *see* learners and learning

quality, learning
features and tools for assessment of, 220–25, *221, 222–4*
strategies for ensuring outcomes of, 92
see also factors enhancing e.g. reflection, critical
questionnaires
use as information about new child, 200
questions and questioning
as strategy to discover child thoughts and ideas, 125–8
role in ability assessment, 37–41

reading and writing
importance of paced development, 131
recapitulation theory of play, 138
records
role in learning assessment, 201–3, 204–5
use as information about new child, 200
see also stories, learning
recreation theory of play, 138
reflection, critical
role and importance in education, 209–25, *221, 222–4*
Reggio Emilia (Italy), 10, 14, 95, 121, 131, 203, 204, 205
relationships, learning
role and importance of reflection concerning, 211–12
repetition and reinforcement
importance for child brain development, 6
research (action research)
use as method of critical reflection, 212–15

Researching Effective Pedagogy in the Early Years (Siraj-Blatchford), 121
Researching Effective Pedagogy in the Early Years (REPEY) Project, 122
resources
nature of for 'play', 146–7
requirement for and organization of, 101–2, 107–10, *108, 110*
role and importance of reflection on, 210
use review, 113–14
see also particular e.g. spatiality
responders and responses
adults as in supporting play, 157
Risley, T., 18
Roberts, R., 29
Robinson, M., 9
Rogoff, B., 58
Rose Review (2006), 49
rough and tumble play, 140
Rousseau, J-J., 51, 54
routines, learning environment
impact on child ability development, 34–6
Rowland, S., 72, 161
rule dominated play, 140
rules, classroom
scope for negotiation, 176–7

sanctions, classroom
scope for negotiation, 176–7
Santer, J., 137–8
schedules, assessment
Ofsted grade descriptor, *221*
schools *see* environments, learning
'security'
need for in learning groups, 135

self-analysis and evaluation
use as method of critical reflection, 216–20
use of videos for, 215–16
self-image
importance for learning success, 29–30, *29–30*
Selleck, D., 166
Shaffer, D., 10
Sinclair, J., 168
Siraj-Blatchford, I., 121
skills
learning of among young children, 11–12
need for outdoor resources to encourage, 101–2
salience of intended for education planning, 64
society and socialization
application of control to learner, 168–70
influence on child play, 141–2
socio-dramatic play, 139
solitary play, 140
spatiality
in environment design, 101–2, 104–6, *105, 106*
use reviews, 113–14
speaking
educational importance of adult–child, 118–29
educational importance of child–child, 129–31
socio-educational importance, 131
spectator play, 140
spontaneity
as outcome of child-initiated learning, 83
Starting School (Brooker), 30
Statutory Framework for Early Years Foundation Stage, 16–17, 29, 49, 137

Steiner, R., 54
Stewart, N., 58
stillness, learner
    challenge of need for in class
        teaching, 119–20
stories, learning
    role in learning assessment,
        203–4
strategies, learning *see* learners
    and learning
'structured' play, 150–51
summative assessments
    definition and characteristics,
        185–9, 194–80, *197, 198*
    moderation of, 193–4
    recording of, 189–91
superheroes
    influence on child play,
        143–4
symbolic play, 139

talking
    educational importance of
        adult–child, 118–29
    educational importance of
        child–child, 129–31
    socio-educational importance,
        131
Tann, S., 215
teachers and teaching *see*
    educators and education
theories and philosophies
    early childhood education,
        51–7, *54–6*
    of play, 137–9
time
    as consideration in class play,
        153–4, *153–4*
time, organization and
    management
    for child assessment, 200–1
    for classroom teaching, 73–4,
        76–85, *82, 84, 85*
    for observation, 73–4

impact on child learning
    ability, 35–6
importance of for play, 146
of educator in child- and
    adult-initiated learning, 86–9
purpose in independent
    learning, 89–92
scope for negotiation, 178–9
timetables and timetabling
    impact on child learning, 34–6
*Time to Play in Early Childhood
    Education* (Bruce), 137, 140
Tizard, B., 117, 118
Tompkins, M., 181–2
tools, assessment
    characteristics of external,
        220–5, *221, 222–4*
topic work
    planning of, 62
    scope for content negotiation,
        180–81
transitions, childhood
    from home to and within early
        years settings, 164–5
typologies and models
    child development needs, 2–4,
        3
    independent learning
        environments, 76–8
    successful play, *158–9*
    teaching, 72

values, personal
    implications for successful
        conversation, 128–9
Vermes, S., 41
videos
    use for self-reflection and
        analysis, 215–16
visits, home
    role in learning assessment,
        199–200
    salience for early years
        transition, 165–6

use for information about new
   child, 200
Vygotsky, L., 13, 19, 22, 53, 58–9,
   117, 152, 165

Warham, S., 173–4
wars and weapons
   influence on child play,
      143–4
weather
   consideration in learning
      environment, 100–1
Wells, G., 16, 18, 117, 118

White, J., 98, 99–100
Why Love Matters (Gerhardt), 10
Wilkinson, A., 129
Willes, M., 169, 170
Wood, E., 53, 122
worksheets
   role and use, 90–2
writing and reading
   importance of paced
      development, 131

Young Children Talking
   (Chilvers), 131